D1740040

Uncommon Alliances

Cultural Narratives of Migration in the New Europe

Nataša Kovačević

EDINBURGH
University Press

Edinburgh University Press is one of the leading university presses in the UK. We publish academic books and journals in our selected subject areas across the humanities and social sciences, combining cutting-edge scholarship with high editorial and production values to produce academic works of lasting importance. For more information visit our website: edinburghuniversitypress.com

© Nataša Kovačević, 2018

Edinburgh University Press Ltd
The Tun – Holyrood Road,
12(2f) Jackson's Entry,
Edinburgh EH8 8PJ

Typeset in 11/14 Adobe Sabon by
IDSUK (DataConnection) Ltd, and
printed and bound in Great Britain.

A CIP record for this book is available from the British Library

ISBN 978 1 4744 3588 8 (hardback)
ISBN 978 1 4744 3590 1 (webready PDF)
ISBN 978 1 4744 3591 8 (epub)

The right of Nataša Kovačević to be identified as the author of this work has been asserted in accordance with the Copyright, Designs and Patents Act 1988, and the Copyright and Related Rights Regulations 2003 (SI No. 2498).

Contents

Acknowledgements

I would like to thank, first of all, EUP literary editors, Michelle Houston and Adela Rauchova, for being enthusiastic about this project and providing helpful suggestions and encouragement along the way. The anonymous readers' exhaustive feedback helped me refine the theoretical framework and address the cultural narratives more effectively. I am also grateful to colleagues who took the time to read chapters or discuss book ideas, especially Tatjana Aleksić, Abby Coykendall, Beth Currans, Craig Dionne, Carla Harryman, Rob Halpern, Christine Neufeld and Barrett Watten. My sabbatical in 2014–15, with a generous research support from Eastern Michigan University, helped me gather material for the book and work on the manuscript draft. Finally, I greatly benefited from the feedback I received from panellists and audiences at conferences where I presented various chapter ideas. This book developed in the interstices between two lives, in the US and Serbia, Southeast Michigan and Belgrade, places which nurture me intellectually and emotionally. I thank my friends and family in both places, especially: Jasmina, for teaching me to love books; Ivan, for being an excellent playmate; Myshkin, for always supporting me in style; and Nemanja, for being in both of my lives.

Section three in Chapter 2 is a revised version of the essay 'Europe as host/hostage: on strange encounters and multicultural love in contemporary European cinema', published in *Interventions: A Journal of Postcolonial Studies* 14:3 (2012). Section two in Chapter 4 reworks an earlier essay 'Storming the EU fortress: communities of disagreement in Dubravka Ugrešić', published in *Cultural Critique* 83 (2013).

For Jasmina

Introduction

In China Mieville's *The City and the City* (2009), policing citizens to 'unsee' one another is the only way to differentiate between Beszel and Ul Qoma, two cross-hatched cities that exist in the same space. Such 'unseeing' is repeatedly threatened by underground rumblings about the cities' potential unification and even by the rumoured existence of a shared in-between: the third city of Orciny. Nonetheless, such possibilities remain mythical and inconclusive. In fact, all theories of unification in this novel are necessarily a chimera, relying on the nostalgia for a 'pre-Cleavage' time that never was: even the historically remote event of Cleavage is never conclusively defined as an act of either joining or separation. Mieville's deliberately deconstructive use of the term cleavage to signify both joining and separation suggests that what divides the cities is also what they have in common. They exist as long as they can perpetuate the myth of circumscribed identities within neatly demarcated boundaries, which gesture to the city that lies beyond.

The specific dynamic that Mieville depicts in the novel suggests a post-Cold War cleaving of Europe and its peripheries along the lines spelled out by neo-liberal capitalist restructuring and movement of labour. Cleaving as a project of both erasing and creating real and symbolic borders marked a traumatic rift at the heart of the European unification project, too, 'unseen' by the idealistic proponents of its rhetoric. While Mieville's Bezsel is technologically outdated, geopolitically isolated and economically depressed, the more glittering Ul Qoma is the poster child of neo-liberal development: confident, dynamic, attracting foreign investment and awash in consumer goods. This situation metaphorically captures intimate social inequalities of neighbouring Balkan states; contiguous Western and Eastern European states; and cross-hatched citizen-immigrant, wealthy-impoverished spaces throughout European metropolises. It is irreducible to any of these coordinates; rather, its different manifestations must be thought together to cognitively map the logic of borders in a tenuously unified Europe.

In *The New Old World*, Perry Anderson castigates self-satisfied European elites who choose to 'unsee' these proliferating inequalities and instead praise the European Union's idealised image, which hovers above its members like the mythical possibility of the city of Orciny: 'the Union is now widely presented as a paragon for the rest of the world, even as it becomes steadily less capable of winning the confidence of its citizens' (2009: xv). One reason for this self-satisfaction, which preceded its current economic and political crisis but nonetheless survives with somewhat abated vigour, is the belief that 'Europe embodies a higher set of values than the United States, and plays a more inspiring role in the world' (ibid.). This suggests the legacy of European colonialism, the Holocaust, as well as Cold War divisions have been relegated to the past. Europe appears as more peaceful and humane in comparison with the United States, periodically haunted by militant rhetoric and embroilment in a series of wars. Europe reconstituted its political legitimacy in a relatively short time, buffering itself against instability and poverty prevalent in other parts of the world; at the end of the century which saw its greatest upheavals and cataclysms, it also became united, ready to move on.

Europe's buffering against world events, however, is increasingly impossible, as evidenced by recent violent attacks across its cities as well as a steady arrival of refugees from Africa and Asia. Although Europe is becoming less European, it continues to separate itself from the world both discursively and physically. For instance, Anderson quotes New Labour politician Mark Leonard who claims that the twenty-first century will be the 'New European Century' (47). As a synthesis of freedom, stability, welfare and social democracy, 'the *European* way of life will become irresistible' as 'the *world* becomes richer and moves beyond satisfying basic needs such as hunger and health' (47, my emphasis). Leonard suggests a de facto revival of Eurocentrism, as if it were not already in place given Europe's political and economic organisation of 'the world' for many centuries. Nonetheless, this version of Eurocentrism, while continuing to uphold Europe as an exceptional paragon for the rest of the world, is no longer underpinned by political and military occupation. Rather, it is an embodiment of a new, consensual empire, irresistible to its participants as it entails their willing emulation and desire, much like Beszel and Ul Qoma mimic the mechanisms of free-market development to receive external accolade and funding. This empire seems all the more appealing because it is multicultural and inclusive; as historian Tony Judt notes, 'a community of values held up by Europeans and non-Europeans alike', the EU is 'an exemplar for all to emulate' (Anderson 47).

Rather than praising Europe as a successful multicultural exemplar, I propose that we approach this instance of 'worlding' not only as a fallout of Europe's colonial legacy, but also as a crucial component to its consensual empire, which relies on continued economic domination abroad and the perpetuation of racial and ethnic hierarchies at home. In analysing the EU as neither a fully postnational formation free of old national antagonisms nor a simple link in the chain of transnational economic interests, this book focuses on the synergy of systemic social and cultural exclusions on national and Europe-wide levels, reflected in its economic and immigration policies towards former colonies as well as Europe's peripheries and margins. The EU is neither just a super-nation – an assembly of nations – nor has it completely transcended the apparatus of the nation. Irreducible to either, it creatively sets both into play, while its increasing participation in neoliberal capitalist restructuring radically shapes the world still linked to it by (post)colonial ties. As its point of departure, then, this book takes a critical stance towards self-congratulatory multicultural imaginings of community in the EU that occlude neocolonial relations of dependence and exclusion; it analyses how the discourse of multicultural racism interacts with discourses of traditional biological racism; it considers the far-reaching effects of discrediting leftist politics or any other models of community not based on liberal citizenship that assumes multiculturalism. Since the EU slogan 'united in diversity' markets the union as a democratic, egalitarian, postcolonial encounter between Europeans and non-Europeans (or postcommunist semi-Europeans), we may ask to what extent it is different from or similar to old European colonial empires.

I combine the legacy of postcolonial theory as it was developed in decolonised locales with EU discussions of multiculturalism and globalisation in order to understand the current situation of Europe's postcolonial and postcommunist peripheries and migrants. This becomes especially significant in light of EU participation in what

Michael Hardt and Antonio Negri have described as a decentred logic of Empire: multinational establishment of the right to intervene, evident in world conflicts of the post-Cold War era. To complicate the EU's positive self-image,[1] we must question the EU union with NATO, its at least partial support for US-led wars after 9/11 and its radicalisation of anti-immigrant sentiment in the wake of violent attacks on its soil and the current crisis. If official multiculturalism dangerously overlaps with internal colonialism affecting migrant minorities, I am invested in exploring avenues of critiquing the EU 'imagined community' and in devising strategies for resistant, anticolonial ways of being.

In the chapters that follow, I address questions of migration, exile and multicultural communities in the EU via readings of cultural texts – performance art, literature and film – which offer imaginative possibilities of what, in *The Inoperative Community* [1986] (1991), Jean-Luc Nancy calls a (non)community of 'being-in-common' beyond dominant multicultural identity politics, interrogating difference as a cultural or ethnic property. A burgeoning field of studies grapples with EU multiculturalism,[2] especially as manifested in literature, cultural narratives and artistic exhibitions, but none of them offer a comprehensive theoretical analysis of the politics of community, nor are they sufficiently rigorously critical of EU neo-liberal capitalism and increasing social gaps between EU citizen elites, on the one hand, and postcolonial and postcommunist migrants, on the other. Moreover, few literary or cultural studies have explored the possibilities of EU identities that are neither broadly 'European' nor consistent with official liberal multiculturalism. Given that right-wing politics are gaining ground across the EU, it is imperative to think new, dynamic modes of transnational affiliation that complicate the static politics of the nation or even of multicultural identity groups. Thus, I analyse Europe's new reflections in the mirrors held up by imaginative texts which both explore the limitations of the official state of affairs and offer possible alternatives. While I do not accept the EU as an unquestioned good or a historical inevitability, I do not advocate a return to an allegedly originary or natural community of the nation state either. If the EU gestures, at least, to the promise of cosmopolitan citizenship and transnational 'contaminations' of all kinds, I wish to remind of mythical Europa's non-European, migrant background, taking cues from critical cultural narratives which reflect on (im)possible forms of democracy, hospitality and egalitarianism.

Europe, the impossible object of desire

> The fight over who or what is granted free global movement and the ways in which mobility, geographically and socially, across national and internal borders, is restricted and contained, follows patterns that are shaped but not determined by the logic of the nation-state. Movements of resistance, in the United States, Europe, and elsewhere have responded by creating structures both below and above the level of the nation in order to circumvent and counter their marginalisation. In order to grasp this complex interaction of commonalities and exclusions, scholarship will have to follow and move beyond the national paradigm and, in the European case, beyond the 'postwar' moment. (Fatima El-Tayeb 2008: 666)

While the enlarged EU is trying to make sense of itself politically, legally, economically and sociologically, literary and cultural studies remain, for the most part, circumscribed by either narrowly defined literature departments based on the nation state or a common language or in somewhat broader, but still limited, versions of national postcolonial studies and comparative literary studies. The institutional space in which to speak of literature and culture dealing with the EU is limited to European studies centres and departments, frequently to a few courses within the larger interdisciplinary programmes. Indeed, Europeanising the study of literature and other cultural narratives is a daunting, perhaps impossible task, not least because it hazards generalisations and suffers from the lack of linguistic expertise necessary for such a comprehensive project.

Moreover, one of the greatest complaints about the EU is that its discourses are dry, unimaginative and stripped of the possibility of affective affiliation, which makes them an unappealing object of cultural study. This could explain why, as Rita Felski observes, the scholarship on contemporary Europe has been developed largely by social scientists, overshadowing the role of 'the art historians, the literary scholars, the philosophers, the cultural critics' (2012: v). Also, the EU is often seen as little more than an economic skeleton yoking together nations steeped in their own separate mythologies and histories. Perry Anderson emphasises that the EU has arisen as an agonistic affiliation among nation states after World War II, and that this national(ist) foundation of the EU is in constant discord with federalist visions that push for a decentred European perspective.

Similarly, Yasemin Soysal wonders about the ways in which a common European identity can be forged given the domination of local models and national(ist) curricula. She describes how the German educational curriculum, for instance, downplays the nation in light of de-Nazification policies and instead promotes European values; in contrast, the French curriculum equates European civilisation with France and glorifies French national achievements (2002: 276–8). A corresponding anxiety about the possibility of European identity informed Anthony D. Smith's reflections, on the eve of Europe's unification, about European education models overtly promoting national ideals, which would make it difficult to create transnational affiliations among the working classes, peasantry and other broad segments of the population beyond the EU elites and technocrats (1992: 72). These arguments suggest that a cross-national study of EU literature and culture might not only be difficult but also misguided, since the dull project of European unification, unlike its nation states, has failed to win the hearts and minds of its residents.

A quick search on literary productions of the 'new Europe' predictably yields traditional national studies of Spanish, French, Irish and other literatures; studies of the European periphery, tellingly grouped together as 'postcommunist literature' or literature of 'the other Europe', and finally, national minority and postcolonial literary studies (such as Maghrebian French or Turkish German), which are sometimes combined in edited collections.[3] But just as 'postcommunist studies' has become a productive field of literary research, I argue that a similar logic should apply to EU literary studies. Postcommunism has become an umbrella theoretical concept that allows for fruitful discussions of (un)common memories, experiences and cultural production in the context of communist takeovers which effected a supranational, radical restructuring of one part of Europe. Similarly, the European Union is a contemporary unifying element behind not only material restructuring of much of Europe, but also symbolic reinscriptions of (post)national identity and community, which in turn engender new ways of thinking and writing about this space.

Here I am reminded of a humorous anecdote recounted by post-Yugoslav writer Dubravka Ugrešić about an Indian who moves to New York and writes a novel about Hungary. While a Hungarian intellectual complains that the novel is too Indian, a British publisher hopes that the writer will compose something truly Indian, or live up to what Ugrešić calls his multicultural 'identity kit' (2008: 146–7). The anecdote illustrates that there are already such proliferating literary examples, both in the EU and elsewhere, which do not fit into either the politics of the nation or multiculturalism as traditionally conceived. They write, as Azade Seyhan (2000) says, 'outside the nation', but in case of the EU, many also cognitively map Europe's official policies, aspirations and fears in this growing multi-ethnic and multiracial community, which commonly, if differentially, affect its member states. Reflecting on the necessity of writing outside the nation, Ugrešić concludes 'A language which would include the overlapping interests of numerous groups, trans-local solidarities, cross-border mobilisations and post-national identities does not exist yet' (2008: 149). This book hopes to contribute to the creation of such a language to make sure that Europe, in Rita Felski's words, 'emerge[s] as a theoretical problem' (2012: vi). While it also aims to reorient the discussion of Europe towards humanities, to offset its insufficient contribution to European studies in Felski's appraisal, this task would be impossible without drawing on the ample research in social sciences: numerous sociological, anthropological and political science studies ground my discussion of cultural narratives. In other words, my book poses Europe as a theoretical problem by fostering an interdisciplinary conversation between humanities and social sciences.

Despite laments over European identity's elusive, ghostly[4] or even non-existent nature, and the continued prevalence of national affiliation, both Europe as an idea and the EU as its political praxis do exist and infiltrate themselves in myriad ways in the daily lives and imaginations of European residents. The frequent observation that the EU is primarily a technocratic, neo-liberal, top-down project might explain the perceived indifference among the general populace. However, the complaints about the EU's democratic deficit should be taken seriously, especially as they imply that the circles of EU decision-making are not sufficiently accessible to populations on the ground. This deficit has been sharply highlighted during the popular referenda opposing the EU treaties and widespread anti-austerity protests. In most academic discussions, the nation state appears as a mooring point for unified Europeans, to which they return for allegedly authentic identity. This authenticity presumes that a federalist union with other nations will destroy some imagined specificity, give control to powers beyond the nation that cannot be easily reached

or imagined and possibly even 'contaminate' the nation with outside (multicultural) influences. This vein of reasoning, according to
Ariane Chebel d'Appollonia, accounts for a broad series of 'pro-
national European nationalisms' where the EU might be accepted
only as a further fortification of already existing, self-contained
national identities (2002: 180). Such European nationalists attempt to
'rescue' the victimised, beleaguered nation from the Goliath, 'widely
perceived supranational technocratic tendencies of the Union' (181).
Contrasted with this tendency, which relies on the 'false sacralisation of the nation', is cosmopolitan Europeanism which relies on
the 'false sacralisation of Europe' as a gathering of universal, Enlightenment values that transcend the nation (171).

However, the two visions, cosmopolitanism and nationalism, are
not mutually exclusive, as it might at first appear. This is not only
because the EU accommodates both cosmopolitan and national symbols in its official discourses and celebrations, but also because both
visions share a similar conceptual framework and philosophical sup-
positions. Most official accounts and histories of the EU rely on a
messianic progress narrative, which entails overcoming initial difficulties and past dilemmas, teleological movement to a brighter future
and downplaying rough patches along the way, including war, racism
and violence. This narrative closely echoes any traditional history of
the nation state.

As Nico Wilterdink observes in a probing theoretical analysis of
EU historiography, the attempt to intellectually forge a European
collective identity has led to the creation of a de facto nation of
Europe and a propagandist 'Euro-nationalist' narrative that justifies European integration. Just like a traditional account of the birth
of a nation, Euro-nationalism also focuses on teleological progress
from Europe's distant past to the present, 'uninterrupted cultural
traditions', 'unique characteristics and special achievements that
command the admiration of other nations', and 'major historical
figures and important events' (1993: 122). Simultaneously, Wilterdink argues, Euro-nationalism ignores the relations of power that
have determined intellectual and artistic achievements and downplays 'wars, oppression, and genocide' that do not fit into the ideal
national image (123).[5] Thus, it is epistemologically problematic to
juxtapose the EU to the nation state, as if they cancelled each other
out. In the best-case scenario, we are dealing with a false opposition,
and this book treats it as such.

If there is something called Europe, then, and if its images and principles gain real currency in the daily life of Europeans, we must explore how Europe imagines itself, given that the apotheosis of Euronationalism is not separate from the popular ideology of the nation state itself. 'Europeanness' is implicitly, yet consistently, invoked in setting up civilisational boundaries, fortifications from within and without the EU and various acts of policing non-European difference. Appropriating the almost invariably positive term European often becomes a populist, defensive strategy in moments of real or perceived crisis, to denote certain practices and groups as cosmopolitan, progressive, resourceful and distinct from their implied opposites. That Europe is a project of symbolic and not just economic fortification is evident from the official adoption of a *Declaration on European Identity* as early as 1973, which enshrined the Union as a bastion of individualism, democracy, law, justice and human rights (Passerini 2002: 194). While there have been many vociferous challenges ever since to the whitewashed Eurocentrism in these and other narratives of European identity,[6] we can also imagine how these symbolic coordinates of Europe filter into material, legal apparatuses of the EU, examples of which I will discuss later on.

As I write this, the EU is undergoing its most serious crisis yet, which coincides with the largest electoral gains by anti-immigrant, moderate to extreme right-wing parties across the continent since the 1990s.[7] Europe is the desired safe haven for economic migrants, war refugees and asylum seekers from the former colonies and postcommunist Eastern Europe. For some Europeans this promotes diversity and progressive politics, which undermines old Eurocentrism, while for others this threatens to destroy European values and standard of living. According to recent polls, when it comes to Eastern Europeans (as we witnessed in the hapless conversation between former UK Prime Minister Gordon Brown and prospective voter Gillian Duffy), fears are related to job competition and when it comes to non-Europeans, it is racial and cultural difference that occasions anxiety (Taras 2008: 92). Nonetheless, as we will see in the coming chapters, these anxieties cannot be so clearly delineated and categorised: for instance, economic fears of Eastern Europeans interact with the long historical legacy of racist attitudes to these peoples as less developed, civilised and democratic. Although each country in Europe deals with immigration in irreducibly different ways – tentatively speaking, some models include French assimilationism, to German 'equal but separate' approach, to British multiculturalism[8] – by analysing it on a purely national level we will overlook the extent to which this is becoming a European phenomenon, crucial to its contemporary articulations of identity and unity.

Thus, the most diverse groups of immigrants who happen to be from predominantly Muslim countries are increasingly treated as homogeneous 'Muslims', which not only reduces the complexities of their situations and backgrounds, but also calls attention to them as a 'problem' everywhere in Europe. Commenting on this recent reduction of identity markers for diverse populations of Pakistani, Turkish, Algerian and other backgrounds, Aamir Mufti warns:

> We need to be alert to the likelihood that the emergence of 'the Muslim' in Europe, to the exclusion of all other possibilities of self-description, linked though it is to massive social storms swirling beyond the continent, is in a strong sense a *European* phenomenon – that is to say, it is a spectre conjured up by the European project itself. It marks *the reinvention of minorities in Europe* in the decades following the dispersal and decimation of the continent's Jewish minorities. (2007: 22)[9]

It is productive to think about this discursive shift in light of Europe's past treatment of another seemingly homogeneous group, Jews. Matti Bunzl argues that there is a crucial difference between contemporary Islamophobia and historical anti-Semitism because Jews were seen as being racially distinct from ethnically pure European nations, whereas Muslims today are seen as threatening European cultural and religious identity (2005: 502).[10] While the veritably European dimensions of shared racist and xenophobic sentiments call for a rigorous inquiry into contemporary articulations of Eurocentrism, we must not forget how the nation itself promotes the cultural exclusions that replicate this discourse of European civilisation under attack. Ray Taras notes that European Jews were seen as outside the national body precisely because they were 'too' cosmopolitan, nomadic and scattered (2008: 96). If we extend this 'cosmopolitan' gesture to the horizontal naming of Muslims, which dehistoricises and uproots them, then they effectively become outsiders both in Europe and in the host nation. Especially in times of national crisis and upheaval, they are portrayed as nomadic migrants even when they have been living in the country for several generations. This symbolic migrant status suggests that they have always 'only just' arrived, excluding them from the common European history. This was evident, for instance, in the 2005 French *banlieue* protests: as Fatima El-Tayeb argues, the 'rioters' were portrayed in the media as a violent underclass that the nation doesn't recognise as its own, while, ironically, they were protesting precisely because they were French citizens asserting their rights (2008: 664).

The symbolic exclusion emerges also when Muslims and any other migrants and refugees are portrayed not as active political participants building the future of a common Europe, but rather as a 'test' of European tolerance or a 'problem' which Europe has to solve.[11] If migrants, whether postcolonial or postcommunist, are the problem, it is often up to them to shed whatever doesn't make them European: to de-culturise in order to assimilate to a monocultural community or to transcend their culture in favour of civic duty to a multicultural community.[12] In place of abolished national borders, Europe is erecting invisible borders based on visible minority status that can be implicitly racialised, but also determined by one's class or culture.

In dominant discourses, European identity is rarely treated as a theoretical problem or radically subjected to deconstruction; instead, even when Europe admits to its inherent violence, it portrays itself as having transcended it by learning from past mistakes. In the decades following the Cold War, which are the primary focus of this book, Europe has consolidated a common identity around its negative apotheosis, the Holocaust. The Holocaust is treated as a founding event of modern Europe, giving all Europeans who experienced the cataclysm of World War II common political and ethical guiding principles. While commendable, as I argue in Chapter 3, this overt focus on overcoming the Holocaust perhaps unwittingly extracts it from European history as an exceptional event unrelated to other nineteenth and twentieth century disasters, such as the genocides of colonialism and decolonisation. El-Tayeb argues that Europe tends to compartmentalise major historical events, '[provincialising] world wars, [externalising] colonialism and [dehistoricising] migration' (2008: 660), and such historical disassociation results in what Mufti describes as the contemporary failure to see migration as an 'after-life' of European colonialism (2007: 23).

The belief that Europe has been ethically humbled by its participation in the Holocaust and consequently matured into a global beacon of peace paradoxically helps to justify its renewed militarism under the auspices of NATO by invoking the Holocaust, especially the urgency of preventing any new Auschwitz. This, European, discourse of ethical legitimacy underlies much deadly humanitarian imperialism – including the bombings of Serbia, Iraq and Afghanistan – while aligning the Union ever more firmly with US foreign policy. A telling example of this ethical convergence on the European level was the first 2001 National Holocaust Memorial Day in the Great Britain, attended by Prince Charles and Tony Blair. As Lothar Probst describes:

> The commemoration ceremony, broadcast on television, started with a girl from Kosovo who lit a torch of memory. After that, two survivors of the Holocaust described the hell of the concentration camps, followed by reports of a teacher who escaped Pol Pot's massacre of intellectuals. (2003: 55)

Beyond commemorating victims of various genocides, this solemn parade of world misery legitimised Blair, and by extension his NATO partners, as a moral force committed to preventing new holocausts.

Non-imperial empire

While the discourse on European exceptionalism solidifies a new European identity, both reliant on earlier Eurocentrisms and seemingly edified by Europe's violent past, many economic and political practices of the EU continue to absorb the advantages of colonialism while conveying the image of equitability and concern about the world at large. Therefore, my book addresses not only the symbolic coordinates of Eurocentrism but also the material effects of neocolonialism in the era of neo-liberal capitalism consolidated by the EU's consensual empire. Externally, Europe's former colonial countries maintain relations of dependency and unequal power with the former colonial outposts; within the EU, relations of internal colonialism proliferate with respect to postcolonial, postcommunist and other migrants, where discrimination based on race, culture and/or religion increasingly overlaps with class contempt.

A meaningful, comprehensive denunciation of colonialism on moral and legal grounds has not taken place across Europe. While the EU prides itself on its overcoming and denunciation of the

Jewish Holocaust, the strategy of cautious silence or half-admission of colonial abuses is not merely a pragmatic attempt to stall requests for compensation. Indeed, it suggests that formerly colonised peoples cannot truly be heard in global political forums or taken seriously as damaged victims seeking a fair recognition of crimes committed against them. A virtual refusal to come to terms with colonialism was reflected in the EU's united front at the 2001 UN Durban World Conference against Racism and Xenophobia. The draft of the Durban declaration, as envisaged by the African bloc, would have included a detailed recognition of the various consequences of colonial crimes and demanded financial reparations for colonialism and the slave trade. Because EU countries (represented by Portugal), along with the US, opposed such provisions, the subsequent declaration omitted any references to financial compensation. In safely vague ethical terms, it stated:

> We acknowledge and profoundly regret the massive human suffering and the tragic plight of millions of men, women and children caused by slavery, the slave trade, the transatlantic slave trade, apartheid, colonialism and genocide, and call upon States concerned to honour the memory of the victims of past tragedies and affirm that, wherever and whenever these occurred, they must be condemned and their recurrence prevented. We regret that these practices and structures, political, socio-economic and cultural, have led to racism, racial discrimination, xenophobia and related intolerance. (*World Conference against Racism* 2001: 17)

That the concerns of the hundreds of millions of victims of Euro-Atlantic colonialism were eventually overshadowed by US victimisation in the wake of the 9/11 attacks (which took place three days after the conference) is indicative of the ways in which the (in)admissibility of suffering is affected by contemporary relations of power, determining whose lives are grievable, as Judith Butler explains in *Precarious Life: The Powers of Mourning and Violence* (2004). This event also foretold Africa's lack of bargaining power at the 2009 follow-up Durban conference, which also featured a relatively united EU front; by this point, African countries had given up requests for reparation.

The absence of a responsible confrontation with the legacy of colonialism enables Europe's continued economic and political policies of dependency and inequality in the former colonial locales, which are significant sources of its immigrants. As Étienne Balibar observes, it has been difficult to argue for the centrality of the 'postcolonial phenomenon' in Europe, because it has a 'fantastic need to preserve the colonial myths as an imaginary protection against decline, and a symbolic barrier against the integration of migrants of colonial descent into the "legitimate" community of citizens' (2016: 169). Such a compartmentalisation of the issues of colonial occupation and postcolonial immigration applies even more to those dominions that never fully gained independence. Neglected in discussions of European identity, for instance, are the various territories in the Pacific, Africa, South America and other continents which still technically belong to various EU nations and enjoy all EU rights but remain virtually invisible in discourses about European achievements. Moreover, such non-European European territories often serve as lines of defence, literal and symbolic, of European borders, since they are employed as military grounds for preventing illegal immigration to Europe 'proper'.[13] Thus, the EU exists suspended in an irresolvable philosophical and political aporia that depends on 'mobile' borders, in Balibar's terms (2016: 166), and on the convenient application of the signifier 'Europe': while the EU refuses to officially acknowledge countries that are outside its conventional geographic borders, its flags nevertheless adorn and claim many lands and resources that lie beyond. Commenting on this aporia, Peo Hansen asks, 'what are we to make of those member states that divide their location between continents; that is, those member states that are both European and African, both European and South American, and so on?' (2002: 490).

It is certainly in the EU's interest to promote the raising of living standards, stability and government cooperation in the former colonies, particularly those physically close to its borders, in order to stem the flow of migrants. The EU has therefore sought to foster political and economic partnerships, coming across as flexible, multilateral and open to dialogue. Since the publication of the so-called *White Paper* on economic performance and competitiveness in 1993, the EU has been fighting the world market war 'by other means'. At the time, in order to be competitive with the US and Japan, it tied to itself proximate international markets, creating a Euro-Mediterranean partnership, among others. This regional partnership encompasses numerous Mediterranean countries, from Lebanon to Tunisia, from Croatia to

Spain, seemingly decentring the EU and its interests. However, as Nivien Saleh explains, it is essentially a partnership that benefits the EU, as it 'locked the partner states into far-reaching market liberalisation without obliging itself to similar structural changes in Europe's agricultural sector. That the commission succeeded in doing so was due to its superior bargaining power' (2007: 80).

The EU employs various mechanisms of economic coercion, which appear consensual as they are often accepted and welcomed by its partners. Tunisia, for instance, cannot afford to reject EU terms and lose the enormous market that is the EU, whereas the EU will not be crucially affected by losing the marginal market in Tunisia. We thus arrive at several questions, which can only be answered if the postcolonial theoretical framework itself is revised to account for a structure like the EU: What is the nature of this new, consensual EU empire? How does it manage to appear consensual even when it is coercive? How is it possible to know where, between the extremes of desperate, powerless poverty and enchantment with Europe as a civilised non-empire, this infuriatingly polite consensus takes shape? How do we place into conversation, on the one hand, young Algerians who greet former French president Nicholas Sarkozy visiting their country by chanting 'visa, visa', and on the other, the government of Morocco that misunderstands Europe's terms by applying and getting rejected for EU membership?[14] The hegemonic desire for Europe likely depends on the widespread conviction that this is the best economic and political option and anxiety that there is no viable alternative to the EU, especially for peripheral European countries. Finally, much real and symbolic capital is purchased through affiliation with the EU, through being recognised for embracing European ideals.

Nevertheless, there is always a dose of romanticism associated with the new Europe that exceeds even this type of pragmatic explanation. British diplomat and EU official Robert Cooper's 2001 piece 'The next empire' is a case in point. In this apology for imperialism, Cooper laments the devastating policy of old European colonialism and argues against the nation state as a unit of governance because, especially in decolonised locales, it often subsists on corruption, economic ineffectiveness and anarchy. Because the need for 'outside authority' is greater today than it was in the nineteenth century, Cooper argues for a new and improved empire, represented by the IMF and other 'objective' world institutions. He proposes a 'system in which the strong protect the weak, in which the efficient and well governed export stability and liberty, in which the world is open for investment and growth' (24). His unsurprising conclusion is that the EU can offer such guidance to the weak, and this is described as 'voluntary imperialism' that entails a 'temporary loan of sovereignty' rather than its loss. In return, the EU offers democratic participation and economic stability; this ideal improvement over old empires of genocide and exploitation is dubbed a 'co-operative empire' or a 'commonwealth' (26). Similarly, in 2007, then President of the European Commission José Manuel Barroso praised the EU as a 'first non-imperial empire', based on a 'voluntary surrender of sovereignty, not military conquest' (Waterfield 2007: n.p.).

Empire is thus transformed into a model of sovereignty that is necessary as well as desirable, based as it is on alleged voluntarism and temporary loss of independence. Cooper's assertion that 'today there is no violence, only money' obscures the social violence of much financial restructuring under the auspices of the IMF, the World Bank and the EU (2001: 25). Europe is also seen as a benign empire by Jan Zielonka, who favourably contrasts the EU with nineteenth-century conquering, centralised, exploitative powers, while portraying it as a neo-medieval empire: 'a polycentric polity penetrating rather than controlling its environment. A multiplicity of overlapping military and police institutions' which will increasingly turn to a 'multilevel governance system of concentric circles, fuzzy borders, and soft forms of external power projection' (2007: 1). This empire, which Zielonka describes as a patchwork or maze of multiple allegiances rather than a fortress of absolute sovereignty, embraces new members by inviting rather than coercing; indeed, postcommunist countries accepted the invitation 'quite eagerly' (13). While Zielonka admits that the EU aggressively imposed accession rules to the East and that an enormous power discrepancy between old and new members existed both pre- and post-accession, he does not criticise the overall logic of a consensual empire that brings 'some order to unstable neighbours' or converts 'barbarians into "good" citizens' (13).

The focus on consensus and cooperation which passes for better imperialism, but imperialism nonetheless, has been highlighted in seminal texts that analyse the hegemonic structures of neocolonialism. In *Empire* (2000), Hardt and Negri argue that contemporary imperialism, which they see as a decentred, multicultural, overtly international yet unequal system of global governance 'is not formed on the basis of force, but . . . of presenting force as being in the service of right and peace'. Empire thrives on 'expanding the field of consensus' worldwide (15). For Jacques Rancière, who is concerned with the possibility of radical political subjectification for migrants and exiles beyond paralysing discourses of victimhood and 'not belonging', one must actively break the 'logics of consensus systems', which efface traces of fractures and dissensus and keep political action 'trapped in a pincer movement between state managerial police and the world police of humanitarianism' [1995] (2004a: 137). Perry Anderson (2009) criticises the politics of neo-liberal consensus that reigns over the EU, suggesting that its self-congratulatory discourses cast disagreement and debate as unwarranted breaches of decency.

If this new empire coerces through expanding the field of consensus, my book is committed to exploring dissent in that it seeks new forms of political subjectification which would challenge traditional identitarian loyalties and pinpoint possibilities for solidarity among those who desire transnational forms of belonging and egalitarian participation. It is especially crucial to break the consensus within empire itself in order to highlight and contest the conditions that make the practices of internal colonialism possible. The EU is not only safely guarded from the non-European world; indeed, its privileges are restricted through a number of concentric circles within and without, effectively locating the heart of new Europe in old colonial empires of Western Europe. At the outer edges of empire lie so-called third countries which have signed agreements with the EU to accept any asylum seekers that the EU refuses. The EU also keeps outsiders at bay through a system of custom tariffs and Schengen regimes. Just outside the EU border, prospective members must abide by accession treaties that largely rely on old colonial standards of civilisation, rule of law and development, defining Europe's margins as not-yet European.[15] Inside, workers from new EU member states can hit a wall, up to seven years, if they want to take advantage of the provision for the free movement of European labour. Such Europe-wide circles of inclusion/exclusion importantly interact with social hierarchies within each EU state individually.

While the neo-liberal turn has increased existing income discrepancies across the EU, my concern is primarily with the ways in which class inequalities interact with ones based on race and culture. In particular, in times of economic crisis, the term European is used to validate so-called true Europeans and put a face, sound, smell or another source of eccentricity to a non-European 'other'. This mechanism of civilisational differentiation applies especially to postcolonial and other non-European minorities and newly arrived postcommunist Europeans. It is used within these communities as well, as I argue in Chapter 4, to separate hard-working and law-abiding non-European minorities from 'terrorists' and 'fanatics'; or in the case of Eastern Europe, to distinguish between semi-Orientals with a passive, corrupt, communist mentality and real Europeans who have embraced the entrepreneurial spirit and individual respon-sibility. These types of cultural attacks justify the devastating con-sequences of Europe's economic restructuring and discriminatory job practices in both Europe's neocolonial metropolises and East-ern peripheries which create virtual pockets of internally colonised minorities.[16] Such (non)citizens have limited access to neo-liberal prosperity, education, mobility and consumer goods or democratic validation within societies in which they live.[17]

The EU appears as progressive because it provides increased economic opportunity to professional elites and educated middle classes. This upward class shift is also reflected in the fact that the EU no longer favours immigration of unskilled, uneducated labour as it did in the period of vast re-industrialisation after World War II, preferring, instead, specific university-educated cadres. Stephen Gill portrays these privileged workers as an 'oligarchic bloc' whose wealth is connected to global financial capitalism and who share the '*mentalities* of an emerging market civilisation of commodified production and consumption' (Cafruny and Ryner 2003: 6). The EU, the empire of capital, thus combines neo-liberal classism with Orientalism, which, as Ezequiel Adamovsky argues in his discussion of Euro-Orientalist attitudes to Eastern Europe, is a crucial part of liberal-bourgeois ideology (2005: 609). While Adamovsky primarily shows how this narrative of Western superiority regulates differen-tiations between the professional elites and less privileged classes in postcommunist Eastern Europe, its framework also applies to West-ern Europe, with symbolic hierarchies between European elites and impoverished non-European residents who are often not perceived as legitimate members of the national community. This is not to claim that social conditions in Bulgarian sweatshops and French *banlieues* are the same, but rather that, as singular actualisations of discrimina-tory EU politics and culture they must be brought into conversation. Europe today is an increasingly nihilistic empire because it places its bet on abstract market indicators such as economic growth and GDP, overlooking the variegated lifeworlds of its most vulnerable residents, whose declining education and life expectancy, and rising income inequality and exposure to violence cannot be meaningfully represented in public discourse.[18]

Moreover, postcommunist transitions to neo-liberal capitalism are characterised by semi-success, resulting in a rise of economic disparities between Eastern and Western Europe following de-industrialisation and liquidation of Eastern Europe's productive capacities. This process cannot be disconnected from the outsourcing of industrial labour from metropolitan Western European centres that resulted in scores of unemployed and impoverished citizens of postcolonial backgrounds. I suggest that we think contemporary European unification by placing into conversation postcommunist transitions and the disenfranchisement of postcolonial immigrant labour, as both events have been affected by similar neo-liberal policies. The EU thus establishes borders against and among a variety of second-class populations that have overlapping concerns. As Anikó Imre notes, these populations, be they Arab, Polish or Roma, become jointly racialised and classed through their excessive transgression against 'common European values', often through their 'spectacularly' bad cultural and political practices (2014: 133).

As Chapter 4 demonstrates in more detail, my book brings into conversation 'Second' and 'Third' World experiences of (post)coloniality so as to deconstruct the 'First'–'Third' World paradigm which has become dominant in postcolonial studies. Eastern European histories particularly illuminate the internal hierarchies that complicate the image of Europe as a coherent entity. For instance, while quite a few Western European states had overseas empires, much of Eastern Europe was in a colonial or semi-colonial position. We can consider Eastern European countries 'inter-imperial zones' where national histories were shaped by multiple imperial legacies, with a number of European and Asian empires (Austro-Hungarian, Russian, Ottoman) vying for either simultaneous or consecutive colonial control (Doyle 2014: 163). This is further complicated by the fact that Russia (like Spain or Italy), for instance, represented both an imperial power and an undeveloped colonial periphery in the eyes of its Western neighbours.

In this context, it is more productive to think about 'multiple Europes', the paradigm that Manuela Boatcă develops in order to challenge the notion of a 'single Europe' and highlight European countries' 'different and unequal roles in shaping the hegemonic definition of modernity and in ensuring its propagation' (2013: n.p.). For Boatcă, 'multiple Europes' entail various imperial and non-imperial Europes, so that the 'centre of modernity' is associated with the north-west hegemony of Europe ('heroic Europe'), while the Balkans and Eastern Europe become its inferior imitators ('epigonal Europe'). Because 'heroic Europe' ideologically sets the blueprint for the contemporary idea of 'Europe', monopolised by the European Union, my book focuses primarily on its colonial relationship vis-à-vis the 'epigonal' Eastern periphery, rather than on the earlier imperial legacies that have shaped this space.

I call attention to the EU also because coloniality in this space is often discussed in terms of past imperial legacies, most recently Soviet rule, so that the 'hegemony of anti-communism . . . results in naturalisation of the region's dependence from the European core' (Zarycki 2014: 31). This accounts for the EU's consensual enlargement, where Eastern Europe's assumption of belonging to the European racial and cultural family occludes colonial relations of dependence and justifies discrimination towards internally racialised minorities.[19] Unlike non-Europe, then, Eastern Europe hasn't been epistemologically constructed as entirely distinct from or oppositional to the European core. The difficulty of analysing coloniality in this space stems from its status as a semi-periphery rather than periphery, as quasi-Europe rather than non-Europe,[20] subjected to the violence of discursive 'hierarchies which are seemingly blurred, not easily admitted, implicit rather than explicit' (ibid. 5).

Mapping (un)common European belonging

The upheaval surrounding the French soccer team's mutiny against their coach and the ensuing démarche from the 2010 World Cup calls to mind Frantz Fanon's reflections on the paradoxes of racist thinking in *Black Skin, White Masks*. Writing about the ineluctable 'fact of blackness', Fanon says that one is praised as a black teacher or doctor to lend support to the colonial culture's liberalism, its alleged acceptance of the possibility of black intellectual advancement. However, as soon as this teacher or doctor makes a mistake, 'blackness' will be employed as a weapon: he (sic) is incompetent precisely because he is black [1952] (1967: 117). When France won the World Cup in 1998, its multi-ethnic team composed mainly of players who trace their background to the former colonies was hailed as an example of France's successful multiculturalism, its ideal of what was possible beyond the gloomy statistics of urban *banlieues*. After a similarly multi-ethnic team clashed with their French coach at the 2010 World Cup, their failure to deliver on French soccer hopes was blamed on their minority racial and ethnic status.

While many politicians, journalists and public intellectuals were cautious not to invoke either immigration or race, some 'blasted the players as "scum," "little troublemakers" and "guys with chick-peas in their heads instead of a brain"' (Erlanger 2010: n.p.). Conservative intellectual Alain Finkielkraut, who had already attracted criticism for complaining that the French team was too black, dismissed the soccer players as a gang of hooligans, little better than youth rioting in *banlieues*. This uncomfortably easy slippage of liberal multicultural rhetoric into racism and the degradation of the players' class mobility through a discursive return to the *banlieues* illustrates the limitations of the current models of multiculturalism in Europe which, whether of the assimilationist or pluralist variety, rest on a horizontal, static and interchangeable attribution of difference. Difference is assumed to be 'experienced' through official celebrations of different races or cultures, or through equally abstracted collective disparagements of what is perceived – and grouped – as 'other'. In both scenarios, we are dealing with cultural stereotypes, because, as Rey Chow argues *The Protestant Ethnic and the Spirit of Capitalism* (2002), we cannot define a culture without stereotypes, whether negative or positive.

I do not suggest that the EU should dismantle its multicultural lobbies, representative bodies or affirmative action policies where they exist, merely because they are based on pinpointing and offering help to different minorities.[21] Rather, multiculturalism need not exhaust imaginative possibilities for conceptualising a community immersed in a variety of religions, customs and languages. Identity politics that underlies multiculturalism is not only problematic from the perspective of poststructuralist challenges to traditional Western concepts of a self-present subject, an individual with a presumed essence and interiority, but also frequently acts to segregate and isolate rather than connect, both various minority groups and minority and majority groups.[22]

Assimilationism doesn't preclude the occasional labelling of nationals of immigrant background as 'inauthentic' nationals, just as pluralism can signal respect for cultural differences as well as maintain the segregation of 'others' from one another and from mainstream society.[23] Also, if multiculturalism hopes to achieve any radical transformation of European society, it must tackle the material inequalities associated with global capitalism and the legacy of colonialism: it must return to the question of class and consider this in a supranational context in which it unfolds, underpinned by the legacy of colonialism.

But even here we preserve the pesky fetish of culture, taken for granted and privileged over any other approach to understanding alterity: culture becomes a given, unified discourse about a group's identity, sacralised and internally consistent. As Seyla Benhabib cogently argues in *The Claims of Culture* (2002), the blockage of other (for instance, gender) claims to justice by waving the flag of cultural difference erases the history of power within any so-called cultural group, especially the privileged segments within any society who shape hegemonic cultural rules to be observed by all others. While this is not an argument against preserving the practices of one's culture, it is an attempt to dethrone its supremacy in favour of other types of fluid community affiliation and intimacy. Because culture, if such a thing exists, is asymmetrically negotiated, practised and disseminated, perceiving it as some-thing that the other simply 'has' and can 'use' to participate in the multicultural nation becomes a superficial approach to difference. This presupposes that difference can simultaneously be both singularly represented, embodied, as well as circulated as an iterable, recognisable, disembodied currency on the market of cultural diversity.

As Sara Ahmed argues, if one is to be legitimised by the multicultural nation, one must be in possession and use of such a currency: one must share one's difference liberally and, in return, love the other's difference. This multicultural mandate to love difference, Ahmed cautions, depends on the ideal image of the nation as egalitarian and tolerant, and thus implicitly on potential failure, by some, to love. In this self-serving gesture, the nation can legitimately scapegoat those who fail to share and/or love difference, accusing them of pathological narcissism (2004: 137–8). While Ahmed importantly deconstructs the repressive supplement of multicultural celebrations of diversity, I turn my focus to the problematic of understanding communication and intimacy within the nation primarily through the filter of cultural difference.

Culture both allegedly enables participation in the multicultural nation, mingling with others, and becomes a culprit for the failure to participate, keeping to oneself and a disinterest in others' differences. Difference *as* culture is what is visible, audible or in some other way representable by one's body, including one's technologies of speaking, writing or ritual – the racialised and gendered body itself is inscribed through the technologies of language. Culture, rather than anything else, thus becomes the prime mover of connecting with others, or conversely, the prime obstacle to communication. (How often do we hear that 'someone' seeks friends 'from other cultures'? Or that 'they' get along 'in spite of cultural differences'? Or that a marriage couldn't survive 'a vast cultural divide'?) This obsession with overcoming the cultural divide, or Samuel Huntington's clash of civilisations, overshadows other asymmetrical relations of power in the global playing field.

While not losing sight of culture, but rather treating it as a fluid and performative rather than essential or primary form of identification, the coming chapters interrogate the transcendental ideals of Europe still at work, offering readings of the burgeoning literature, film and artistic performances that both trace the contours of multicultural interactions and expose the limits of its 'grounding' identity politics. I trace the development of such cultural narratives over the last two decades, contemporaneously with the EU's expansion and consolidation. Being interpellated in a 'coercively mimetic' ethnic identity in the era of multiculturalism, for Chow, is also a way to achieve recognition, legitimacy and empowerment within a community and forestall what Slavoj Žižek defines as the terror of a 'radically open field of significatory possibilities' (Chow 2002: 110). If (multi) cultural production necessarily does away with this terrifying freedom – and helps one make sense of oneself through (both consensual and coercive) self-identification in the Imaginary – then it can also be replaced and/or combined with different forms of signification, new avenues of political subjectification. What emerges along the seams of a collapsing Imaginary order may not be necessarily destructive and abyssal, even if it is traumatic, but also productive of new forms of empowerment and potential affiliations. I am especially interested in alternative imaginings of community in Europe that glimpse the (im)possible ethics of hospitality and friendship, un-grounded and invested in being-in-common in a variety of ways despite not having common features (race, ethnicity, religion) or a teleological goal.

I set the stage for this line of inquiry in Chapter 1, which focuses on artistic interventions that performatively mirror the EU's preoccupation with representing itself as a progressive, postmodern state whose 'united in diversity' ideology aims to supplant national allegiances. Performance art opens up radical critiques of the traditional accoutrements of the state as such, including questions of exclusionary borders, definitions of political community and affective identifications and notions of belonging, all of which apply to the EU. Neue Slowenische Kunst's project NSK State in Time, Schleuser's marketing of 'professional human smuggling', and David Černy's installation *Entropa* inhabit politics as a space of art, replicating and exposing the limits of the EU state and any transcendental signifiers used as grounding concepts for the organic community this state claims to represent. Implying that a supranational Europe restages twentieth-century traumas of totalitarian politics, these artistic interventions embrace diasporic, displaced perspectives that not only interrogate extreme identity politics, but also confront Europe with its repressed heritage. However, while Černy and Schleuser stage trauma as the content of various state fantasies which need to be exorcised, NSK implies that trauma is contained in the very mechanisms of the state for which there is no cure. Finally, Černy's and Schleuser's innovative representational aesthetics gesture to a new conceptualisation of European community, which would take into account the variously disenfranchised multitudes unrepresentable by either discrete national or EU ideals. NSK, on the other hand, warn that representational strategies of even seemingly progressive political aesthetics always-already contain the potential to alienate the social body and impose a violent hegemony, as they did in the twentieth century.

Building on Schleuser's critique of European borders, Chapter 2 focuses on the necropolitical regime of external border policing immanent to the existence of the EU as a political and cultural space. Drawing on Achille Mbembe's 'Necropolitics' (2003), I address this zero degree of neo-liberal governmentality as the repeated creation of illegal migrant 'death worlds', or violent states of exception, in the name of protecting civilisation. Contemporary literature and film's recurrent preoccupations with the impossibility of a 'good life', disenfranchisement and human rights abuses in borderland states of exception suggest that an invisible war on migrancy has become immanent to the EU construction of sovereignty. These texts treat the borders as a threshold into 'Fortress Europe' rather than any specific EU country, portraying prospective migrants as new communities taking shape in the process of crossing, their solidarity based on a shared predicament rather than ethnic or racial background. Mahi Binebine's *Welcome to Paradise* (1999) and Laila Lalami's *Hope and Other Dangerous Pursuits* (2005) imagine spontaneous communities among various African migrants crossing the Strait of Gibraltar, juxtaposed to phantasmatic narratives of death and cannibalism that subvert the idealisation of Europe. Their hospitality to one another, along with mutual aid and compassion, announces the possibility of a future common cause in redefining European politics. In turn, the films *Eternity and a Day* (1998) and *Terraferma* (2011) imagine alternative, private hospitalities offered to illegal migrants in states of exception characterised by living on symbolic as well as economic margins of the EU. Disenfranchised European citizens who aid migrants challenge the government's monopoly on extending hospitality.

Chapter 3, in turn, analyses ways in which the history of colonial violence to Europe's 'others' perceived as external remains insufficiently acknowledged in hegemonic discourses and divorced from the analyses of contemporary violence to non-European migrant populations. The discursive erasure of colonial violence dates back to the beginnings of Europe's unification: as the post-war European Community proclaimed opposition to tyranny and totalitarianism, its member states carried on extensive military campaigns and committed numerous atrocities in their colonial empires. Addressing these historical omissions, novels such as Leila Sebbar's *The Seine Was Red* (1999), Jamal Mahjoub's *Travelling with Djinns* (2003) and Bernardine Evaristo's *Soul Tourists* (2005) make a case for a supranational focus on Europe's historical hospitality to 'others', especially the hospitality of official historical narratives to the existence and contributions of 'others' to the imagined communities of both the nation and Europe. They re-narrate distant and recent histories of the continent as always-already 'creolised', to borrow Françoise Lionnet and Shu-Mei Shih's (2011) term, where cultural and ethnic groups are never separate and distinct to begin with, but are mutually constituted and evolve through hybridisation. The novels develop contested histories as a site of dissensus (Rancière), which negotiates rather than blocks European unity, resulting in fragmented but relational histories that take non-European perspectives to bear upon European history. Simultaneously, these narratives move beyond the binary conception of European/non-European history, as non-European legacies are not treated as either a potential replacement of or supplement to the 'idea' of Europe.

The penultimate Chapter 4 creates connections between postcolonial and postcommunist migrant experiences in the EU, building common ground through their shared economic alienation from European prosperity and cultural exclusion from Europe's hegemonic value systems. After the EU's expansion into formerly communist countries, new economic migrants from the East have entered contact zones with established migrant populations from Europe's former colonies and faced similar prejudice to which postcolonial migrants have been subjected, often including a racialised component. To foster a dialogue between postcolonial and postcommunist studies over such shared as well as divergent experiences of colonisation, I employ a unified interpretive framework that explores worldwide effects of the Cold War ideology and undermines the traditional divide between 'Third' and 'Second' World studies. Enveloping Mike Phillips's novel *A Shadow of Myself* (2000) and Dubravka Ugrešić's novel *Ministry of Pain* (2005) and essay collection *Nobody's Home* (2008) in this interpretive contact zone, I ask how the experience of communism and decolonisation can be thought together in a united Europe, posing alternative imaginings of community that unsettle both mainstream multiculturalism and neo-liberalism. Phillips's novel interweaves the histories of African struggles for independence and Eastern Bloc communism to shed light on often neglected connections and interrogate the dominant imaginings of Europe today. In turn, Ugrešić uses the experience of Yugoslav socialism to remobilise discourses of class and identify neo-liberal mechanisms of exclusion that jointly marginalise postcommunist and postcolonial minorities in times of EU crisis.

The EU is often negatively compared to former Yugoslavia in that the breakdown of social solidarity and welfare state that resulted in Yugoslav civil wars is seen as prefiguring the EU's own demise. In Chapter 1, I show how NSK State in Time's analogies between the EU and former Yugoslavia imply, paradoxically, that former Yugoslavia's sociality-in-common is only possible when not monopolised by hegemonic representations of the state. In the concluding Chapter 5, I develop analogies between Yugoslavia and the EU that are not pessimistic, but rather cast the community that survives former Yugoslavia as an unofficial, uninstitutionalised community that offers alternatives to dominant state mythology, built around the absence of a common identity and a critical attitude to the state. After surveying the prominent artistic and cultural phenomena of re-membering former Yugoslavia, I focus on the Subversive Festival in Zagreb, which revisits the breakup of Yugoslavia by placing it in the context of European and global socialist initiatives and histories. Common threads in this remembrance of Yugoslavia – as cosmopolitan community shaped by common historical experiences; as being-in-common despite the absence of a common identity; and as a politics of dissensus (anti-fascism, anti-capitalism and Non-Alignment) – merit further analysis and discussion. By way of analogy, we might imagine the effects of such a politics of dissensus within the EU, where even the label European would no longer signify Eurocentrism and where the identity politics traditionally associated with individual European states would be critically assessed. Lastly, invoking Yugoslavia also represents a refusal to abandon the politics of socialist equality, the welfare state and solidarity, which underwrote the European unifcation project itself for much of the twentieth century.

As this thematic overview announces, the book places in conversation the historical theorisation of discrimination in postcolonial criticism and the challenges to liberal conceptions of the individual subject and its collective manifestations (such as nation or people) in poststructuralist criticism so as to overcome the impasse of the ontology of identity where the line blurs between postcolonial multiculturalism and neocolonial racism. I explore the imaginative possibilities of what Jean-Luc Nancy terms 'being-with' or existing *as* communication, which posits as primary the social aspect of existence, the being-together of singular presentations of alterities which collide, communicate and co-appear to one another. Community does not have to start with an individual who is then emancipated into belonging to a collective or a cosmopolitan awareness; rather, community can be seen as this 'praxis of staging' of the 'with' as a crucial aspect of existence [1996] (2000: 69).[24] Being-together is being singular-plural, necessarily exposed and exterior to one-self.

This type of being-with is a manifestation of what, throughout *Inoperative Community*, Nancy terms 'community without communion'. Rather than thinking of political community as a nation state or even a multicultural superstate like the EU, which still relies on the myth of common origins and shared ideals, the real challenge today is to conceive of community without a communitarian essence, and with an excess that cannot be recuperated into a supposed organic unity. For Nancy, this 'inoperative community' also doesn't 'work' according to the contemporary 'techno-economical imperative', which seems to be the only incentive to organise social existence (1991: 23). Its unworking, which neither starts with an origin (Europe as a cradle of democracy) nor teleologically moves towards a goal (Europe as a global economic and democratic power), 'encounters interruption, fragmentation, suspension' (31). The inoperative community echoes what Jacques Derrida describes in *The Politics of Friendship* [1994] (2005a) as the seemingly counterintuitive – and (im)possible – friendship to those with whom an 'I' has no filiation, whether biological, political or cultural. It is the vision of a community where, politically, one can love even those who refuse to love back, rather than designating them as the stain on the multicultural fabric of society, as described in Sara Ahmed's critique of liberal multiculturalism. For Derrida, who is concerned with the contemporary notions of borders and hospitality to alterity in European political discourse, such a politics of friendship also entails the thinking of unconditional hospitality, which would expand the existing rules of the 'restricted economy' of hospitality, offered on condition that guests behave well, are fully known and controlled or observe their proper place in society.[25]

While poststructuralist thought predates the founding of the European Union in its contemporary form, most theories of community shaped by poststructuralism referenced in the book develop either as Cold War divisions disintegrate or in the post-Cold War era, concurrently with the search for new European identities that accompanied the EU's own consolidation and expansion. Despite poststructuralist critics' European backgrounds, many further profound critiques of Eurocentrism, as we shall see in the coming chapters, especially as some of them have been subject to marginalisation and discrimination in their home countries due to their ethnoreligious identities. I draw on their philosophical contributions to critiques of European (post) colonialism, racism, fascism and anti-Semitism, while acknowledging the blind spots in some of their theories of community, primarily in terms of gender exclusion (for example, community conceptualised as a fraternity).[26] While poststructuralism is useful in envisioning alternative communities, un-grounded in identity politics, it is also productively interrogated and refined in my book by postcolonial thinkers who use its tools to deconstruct multiculturalism and racism, such as Spivak, Ahmed and Rosello.

Art that stages the potential as well as the aporias of the aforementioned alternative communities, non-identitarian affiliations and hospitable passages across the borders of Europe simultaneously acts as an incentive for resolving the issues that it takes up. As it calls attention to the contemporary problems haunting the EU superstate, it also gathers communities that become politically invested in the aesthetic paradigms that it innovatively infiltrates into existing 'distributions of the sensible' (Rancière [2000] 2004b: 12). This praxis of community staging is perhaps most readily apparent in highly public performance art and artistic-political events discussed in this book, which incited lively debates among temporary communities they engendered, including accidental and intended general audiences, political officials and art critics. However, this political dimension is contained in other genres as well, including literature and film, where aesthetics overturns the reigning regime of the sensible, an established system of forms of social experience that determines who can speak and in which role, as well as what, precisely, can be seen or heard. Aesthetics is indivisible from politics because politics, as Rancière suggests, is dynamically informed by new aesthetic forms explored in art: 'the logic of descriptive and narrative arrangements in fiction becomes fundamentally indistinct from the arrangements used in the description and interpretation of the phenomena of the social and historical world' (2004b: 37).

Art, therefore, invades politics through figurations of enunciatory possibilities among its political subjects. If community is exposure, exteriority or figuration, whether using symbolic or any other aesthetics, then art necessarily calls into question existing representations of community and helps to expand its cognitive possibilities. It contributes to the formation of 'political subjects that challenge the given distribution of the sensible. A political collective is not . . . an organism or a communal body. The channels for political subjectivisation are not those of imaginary identification but those of "literary" disincorporation' (2004b: 40). This is crucial to the strategy of disagreement and disidentification from one's habitual group, which challenges the established reign of consensus.

This materialist conception of the significance of artistic intervention has also been inspired by Gilles Deleuze and Felix Guattari's notion of art as the production of new sensations – affects and precepts – as intensities with their own being which exceeds the 'subject' who experiences art, so that 'we' are no longer 'in the world' but rather 'we become with the world; we become by contemplating it' (1996: 169). This nonhuman becoming of art brings into contiguity 'sensations without resemblance', creating zones of 'indetermination, indiscernibility' (173), echoing Mary Louise Pratt's (1992) notion of the 'contact zone' as an uncertain convergence point of a (post)colonial encounter from which something new can emerge. This, however, does not occur according to the logic of mimesis as resemblance or identification with 'the other' understood as a liberal subject, but through the contiguity of becoming-together, the splitting of consensus and opening out into the realm of infinite – and potentially dangerous – possibilities. Art is the mobilisation of intensities through which we transform both 'our' body and the world. Writing on this dynamically materialist conception of art in Deleuze, Elizabeth Grosz observes:

> What painting, music, and literature elicit are not so much representations, perceptions, images that are readily at hand, recognisable, directly interpretable, identifiable, as does the cliché or popular opinion, good sense, or calculation; rather, they produce and generate sensations never before experienced, perceptions of what has never been perceived before or perhaps cannot be perceived otherwise. (2008: 22)

While Deleuzian articulations of art as a generation of sensation and affect moves away from the (overly intellectualised) notion of concept, image and representation, I want to underscore, vis-à-vis the earlier discussion of Rancière, the importance of this generative dimension of art as well: the new aesthetic possibilities that affect the future mappings of the social field. My book is committed to exploring alternative conceptions of the community and citizenship in Europe which not only complicate identitarian, multicultural politics, but also entail an opposition to all forms of institutionalised and reactive violence of (post)colonialism and neo-liberal capitalism. The narratives that offer imaginative possibilities for affective solidarities among disparate groups around shared concerns can help articulate a new, anticolonial Europe resignified from the bottom up and reflecting a progressive transnational public sphere. I treat such narratives neither as broadly diasporic nor as narrowly hybrid, since such approaches create connections primarily between 'original' and 'adoptive' countries/cultures as well as among the 'diaspora' of the same cultural or other filiative group, while keeping groups that are already segregated by some multicultural standard symbolically isolated from one another. Rather, I approach these narratives as singular contributions to a subaltern transnationalism which emerges in a new form after the Cold War, with differential re-colonialisations of both postcommunist and postcolonial populations and territories.

As Étienne Balibar notes, colonial 'administrative methods and habits' were naturalised in Europe 'when dealing with immigrants not merely from the former colonies but also from the "South" (for example, Turkey or Portugal) and Europe's "Oriental" margins (for example, communist Eastern Europe)' considered as external to Western values (2003b: 39). The contemporary discourse of 'imperial unification', in which assimilation and differentiation are only apparently contradictory, carries out the new civilising mission of categorising and managing 'cultures' and 'ethnicities' which then compete for the status of an 'emancipated' nation (ibid.). This horizontal gesture of official multicultural imperialism, then, also fosters divisions among the managed ethnics, conducive to the global capitalist divisions of labour as well as antagonisms between domestic and immigrant labour. Within and without the EU, postcommunist, postcolonial and other populations waiting in line to be 'emancipated' are also united through an erasure of complex histories – for instance, by downplaying Europe's colonial tradition or by reducing communist legacies to narratives of authoritarian oppression – in favour of a teleology of capitalist development as the only chance at liberation from the past. It is therefore important for literary-critical production to resist replicating the divisions of this hegemonic regime and work on creating innovative connections among heterogeneous groups.

My project, then, moves flexibly between national and transnational affiliations, individual and community concerns, without presupposing a teleological move from the former to the latter. The individually 'rooted' narratives under consideration contextualise, and thus relativise, the nation with its imagined spaces and historiography within the EU, and by extension, a transnational milieu. The traumatic nodes of European (un)belonging – hospitality across borders, heeding of colonial history, politics of friendship beyond multiculturalism, radical subjectification of the disenfranchised – are not located along the lines of identification with alterity, as the articulation of a common human essence. Rather, they emerge in an (un)common, egalitarian struggle that overcomes the impasse of not belonging (as well as tropes of exile, unbelonging and in-between-ness which often appear in postcolonial and diasporic literary scholarship). Connecting the disparate concerns of the marginalised beyond the logic of ethnic/cultural identity or the framework of the nation state performs what Ernesto Laclau (2007) praises as a populist strategy, which universalises particular struggles via 'popular' demands of the politically undomesticatable *plebs* and disrupts regular procedures that rely on recognised avenues for voicing 'democratic' demands of a legitimate *populus*. Populism thus conceived is inadmissible in regular political channels: it splits the consensus of democratic politics, but because of its sheer volume and force, the *plebs* comes to represent the legitimate part of the *populus*, rather than remaining in the background as those who do not belong, dismissed as only making noise.

The book is an intensification of this noise to the point where it can be understood as legitimate political language. Europe's largest challenge today is a confrontation with that part of itself perceived as unclean, inefficient or in some other way disorderly because it thwarts desired economic and democratic progress. In the name of symbolic health, its mechanisms of political and military control create the illusion of separation from that which is dysfunctional and relegated to countries beyond the borders, immigrant neighbourhoods, socially insignificant jobs or refugee camps. However, Europe's self-immunisation is increasingly proving unsuccessful. Its neocolonial afterlife, perhaps, means that the problems of colonialism will ultimately have to be resolved on European soil itself.

Chapter 1

Performing the State: Artistic Re-Presentations of European Community

This is what is at stake in the new version of [EU] federalism: the relation between legitimacy and people. We cannot avoid questioning the lack of the former without asking who the European people is. Is it the European peace movement? This is insufficient and we are still faced with the dilemma, when we come across the Bismarckian position (with Nietzsche): the state is the people. This solution would create a statist idol and repress social conflict, what Gramsci called a passive revolution. That is not an active revolution, i.e. a party of the movement of the multitude, because in Europe we fear the masses, governments are terrorised by the idea that the masses might participate. (*Étienne Balibar and Antonio Negri* 2004: n.p.)

Like any other state, the EU has had to invent its people: it shores up support for its project by encouraging and disseminating a collective identity beyond what is exhausted by the national mythologies of each member state. Often this is done through a variety of cultural projects that cut across borders and represent the sheer diversity of peoples, styles and current topics, attracting large audiences outside of the restricted circuits of EU technocracy. Nonetheless, such attempts to foster a dynamic, new culture are frequently strained because of the unresolved relationship between the new EU state and the new EU people that Balibar discusses. For instance, it is unclear how we might imagine the EU as a multicultural and egalitarian state, as its official imagery suggests, when it is frequently criticised as a top-down, neo-liberal economic project, promoted by EU technocrats. These complaints about the EU's democratic deficit should be taken seriously: they suggest an ever-widening gap between the circles of EU decision-making and the populations on the ground, as seen after the popular referenda opposing the EU treaty and widespread protests in Greece, Spain and other countries in recent years, where the people refused to be represented by the state, effectively overturning the statist idol.

Perry Anderson argues that, constitutionally, the EU is a caricature of a democratic federation, since its Parliament 'lacks powers of initiative, contains no parties with any existence at European level, and wants even a modicum of popular credibility' (2009: 23). For Rob Kroes, the EU is the 'end of Europe,' where people have no affective affiliations with the political community of 'New Europe' and are in 'anguished search for more meaningful frameworks to define their citizenship' (2008: 25). The EU often comes across as politically disenchanted and emptied out of meaningful collective identifications; symptomatically, it struggles to represent itself. While some think the EU offers too little in terms of affective affiliation, others think it offers too much: stressing the 'united in diversity' motto, for instance, leads to ambiguity and overflow of meaning, which translates into 'an inconsequential celebration of peaceful cultural understanding, rendered even more irrelevant by the limitations within the borders of Europe' (Sassatelli 2009: 35).

This chapter will delve into artistic interventions which parasitically emulate the EU's preoccupation with promoting itself as a progressive, postmodern state whose 'united in diversity' ideology aims to supplant supposedly outmoded national(ist) allegiances. I turn to recent conceptual and performance art which can help us articulate radical critiques of the traditional accoutrements of the state as such; these include exclusionary borders and definitions of political community, along with affective identifications and notions of belonging, all of which continue to be embodied by the EU.[1]

First, I would like to touch on two broad and fluid strains that dominate contemporary representations of the European superstate: narratives of European exceptionalism and narratives of multicultural diversity. While official multiculturalism certainly thrives through programmes, commissions and institutions meant to ensure cultural interactions and sensitivity to 'otherness', I am interested not so much in this institutional dimension as in the guiding mythologies of EU's imagined community – or, how the EU narrates itself.

Simultaneously, it is necessary to interrogate the transcendental ideals of Europe that were historically employed to promote Europeans' civilisational exceptionalism and that still haunt much of its public life: from official political statements to cultural celebrations and the design of the euro currency.

As Monica Sassatelli observes, 'Europe is contemporaneously thematised as a place, a history, a concept and a subjectivity', as the many visual images of Europe suggest, from the mythological representations of the 'abduction of Europa' to anthropomorphic maps where Europa is pictured as a 'powerful queen' (2009: 22). Contemporary Eurocentric imaginings of an exceptional civilisation portray Europe as connected through a deep-rooted cultural and historical unity – a vision of specifically European 'diversity', as it were. Among common denominators of this identity are the legacy of Hellenic philosophy and art, Roman law and institutions and Judeo-Christian religious ethics. They are combined with the experience of the Renaissance and the Enlightenment and the modern discourses of democracy, human rights, freedom and progress.

A beautiful example of both Eurocentric exceptionalism and a top-down approach to collective identity is reflected in the design of the euro currency, commissioned by the European Monetary Institute. The euro is not only a functional, economic tool of financial unity in the guise of a single capitalist market, but also a repository of symbolic ties that make up Europe's identity, embellishing a relatively unromantic process of integration and endowing it with almost magical significance. Jean Baudrillard says that the EU is necessarily mediated and simulated by signs like the flag, anthem and the euro, the 'magic' of symbols that 'make the thing exist' (Sassatelli 2002: 524). In this respect, the European Union is not too different from traditional nation states. The euro currency exhibits a conservative European federalism that both transcends and accentuates individual national traits. For instance, the coins all have a front, European, side common to the countries that circulate the euro, whereas the rear side reflects whatever the individual member state decides represents its greatest historical and cultural achievements. These often invoke easily recognisable, traditional symbols: royalty, coats of arms, heraldic animals, symbolic objects, significant political slogans, historical and cultural monuments, famous artists and freedom fighters and typical natural landscapes (Fornäs 2008: 129–30). In contrast, the banknotes feature abstract and universalist images of connecting: bridges, windows and other gateways portrayed do not exist in reality but nonetheless reflect major European architectural styles, ranging from classical, Gothic and Renaissance to baroque and modernist. As Johan Fornäs observes, missing from these representations are histories of European colonialism, slave trade and contemporary mass migrations; also, while women remain marginal, children and the working classes are altogether omitted (136).

This triumphalist discourse of European cultural achievements also implicitly underlies the annual 'Cultural Capital of Europe' event. In terms of selecting participating cities, this event has become more geographically and artistically inclusive, featuring European cities like Reykjavik and Bergen which are not in the EU, cities like Istanbul that are not entirely European and cities in prospective Eastern European member states. However, this strategy does not question the mythology of European urban sophistication, but rather demonstrates the supposed permeability of its borders in its generous act of acceptance of 'otherness', its universal applicability to cities beyond its reach. The event speaks to the tension between the myth of continental exceptionalism – where cities compete for symbolic belonging to the European community – and the EU's own desire to appear multicultural and diverse. Unlike the euro design, this event emphasises the multicultural: many annual exhibitions, for instance Copenhagen 1996 and Rotterdam 2001, explored the relationship between Europe and non-European minorities, immigrants, various marginalised groups and colonial histories. To an extent, these cultural celebrations have focused on culture as collaboration, process of becoming and negotiation of community, rather than as a static identity marker or object to be displayed.

The 'Unpacking Europe' Rotterdam exhibition, in particular, carried hope for radical interrogations of the concepts of culture and diversity beyond liberal identity politics. In light of these developments, I partly disagree with Gerard Delanty's disparaging critique of this attempt at fostering a European identity as just another 'pathetic exercise in cultural engineering', akin to Euro Disney or the Eurovision Song Contest (1995: 128). However, such artistic interventions at the Cultural Capital event are still contained by the ubiquity and broad valorisation of the label European: even if abstract, this term is nonetheless associated with a positive and unquestioned good.

According to Yasemin Soysal, the emphasis on European 'dialogue, conflict resolution, human rights and intercultural understanding' takes Europe for granted; as a result, 'European project's necessity and furtherance' go unchallenged (Soysal 2002: 272). Because of such a conservative containment, Europe is, in the words of Jean Baudrillard, a project of the elite minorities: a 'pseudo political event' (Sassatelli 2002: 527).

The artistic interventions this chapter discusses – the NSK State in Time project, David Černý's sculpture *Entropa* and Schleuser's campaign to legalise human trafficking – complicate this unquestioned acceptance of Europe as a positive signifier. They present the European Union as a pseudo political event, whose transnational, multicultural image harbours – even depends on – colonial-era discriminatory practices, right-wing militancy and aggressive economic policies. These artists, aside from interrogating the EU from positions that are marginalised and/or diasporic according to Europe's imagined geography, do not make political art, but rather 'make art politically', to invoke Thomas Hirschhorn's distinction (Cohen 2012: 105). Usurping the political space of representation monopolised by the state, they model and replicate various features of political community and discourse which the European superstate engenders so as to draw attention to its own attempts to represent itself, expose its imaginative lack and gesture towards alternative possibilities.

Spectres of *Entropa*: the European Union's crisis of self-representation

The difficulties surrounding the EU's self-marketing as democratic and multicultural became particularly obvious in the unfolding of a seemingly insignificant artistic scandal caused by the often-controversial Czech artist David Černý. Černý's sculpture *Entropa*, commissioned to mark the Czech Republic's presidency of the Council of the European Union in 2009, ostensibly replicated European national stereotypes, igniting a number of diplomatic conflicts, after which the artist admitted it was a hoax meant to test if Europeans can laugh at themselves. This inability to laugh – and the solemnity required of imagery representing the EU – symptomatically forecloses substantial philosophical and political re-thinking of the European community on the supranational level, the urgency of which Černý's intervention, in fact, emphasises. The EU slogan 'united in diversity' makes Černý's references to national stereotypes, anxieties and colonial histories almost obscene and superseded. The sculpture unapologetically stages Europe's dis-avowed racism and identity boundaries, suggesting that the diverse EU 'people' is little more than a sum of solipsistic and xenophobic European nations. Simultaneously, in its extreme replication of Europe's identity politics, this sculpture demonstrates the concep-tual containment of a bottom-up, subaltern transnationalism that cannot either voice or represent itself.

Entropa is an eight-ton sculpture in the shape of a European map, composed of twenty-seven individual country representations as Lego-type building blocks. Černý, EU supporter,[2] considers this a single sculpture that suggests European (dis)continuity, rather than twenty-seven separate sculptures, no matter how distant and hostile the countries portrayed seem to their neighbours. Subtitled 'stereotypes are barriers to be demolished', *Entropa* openly lam-poons member states. Most notoriously, Bulgaria is represented by a squatter-type 'Turkish toilet'; Poland by Catholic priests planting a rainbow flag in a replication of the famous World War II photo of US soldiers raising their flag in Iwo Jima; Romania is a Dracula theme park; Germany is comprised of autobahn strips in the shape that distantly resembles a swastika; Lithuania is a line of soldiers urinating on Russia; and Italy is a group of soccer players perform-ing acts of sexual self-gratification on their soccer balls. Černý's own country is represented by an electronic ticker tape featuring quotes from Czech Eurosceptic President Vaclav Klaus.

What this veritably Frankensteinian sculpture suggests is not so much that the EU is merely a political replication of old Euro-pean nation states, but rather that it is, perhaps, fragmented and unrepresentable outside of the politics of national and/or cultural identity, as the sculpture imagines the EU primarily as a hori-zontal, geographical conglomerate of national blocks and their stereotypical features. The sculpture evokes the EU ideology con-ceptually, suggesting that the EU supplies in the empty space of collective identification the historically discriminatory, transcen-dental ideals of Europe, like the ones the euro currency showcases. These ideals, though different in content, conceptually resemble the old compilations of European national stereotypes as well – in fact, such stereotypes are the obscene, racist underside of embellished national ideals. The difference between the euro currency and *Entropa* is that the former implies a foundational European unity that harmoniously gathers all individual national achievements into a transcendent, supranational civilisation, whereas the latter highlights disjunction, discontinuity and discord: the very constructed nature of Europe as a desired common signifier, permanently elusive. Černý's Europe is entropic and monstrous: evoking the description *Frankenstein*'s Creature, the individual parts do not make up a neatly or aesthetically fitting whole, but rather preserve their quirky singularity and independence, at the cost of egalitarian non-specificity.

Reflecting on the sculpture, Černý says that he and his friends started out with the question, 'What do we really know about Europe? We have information about some states, we only know various tourist clichés about others.' He continues, 'the art works . . . show how difficult and fragmented Europe as a whole can seem from the perspective of the Czech Republic' (2010: n.p.). This democratic deficit on the imaginative level and obliviousness to other countries' diverse quotidian, demotic public spheres reveal how difficult it is for ordinary people like Černý to imagine their role – as well as agency – within the EU. Once the hoax was exposed, Černý admitted that he and his two friends constructed all the sculptures and made up the supposed artistic collective that collaborated on the sculpture, together with their elaborate biographies. These biographies mock Europe's predilection for established artistic credentials and big city backgrounds: some of the invented artists seem rather obscure and exhibit only in rural regions or distant provincial towns, instead of metropolitan cultural meccas. Inspired by *Monty Python's Flying Circus* and *Borat*, Černý and his friends also contextualise each sculpture through absurd yet pompous statements by their creators, posted next to each piece. For instance, the sign for Italian soccer fields reads: 'It appears to be an autoerotic system of sensational spectacle with no climax in sight', whereas the sign for Bulgaria describes the toilet as a 'punk gesture, intentionally primitive and vulgar, fecally pubertal' (Lyall 2009: A6; Bilefsky 2009: A8).

By undermining both cherished national ideals and famed metropolitan centres as major points of national identification, *Entropa* nonetheless suggests that the idealised nation and

metropolis remain dominant mini-units of Europe-wide identification. What is being staged for the audience – and what, perhaps,
contributed to the anxiety over this sculpture – is conceptual and
imaginative impoverishment, an (im)possibility of representing
European community as an immanent, unpredictable, collective
process rather than as prescriptive correspondence to a priori
determined (national or European) transcendental ideals. Therefore, the artist's image of Europe appears as a timid repetition
with an insignificant difference, which contains, instead of giving free reign to, conceptual experimentation with ideas about
community and society. Rather than dividing up Europe through
vertical identity politics of the sovereign nation or culture, Europe
might also be thought through, for instance, common transnational movements, cross-cultural affective affiliations and interactions or social and economic exclusions from national and
European ideals or achievements.[3] *Entropa* obviates such bottom-
up, democratic imaginings of community; for the most part, it
also simplifies the social layers, inequalities and asymmetries of
power within and among European nations. As Fornäs concludes,
Černý depicts the 'naturalisation of national identity', where each
nation is represented 'as a closed unity, effectively cut off from all
others' (2012: 1).

If Černý thus emulates Eurocrats by unimaginatively enshrining
culture and/or nation as a ready-made artistic unit whose 'essence'
must be represented, then he necessarily, always-already trades in
clichés. Though the stated goal of the sculpture is to demolish stereotypes, such an explicitly multicultural commitment to overcoming
negative representations of alterity is often philosophically paralysed
by its own respect of difference understood as a static, em-bodied,
identitarian category. Consequently, even presenting a positively
valorised cultural difference would fall victim to the same problematic of stereotyping: any attempt to define a culture necessarily relies
on rhetorical generalisations and simplifications. Rey Chow argues
that in such multicultural representations, 'however benevolent and
complimentary' the perspective is, the differing ethnic groups under
scrutiny are bound to be

> products of a certain kind of gaze to which they are (pre)supposed
> to play *as*, to act *like*, to exist *in the manner of* something. This
> something may be an idea, an image, or a stereotype, but the point

remains that the objects under scrutiny are dislocated and displaced to begin with, and subordinated even as they appear as themselves. (2002: 100)

Chow focuses primarily on the objectification of an 'ethnic' self to explore the process of Third-World cultural production – 'Asianness', 'Africanness' – from the perspective of seemingly neutral, 'non-ethnic' European sociological discourse. However, I would like to extend this concept to the multicultural production of national identity within the contemporary European Union, which, of course, combines and sometimes overlaps with the asymmetrical cultural productions of minority 'ethnics' within and across dominant national groups. In this process, a group is expected to live up to a positive identity that has been coined through stereotypical generalisations. This virtual self-mimicry becomes internalised through *'unconscious automatisation, impersonalisation* . . . in behaviour as much as in psychology, of certain belief, practices, and rituals', because solidifying a stable identity also gives a group a sense of legitimacy, recognition and empowerment in a multicultural community (Chow 110).

From this perspective, the nations most angered by *Entropa*, Bulgaria and Poland, tried to ban the sculpture from being exhibited not because they thought that any representation of national identity was in and of itself epistemologically problematic. They were offended because, instead of idealised national brands that could be used to solidify one's currency on the European cultural market, *Entropa* delivered unflattering national clichés. Betina Joteva, first secretary for the Bulgarian office to the EU, said of the sculpture: 'I cannot accept to see a toilet on the map of my country. This is not the face of Bulgaria', implying that there *is* a more acceptable face of Bulgaria to be represented (Hines and Charter 2009: n.p.).

Bulgaria's official reaction was much more vehement than, for instance, UK indifference to the fact that their country was altogether absent from *Entropa* (under the pretext of the UK's mythical indifference to the EU). However, Bulgaria, unlike the UK, is in a disadvantaged position on the EU market of multicultural stereotypes: like other postcommunist Eastern European countries, it has had to 'rediscover, redefine, and manifest [its] identity' for Western cultural markets and cultural studies alike, in order to overcome, as Boris Groys argues, entrenched, racist stereotypes about communist art (2008: 156). Bulgaria thus has to find and aestheticise a cultural identity that fits the EU's 'colourful diversity' by avoiding all things communist and oriental associations with backwardness (that is, Turkish toilet practices) (151). Groys offers a sharp critique of Western treatment of communist art and highlights the resulting unequal status of Eastern European postcommunist artists in art markets: under the gaze and pressure of international cultural standards, these artists must engage in acceptable 'rediscovery' of 'essence' and self-mimicry along the lines defined by Chow. In this way, Černý replicates, ad absurdum, this marketing of identity; moreover, as an artist working in both Czech and EU cultural circuits, he addresses the unequal situation of Eastern European artistic production as well as its broader contextualisation in the EU's multicultural politics.

It is intriguing that Černý's preoccupation with the politics of national representation echoes much modernist avant-garde art: at times sanctioned by the extremist political regimes it supported, such art similarly traded in positive and negative European national stereotypes. *Entropa* perhaps unwittingly invokes Italian Futurists' 'Synthesis of War' which praised Italy together with other 'Great War' allies and degraded German culture as rigid and unimaginative. It also recalls British Vorticists' 'Blast Manifesto', which placed itself on the side of aggressive masculinity and fascist discipline, blasting English and French philosophical snobbishness, dandyism and effeminacy.[4] The uncomfortable conclusion that insinuates itself here is that postmodern multicultural marketing of national identity repeats, albeit in a seemingly more benign manner, what Barrett Watten defines as 'nativist' tendencies in modernist avant-gardes: 'conservative, hysterical or paranoid, even protofascist motifs' including 'racial fantasies' and 'hypermasculinism and radical sexuality', which effect an authoritarian revenge of displaced cultural norms (Noland and Watten 2009: 20).

Watten contends that European nativist avant-gardes met their counterpoints in the 'contact zones' of non-European colonies and other peripheral locales: here, European avant-garde sensibilities assumed to be universal were displaced by differential diasporic perspectives and the aesthetics of political and racial alterity (19). As with other artists discussed in this chapter, Černý's own cultural production could be seen as diasporic in this sense, since Czech art is situated as peripheral to European art proper, tasked with carrying out a legitimising 'return' to Europe post-1990, whence it will be judged by European standards. *Entropa* invokes the legacy of European avant-gardes through a defamiliarisation of nativist fantasies while suggesting, simultaneously, that the EU depends on such fantasies, including one of setting up its own 'universal' standards of artistic legitimation. If anything, Černý's *Entropa* results in a satire of conservative values associated with traditional nation states as it evacuates any possibility of positive national identification from which other nations could be judged as inferior. Such a diasporic vision, therefore, consists in the impossibility of return to a particular nation, Czech or otherwise, or to any apotheosis of nativist values. Černý sees Europe without idealisation, linked in an endless chain of mutual suspicions and internal strife. Finally, like the lacklustre biographies of fictional rural artists who built *Entropa*, Černý's diasporic position does not live up to Europe's 'universal' artistic standards.

Discussing his politically incorrect satire, which officially posed as a 'playful analysis' of stereotypes by 'artist-provocateurs,' Černý emphasises 'the difficulty of communication without having the ability of being ironic' (2010: n.p.). Before it was exposed as a hoax, the official booklet for the piece available from the Czech Ministry of Foreign Affairs appealed to Europe's celebrated tradition of prickly, ironic artistic sensibility: 'Self-reflection, critical thinking and the capacity to perceive oneself as well as the outside world with a sense of irony are the hallmarks of European thinking' (ibid.). But in the wake of widespread consternation at *Entropa*, Europe demonstrated that it is unable to laugh at itself; while the sculpture made Černý a folk hero in his own homeland, official Eurocrats, for the most part, haven't embraced its satire and irony. In addition to the impossibility of representing Europe outside of the logic of reified cultural clichés, *Entropa*, then, stages another impossibility: of ironic aesthetic that would undermine the high seriousness and solemnity of official EU discourses and build potential for innovative discursive articulations of community. In postmodern fashion, Černý's irony highlights the necessary displacements and distortions of representational politics as such, pushing the reductive logic of identitarian 'essence' to its limit.

The scandalised responses to the sculpture, which nonetheless weren't uniform,[5] imply that EU political ideology prefers a carefully circumscribed, auto-immunising dose of playful aesthetics. For this reason, Černý insisted on staging his project initially as 'activist art' that 'balances on the verge between would-be controversial attacks on national character and undisturbing decoration of an official space' (2010: n.p.). The EU officials in Brussels expected and embraced apparently mischievous 'activist art' in an auto-immunising gesture that would help affirm their image of aesthetic open-mindedness. European art markets demonstrate similar democratic allegiances precisely by balancing contradictory, controversial and multidirectional art trends, simulating the idealised image of complete artistic freedom. However, as Černý describes, the controversial art that was supposed to pique one's intellectual curiosity while effortlessly gracing official EU space 'suddenly degenerated to an unhindered display of national traumas and complexes' (ibid.).

The excessive disturbance caused by *Entropa* poses the necessity of theorising the line between desirable 'activist art' endorsed by – and in turn legitimising – EU ideology of artistic tolerance and the kind of art that works with as-yet politically incorrect European themes and representational regimes. *Entropa*'s fate reveals the need for greater aesthetic and intellectual space in official EU celebrations for irreverent invocations of national and European traumas, including intolerance of alterity and paranoid fears of one's neighbours. If we reflect on *Entropa*'s portrayal of Holland – a flooded land where only minarets rise above the water – we could also read Černý's sculpture as an attempt to exorcise and cure such national complexes. However, instead of facing and speaking to the ghosts, the preferred mode of exorcism too often banishes their existence altogether. In the case of the euro design, immigration anxieties, the unacknowledged afterlives of colonialism and rising social inequalities are invisible, while *Entropa* offends because it portrays the aforementioned motifs in an exclusively negative way, instead of gradually but surely dissipating their accumulated tensions in a teleological move towards idealised multicultural coexistence.

Entropa also mobilises the question of the relationship between art and politics, particularly when art deals with representations of the EU: to an extent, such art is expected to aestheticise political ideology rather than figure as an event that would create a radical rupture in representational strategies. *Entropa* received virulent criticism also because it was seen as tasteless and useless art, instead of operating, as writer Slavenka Drakulić notes in an essay that defends *Entropa*, as 'a propaganda tool' (2009: n.p.) Drakulić's observation implies that, in official EU circuits, commissioned art cannot simply be for art's sake, blissfully useless and indifferent, as the belief in the possibility of apolitical art might suggest. The contemporary desire for art as propaganda confirms Groys's contention that 'ideologically motivated art is not simply a thing of the past or of marginal ideological and political movements' like communism (2008: 8). He continues, 'Today's mainstream Western art also functions increasingly in the mode of ideological propaganda. This art is also made and exhibited for the masses, for those who do not necessarily wish to purchase it' (ibid.). But while communist art is habitually dismissed on moral grounds, art made under market conditions is rarely analysed as propaganda or subjected to a similar moral scrutiny.

'Professional human smugglers': critique of neo-liberal mobility

While *Entropa* registers the imaginative impoverishment of Europe-wide and individual national ideals that are recycled in representations of the 'new' supranational EU, the German-based collective Schleuser take the EU to task for its paradoxical combination of dissolving and strengthening the concept of state borders. As I argue in the introduction, the 'Fortress Europe' image is strengthened by the many concentric circles of EU external border policing, of which walls and fences erected to stop undesirable immigrants are just one example. On the other hand, the EU carried out an unprecedented dissolution of internal state borders, enshrining the mobility of goods, money and people as its official motto. While some EU countries are reinstating border controls in the wake of recent terrorist attacks on their soil, it seems as if this internal EU balance is being adversely affected by events seen as external to the EU. These events, ranging from the US-led 'war on terror' and the 2008 world economic crisis to uprisings and wars in North Africa and the Middle East, have resulted in increasing pressures on the EU to accept refugees and asylum seekers. Nonetheless, such crises appear as isolated, temporary and/or linked to other global trends that no country, including the EU, can be spared, as if they merely implicate the EU rather than being critically enabled by EU's own politics and economics.

The reinstatement of internal borders in times of such crises – by overhauling the Schengen regime or checking passports at borders – is justified as a temporary, exceptional measure. But as the artist collective Schleuser suggest, the heavy regulation of borders and immigration in the EU which helps preserve the interior as a seemingly self-contained political entity is the condition of possibility of such crises, which become the rule rather than states of exception. Schleuser pose the question of EU borders and regulation of mobility as the defining question for Europe's future political community. They draw attention to the meticulous systems of enforcing the EU's physical and symbolic borders in order to shift the terms of discussion away from the frequent scapegoating of both illegal migrants and their smugglers.

Formed in 1998, Schleuser critique both hegemonic representations of illegal vs legal border crossing and regulations controlling the movement of migrant labour in the EU. Schleuser is made up of three Munich-based artists: Farida Heuck, Ralf Homann and Manuela Unverdorben. Appropriating and détourning state-produced images and slogans in a Situationist style, Schleuser announce that they, pursuant to the ideals of free trade, support the movement of labour and goods in a globalising Europe and seek to professionalise the smuggling of migrants across the border. Their Federal Trade Association for Undocumented Travelling emulates neo-liberal corporate rhetoric through PR campaigns and posters, as well as legitimising 'seals of approval' that confirm their 'expertise' at human smuggling. On their website, Schleuser explain that 'the Seal of Approval confirms general quality criteria' that already exist for the documented travel market and that 'exclude profiteering, or coupling of the travel market with the employment market' because 'Profiteering is, of course, prohibited in Germany' (2007: n.p.). If one legalises the undocumented travel market, one will not only benefit the community by offering services at 'a reasonable price', but also avoid the callous profiteering usually associated with human trafficking. The discourse of legalisation, efficiency and professionalism effectively creates a smokescreen of business legitimacy which obscures the fundamental capitalist dynamics of profiteering.

While outrageously claiming that illegal trafficking should become legal, however, Schleuser are actually not erasing the difference between seemingly opposite things, but rather highlighting already existing grey areas within global capitalism, or what Aihwa

Ong describes as neo-liberal 'exceptions' to business as usual. In this definition, neo-liberalism is a flexible technology of governing used to include 'some citizen-subjects' in 'new spaces that enjoy extraordinary political benefits and economic gain' and exclude 'migrant workers', for instance, 'from the living standards created by market-driven societies' (2006: 5, 4). Thus, even if there were 'honest' smugglers who only charged a cost-based price instead of profiteering in the most reprehensible ways from illegal trafficking, they wouldn't be too different from the legal headhunters who, as Ong demonstrates, recruit Filipino and Indonesian maids to work in middle-class residences in Singapore and Hong Kong or subcontract Indian IT engineers in the US Silicon Valley under overtly exploitative and discriminatory labour conditions.

In Schleuser's case, the exception may not be an employment-market situation which demands that a certain type of ethnicised labour be exempted from existing immigration laws; rather, the exception here is the absence of legal documentation required for safe border crossing. This strategy implies that the EU discourse of mobility is similarly fraught by highly layered and hierarchical modes of actual mobility as determined by the vagaries of the neo-liberal market. Such hierarchical modes of travel, according to which some migrants are welcomed and others are left to die in the Mediterranean, are lampooned in Schleuser's comparison of migration to different classes of travel. Warning prospective customers that the media might misrepresent their superior services, they say 'the media like to compare pears with tomatoes, say, a luxury smuggling with a dumping price package tour' (2007: n.p.).

While professionalising human smuggling might only be the latest grey area to be recuperated into legal business practices, this performative gesture of arguing for the legalisation of *every* moneymaking enterprise, no matter how problematic, also pushes the logic of neo-liberal capitalism to its limit. Once there is no longer an outside to global capitalism, even in the form of apparent illegality, one might be able not only to maximise profits, but also do away with scapegoating. Clearly this is impossible because the system can never absorb every business practice, but also because it depends on the creation of enemies out of marginalised, vulnerable populations, such as human smugglers and illegal migrants. More importantly, Schleuser call not only for the legalisation of undocumented travel but also for its 'deregulation', or exemption from state control:

Deregulation is just as urgent here as in other fields of the economy, since the development of border management is readily presented as a four-stage model in economic terms: 1. Deregulation, e.g. of the Iron Curtain and for the purpose of globalisation; 2. The demand for state regulation to secure markets captured; 3. A demand for subsidy to avert the mistaken decision embodied in regulation; 4. Finally, insolvency owing to lack of competition. (2007: n.p.)

The very unthinkability of such a policy – which subjects the purview of state politics entirely to global economics – highlights the fact that EU state borders, far from being deregulated, are in fact strengthened and vigorously guarded in the era of allegedly free movement. Schleuser thus demonstrate that the EU is not so much a radical interrogation of the project that is the state but rather its apotheosis. Schleuser performatively 'side' with the discourses of global capitalism to emphasise the inconsistencies and blind spots of the current regime of 'regulated' border management. Their overidentification with this discourse comes across as more heartless and startling than the more familiar appeals to compassion through stories of migrant 'victimisation and fateful biographies' (2011: n.p.). Such representative clichés – desperate migrants ill-treated by greedy human traffickers and/or repressive border patrols – inform a variety of liberal perspectives on the topic, without questioning the symbolic value of the imagined safety of the state and the sacrosanct role of its borders.

Consider, by way of contrast, the activist video game 'Frontiers: You've reached Fortress Europe', which was funded by the European Cultural Foundation and designed by the Austrian artist collective 'gold extra' in order to increase public awareness of illegal immigration.[6] Here, 'activist art' complements the work of NGOs in promoting human rights. While the game allows players to identify with either illegal migrants or EU border patrol officers, and highlights the dangers of illegal migration as well as the brutal treatment migrants receive at EU borders, it does not address the very conditions that lead to illegal entry into the EU. Europe is seen as a sentimental object of desire, always elusive but clearly preferable to the stereotypical poverty and civil wars that illegal migrants flee. Europe's historical responsibility and contemporary role in global capitalism that systematically impoverishes other parts of the world goes unmentioned.

Taking a different approach, Schleuser explore marginal interstices of unofficial art and politics, insisting that they are neither
'an NGO plunging in where state agencies cannot reach' nor 'a
group of artists bent on accumulating cultural capital' (2011:
n.p.). They echo and overidentify with EU discourses on borders
and mobility, but like Černý, cannot be comfortably co-opted into
'activist art' because they haunt, rather than complement, both
official political discourses (including those of NGOs) and recognised 'activist artists'. Instead, Schleuser describe themselves as
a 'a working platform', which, often in collaboration with other
organisations, complicates rather than provides clear-cut representations of the symbolic meanings of borders, migrancy, legality
and European democracy. However, Schleuser do help and market
affiliate organisations that give 'direct legal and other assistance
to undocumented migrants and raise awareness of the migration-
control policies and practices of state entities' (Gram 2007: 209).
One of them, for instance, is the 'Refugee Council of Schleswig-
Holstein', which provides help to migrants and also publishes the
quarterly magazine *Der Schlepper,* in which it raises awareness
about the fates of deported migrants.[7]

Moreover, Schleuser parasitically and creatively insinuate themselves into official spaces that figure as both immutable signs of
EU citizenship and national politics as well as transitory spaces
of travel and border crossing. For instance, when the Art Association of Munich suggested that Schleuser 'offices' temporarily
relocate to the Munich Hofgarten, they eagerly embraced the offer,
arguing that:

> Ambience is not unimportant when it is a question of exuding unob-
> trusive influence. The Munich Hofgarten with its historic references,
> its direct proximity to the state's administrative offices and other
> lobby organisations such as the advisory board of the Union (conser-
> vative Bavarian political party), is ideally suited. (2007: n.p.)

The Hofgarten is not only a park surrounded by various political offices but, as a former court garden, also harbours associations
with aristocratic Germany, and, housing a monument to the exe-
cuted members of the White Rose, with the history of Nazi persecution. Schleuser exploit such symbolic re-inscriptions of politicised
space by collaborating with other artists on exhibitions that trace

the tense history of human smuggling – from (un)official channels of border crossing during World War II to the West German tradition of 'Escape Aid' during the Cold War – and compare past laws on international refugees to current treatments of migrants, asylum seekers and refugees.[8] Artistic practice here usurps the political, confidently claiming its designated space, as Schleuser operate as an unofficial 'lobby' which '[tests] artistic possibilities for action in the context of state authority symbols' (2007: n.p.).

Schleuser also explore the significance of actively experiencing certain political and social processes on an aesthetic level. Many of their art installations take place at 'train stations, airports, subways, and highways: public spaces in which travel, mobility, passage, and the public sphere intersect with one another' (Gram 2007: 204). In their 2004 installation entitled *Transitwelle*, small FM radio transmitters were placed in one of Munich's major tunnels. Each microtransmitter 'was set to broadcast on the radio frequencies of the most popular radio stations in the city, thus hijacking for a few minutes the broadcast spectrum of a given radio station' (Gram 205–6). When entering a tunnel, drivers would hear Schleuser programming about German and EU immigration policies and the politics of human passage. This strategy, which relies on temporarily and unpredictably commandeering regular media that disseminate information, takes part in shaping the public sphere in Germany and by extension the EU. It also disorients drivers by blurring established boundaries between those who comfortably traverse public spaces as citizens or legal aliens and those who are subjected to a haphazard, subterranean existence as illegal immigrants. The hidden existence of the millions of illegal aliens in the EU is suddenly brought to public attention in a rather startling and uncomfortable manner: the drivers have no choice unless they turn off the radio, which overtly emphasises their participation in this system. By hijacking the drivers into the world most of them ignore on a daily basis, Schleuser establish an inextricable connection between the official and unofficial, legal and illegal, rule and exception.

To highlight this fluid relationship between legality and illegality, as well as the multiplication of real and symbolic borders within the EU, Schleuser's installation at the 2008 Unfair Fair in Rome invited visitors to use the provided sticky tape to mark any borderline that '[hinders] undocumented traveling or the freedom of movement' (*Unfair Fair Catalogue* 2008: n.p.). Schleuser members are fascinated by EU mechanisms of replacing and multiplying borders: internally, state borders are replaced with 'frontier control posts' deep inside state territory; externally, border checks extend thousands of kilometres beyond the official EU frontier. In the business of human travel, policing responsibilities are expanded to include everyone involved, even 'airlines and shipping companies' (2011: n.p.). Like the drivers in the tunnel project, the visitors to the Unfair Fair were actively encouraged to reflect on the experience of restricted mobility and, by extension, on their own roles in policing and establishing borders. As they mimicked state apparatuses, Schleuser asked them to contribute to archiving such experiences by making a snapshot of the tape they've used, writing a brief description and sending it to the Imaginary Border Academy, a project initiated at the Artivistic gathering of artists and activists in Montreal in 2007. This Academy 'strives to cultivate a non-hierarchical pedagogical approach to understanding, subverting and undermining borders' and is 'a mobile and tactical space where the latter is undertaken'.[9] The Schleuser installation not only demonstrates that mobility is heavily regulated but also that borders themselves are mobile and inconsistent. As a result, any pedagogical and political engagement with them must likewise be adaptable and resourceful.

Schleuser's participation in Unfair Fair suggests their preference for marginal, alternative and unofficial art events. The Unfair Fair was a shadow art fair coinciding with two new official art fairs, ARTEContemporaneamodernaROMA and ROMA, while in no way formally associated with these events; however, it did 'have a strategic relation to the mainstream economy they represented'. The organisers explain:

> Whereas the raison d'être of the contemporary art fair may be characterised by maximisation and accumulation, the conditions of the UNFAIR FAIR relate more comfortably to the states of minimisation and disintegration. The aim of the UNFAIR FAIR is to show the process of artistic production and transitional art works that index broader practices by each of the invited artists. (Unfair Fair 2008: n.p.)

Similarly, the Imaginary Border Academy was created at the 2007 Artivistic gathering which, carrying the designation 'gathering' and not 'exhibition' or 'conference', suggests an interdisciplinary spirit of democratic and non-hierarchical collaboration. This subversive, questioning spirit also permeates the Academy's manifesto on borders, which demands: 'Spaces of clarity, relation, consensus, communication, exchange . . . The opportunity to know our limits and push them' and 'The creation of hybrid zones and identities'. For instance, the Montreal Artivistic project explored the topics of indigenous spaces, ecology and space activism. From the perspective of traditional state apparatuses for enforcing borders, the notions of hybrid zones or even spaces of non-hierarchical consensus and exchange that would complicate fixed boundaries sound controversial; however, it is important to develop such projects aesthetically and philosophically in order to question what Rancière describes as the dominant 'distributions of the sensible' (2004b: 12).

All these examples show that Schleuser's overt target is the racist symbolism surrounding the criminalisation of migrancy and ascription of (il)legality which has been gaining ground in right-wing discourses. Schleuser also problematise the apparently liberal initiatives that argue for everyone's right to unrestricted mobility and work on the basis of human rights or other ethical discourses. The mobility of labour is crucially tied to the neo-liberal capitalist distribution of employment opportunities, and as such, Schleuser suggest, any attempt to champion it needs to be situated in a political context in which people have no other choice but to be constantly on the move, contributing to the brain drain and general depletion of labour in their countries of origin.

According to Hardt and Negri, the ideology of the world market thrives on circulation, mobility, diversity and mixture, while establishing new differences and hierarchies (2000: 150, 154). In that sense, neo-liberalism depends on establishing exceptions in its discriminatory attitude to labour mobility. The contemporary emphasis on 'hybridity' and 'difference' in fact corresponds to the logic of the neo-liberal market; we should instead strive for a stable place of residence or at least the 'right to determine one's own desire for mobility' (155). That mobility should not be blithely translated into 'freedom of movement' is also affirmed by Žižek's astute analysis of the psychological acrobatics that the increasingly insecure neo-liberal market demands of workers: for instance, losing one's job is often euphemised as an opportunity to reinvent oneself professionally (2002: 86). By extension, then, a disastrous situation in one's country of origin could be seen as an 'opportunity' to travel and live in a different culture.

Ole Gram praises Schleuser for their nuanced employment of the term mobility, but is nonetheless suspect of

> Schleuser's radical moral cosmopolitanism in which the right to human travel is seen as the one abject form of mobility that advanced capitalist economies cannot countenance. Schleuser's anarchic embrace of travel can seem dangerously close to a type of anarchistic moral puritanism in which local, familial, or national loyalties are jettisoned in favour of an unthinking celebration of a universal personhood dancing on the ruins of postnational capitalist empire. (2007: 211)

However, Schleuser do not necessarily advocate mobility as an uncontested good; similarly, they are careful not to employ the discourse of hospitality to foreigners as a universal ethical duty because it would be the gentle, obverse way of endorsing the type of neoliberal mobility that enables global capitalism. On the one hand, they take the neo-liberal mantra literally – mobility of goods, money and labour – and overidentify with it to demonstrate its hollowness in the face of restrictions placed on the bodies and affects of people on the move. On the other hand, Schleuser explore the possibility of delinking mobility from the notion of work opportunity: they desire the possibility of undocumented travel 'free of any value'. On their website, they describe illegals as 'free agents' whom Schleuser neither wish to represent nor 'fill a paternal role in championing their interests', distancing themselves from the often paternalist roles played by NGOs. Refusing to ascribe a common motivation to diverse migrant endeavours, one which could serve as the foundation of a human rights movement, Schleuser argue that:

> Migration is autonomous, or in other words that each person decides individually as to why he/she wants to go from point A to point B, to use passage C or to cross border D. Every ABCD of travel is as a matter of course laden with connotations, whether these consist of yearning, denial, utopia, resentments, joie de vivre, poverty, sickness, gaining distinction, making sense, etc. (2011: n.p.)

Schleuser are more interested in the possibility of freely determining the conditions of one's movement, as Hardt and Negri might say. While much movement is still linked to economic opportunity, they argue that it does not exhaust the field of motivations for crossing borders. In this way, xenophobic EU discourses which represent illegal aliens as people who are 'taking our jobs', benefits or other resources reductively circumscribe the field of human possibility to crude economic existence. In contrast, Schleuser imagine the possibility of moving from a restricted to general economy of undocumented travel, to invoke Georges Bataille's concept of expenditure outlined in *The Accursed Share* [1967] (1991). The general economy designates a notion of symbolic or economic expenditure – excess – beyond the restrictive ethics of debt, calculated exchange or productivity. When extended to undocumented travel, this general economy would suggest the possibility of going beyond the criteria of economic rationality, moral exigency or political expediency applied to migrants to evaluate whether they are welcome or not. In a general economy of undocumented travel, a prospective migrant might be approached as a complex person overdetermined by diverse motivations for travel, free of the ascription of value and in control over their mobility.

Perhaps most importantly, Schleuser consider contemporary policies on undocumented travel in the context of European, especially German, history, to rethink the notion of European belonging and foreignness in a continent increasingly gripped by anti-immigrant sentiment. They remind that movement, the ability to escape across a national border into a safe haven, 'was seen as a great privilege' and 'as a lesson of history' given Nazi persecutions in World War II, but since the 1990s, 'government and public administrations in the states of Europe have been acting to dissolve this human right' (2007: n.p.). Schleuser also invoke the term *Fluchthilfe* or 'Escape Aid' which, in West Germany, connoted an ethical duty to help East German citizens escape during the Cold War.[10] They highlight uncomfortable resonances between the current discourse on immigration and the patriotic rhetoric of East Germany which considered 'Escape Aid' a criminal act. In addition, Schleuser draw parallels between contemporary discourses on immigration and the 'terms and images drawn from Third Reich propaganda' which are 'being dusted off' and updated in a Europe that experiences a neocolonial afterlife in the guise of mass immigration (2011: n.p.).

State in time: Neue Slowenische Kunst's community without community

In the final part of this chapter, I explore Situationist-type interventions of Slovenian artist collective Neue Slowenische Kunst, whose strategies, like Schleuser's, include an absurd overidentification with and a *detournement* of both communist and capitalist rhetoric and a collapsing of their differences to create a utopian opening towards a different type of political community. In the performative wor(l)ds of NSK, art demands fanaticism: art becomes both the fanatical, total art of living (with an original philosophical outlook, rhetoric, style of dress and/or habits) and the exposure of the fanaticism of ordinary, everyday life in late communism and postcommunism. The intervention of this avant-garde aesthetics in the last twenty years makes for NSK's uneasy relationship with NATO, the EU and global capitalism.

Neue Slowenische Kunst occupy diverse taboo spaces, and consequently, do not fit into either dissident or mainstream artistic positions. The collective does not aim to gain acceptance by artistic or political establishments, which is a radical stance since so many discussions of postcommunist art have focused precisely on measuring the liberal spirit of the newly democratic states based on their readiness to accept previously controversial artwork. As Groys suggests, postcommunist artistic practices are characterised by an extension of the communist paradise, in which 'everything is accepted that had previously been excluded', so 'it is a utopian radicalisation of the Communist demand for the total inclusion' (2008: 170). Instead, NSK operate on the margins of artistic practice by inhabiting politics as a space of art to interrogate existing models of the state and community. The apotheosis of this project becomes the NSK State in Time, which replicates and exposes the limits of the state and any transcendental signifiers used as immanent, grounding concepts for the community the state claims to represent.

Neue Slowenische Kunst is an 'organised cultural and political movement and school' established in 1984 in Slovenia (then part of socialist Yugoslavia) to unite the music group Laibach, fine arts and painter collective Irwin and Scipion Nasice Sisters Theatre into a single organisation (NSK 1991: 53). Later, other 'departments' were added, such as the design and promotion sector New Collectivism, the Department of Pure and Applied Philosophy and Cosmokinetic

Theatre Red Pilot. Perhaps the most prominent and internationally popular portion of this collective has been Laibach, which put NSK on the map in Yugoslavia in the 1980s and inspired a veritable cult following around the world ever since. Frequently, Laibach concerts paved the way for other NSK actions and exhibitions, so here I will focus mostly on Laibach's role in highlighting NSK's critique of Europe, NATO and global capitalism, as I connect this to the NSK project of a State in Time.

NSK rely on an overidentification with dominant political and cultural discourses that effects its own manipulation of signs rather than assuming an oppositional or marginalised position in society, itself vulnerable to manipulation: 'All art is subject to political manipulation . . . except that which speaks the language of this same manipulation' (1991: 18). In this respect, NSK interviews, website posts, statutes and philosophical statements persistently highlight this manipulation and performativity of language, at once satisfying the public hunger for testimony from NSK about what they 'really' mean and undermining this possibility of separating language as a mask from 'real' thought presumably 'behind' it. In their first public appearance in 1983, on a Slovenian cultural and political TV show called 'TV Tednik' ('TV Weekly'), Laibach appeared dressed in military uniforms, and, addressing the question about the suicide of their first singer Tomaž Hostnik, they testified by opening with a quote from Hitler: 'Art is noble mission that demands fanaticism, and Laibach is an organism whose goals, life and means are higher – in their power and duration – than the goals, lives and means of its individual members' (Groys 2008: 133). This announces one of the subjects of their manipulation, Nazi art, but other subjects are 'industrial production . . . totalitarianism . . . and, of course, disco' (NSK 1991: 44). Such a methodology, also described as the principle of 'monumental retro-garde', freely combines avant-garde symbols of Russian Futurism, Suprematism, Socialist Realism, Western pop music, industrialism and Slovenian nationalist mythology.

As Alexei Monroe asserts, 'Laibach's use of language is terroristic in that it is explicitly designed as a disorienting, alienating device as violent as its sounds and images' (2005: 66). By forming an assemblage of artistic and political elements which preclude the pinpointing of their 'real' attitudes, art and politics collapse into each other, not to imply that Russian Futurism is the same as Nazi art, but to highlight their collusion in what Laibach describe as the goal of their concerts:

> Terror as therapy and as a principle of social organisation . . . the effective disciplining of the revolted and alienated audience; awakening the feeling of total belonging and commitment to the Higher Order . . . by obscuring the intellect, the consumer is reduced to a state of humble remorse, which is a state of *collective aphasia*, which in turn is the principle of social organisation. (NSK 1991: 44)

Laibach necessarily recreate a totalitarian rally atmosphere at their concerts to make strange what Guy Debord [1967] (1995) identifies as 'the society of the spectacle'. At the same time Laibach themselves are spectacular, because they operate on the aforementioned 'principle of social organisation' – and as Jean-Luc Nancy says, 'There is no society without the spectacle because society is the spectacle of itself' (2000: 67). For Nancy, therefore, for a society to exist, it must project itself in some spectacular form, so the Situationist question of doing away with the spectacle altogether becomes replaced with the question about whether it is possible to think society as a different type of community: as a spectacle that is not alienated.

Refuting the conventionally understood distance between art and politics, NSK become a spectral image of society, haunting the 'real' society on which they parasitically subsist, much like Schleuser cannibalise EU discourses on immigration and Černý parodies national stereotypes at the heart of the 'new' Europe. Rather than occupying a dissident, self-consciously marginalised position vis-à-vis either socialist Yugoslavia or capitalist Slovenia (or the global market for that matter), NSK have effectively built themselves up as their own institution with their own artistic support network, which later transformed into a State in Time. Insisting on their Slovene origins during their performances in Yugoslavia could have made them globally marginalised because of the relative obscurity of Slovenia in relation to the more well-known Yugoslavia. However, they made Slovenia globally relevant by their controversial use of German and English languages to speak of national issues, their use of Slovenian (quasi) historical national imagery to comment on the shared European legacies of Nazism and communism and their insistence on blurring the political boundaries between the democratic West and the communist East. In so far as they remain parallel, rather than oppositional to, the state, NSK are indifferent to whether the state accepts, praises, bans or ignores them: all these positions would reinforce the distance between art and politics. They neither limit themselves to politicising their art, nor to aestheticising political positions: for NSK, politics *is* a space of art, which they freely inhabit.

Long before the wall separating communism from democracy fell, Laibach prophetically announced the future of European politics which would become clearer in the 1990s with the establishment and expansion of the EU in a close alliance with the United States. Because of the shared terror and 'collective aphasia' of consumers as a 'principle of social organisation', Europe in the 1980s was equally 'occupied' East and West, but its future became an even more dystopian vision of American spectacular consumerism, the 'United States of Europe'. Laibach conducted the first 'Occupied Europe Tour' in 1983–5 and printed Ronald Reagan's 1985 speech on the back cover of the tour album: 'It is my fervent wish that in the next century there will be one Europe, a free Europe, *a United States of Europe*' (NSK 1991: 37). The realisation of this wish arrived first through the expansion of NATO and then a gradual, conditional acceptance of the former communist states into the neo-liberal circuits of the EU.

In the midst of the wars in former Yugoslavia in the 1990s, Laibach deflected Europe's fixation on this area as the sore spot of European politics by launching a second 'Occupied Europe' tour, this time adding NATO to the title to imply that Europe everywhere is occupied, just like it once was by German Nazi troops. One of the tracks on the tour album was 'Geburt einer Nation', invoking the American white supremacist film *Birth of a Nation*. Significantly, Laibach held two concerts in Sarajevo, just as the Dayton peace agreement was being signed; doubling the political developments, they said that this concert showed that NATO would come to Bosnia one way or another (*Laibach: A Film from Slovenia*). At the concert, Bosnia's entry into this type of 'democracy' was appropriately critiqued through the manipulation of Nazi art, echoing the statement that 'Nazi-fascism under the disguise of democracy is the *rule of financial capital itself*' (NSK 1991: 57).

In the face of Yugoslavia's disappearance following the wars and in a gesture that parasitically emulates the appearance of supranational formations like the EU, NSK created their own deterritorialised State in Time in 1991, which, according to music critic Gordan Paunović 'still seems like the perfect solution to the Yugoslav problem' (Monroe 2005: 253). This utopian qualification is indeed justifiable: by creating a state in time rather than space, NSK implicitly provide a mooring point for all the Yugoslavs who have become extra-terrestrials by not being able to align themselves with a definitive post-Yugoslav national identity. It would appeal to all anti-nationalists, refugees and offspring from mixed marriages. But the State in Time is also a global state, interrogating and traversing the traditional understanding of borders everywhere: practicing a policy of absolute non-discrimination, NSK issue passports to anyone who applies and open embassies and consulates wherever they are invited, inhabiting such eclectic, traditionally apolitical spaces as the National Theatre in Sarajevo, an apartment kitchen in Umag or a hotel room in Florence. On the NSK website, this project is described as 'a utopian state without a concrete territory, but with several thousands of citizens plus formal national symbols such as a flag, stamps, emblems and a passport that everyone is free to obtain' (n.p.).

In the Q&A section of the Laibach website, we are faced with a provocative question: 'Is the NSK state a work of art?' to which the NSK reply:

> It can also be understood as a work of art. It is up to each and every individual how does he understand [*sic*] or he wants to understand the idea and the content of the NSK State. It can have many meanings for some people or absolutely no meaning to the others. (ibid.)

The State in Time is necessary as a conceptual alternative to territorial states bound by borders and identity politics, which NSK claim should disappear. However, although they have frequently dubbed themselves politicians rather than artists, the implication that their state is a work of art – and that NSK produce 'Art in the image of the State' – evokes not only the inspiration that the State's ideals draw from artistic aesthetics but also the responsibility that avant-garde artists carry in imagining and collaborating on projects made for an ideal state. Thus, echoing similar concerns as Černý's *Entropa*, NSK highlight their own collusion in the historical traumas 'of avant-garde movements by identifying with it in the stage of their assimilation in the systems of totalitarian states' (ibid.) For NSK, the political and artistic avant-gardes define their fraught relationships as they 'operate and create within a collective. Collectivism is the point where progressive philosophy, social theory and the militarism of contemporary states clash' (ibid.). In an attempt to understand the totalitarian side of artistic collectivism, therefore, NSK offer themselves up as their own scapegoats, as Žižek famously claims in *Laibach: A Film From Slovenia*.

By revisiting and incorporating past artistic forms and conceptualisations of the collective, NSK State in Time also seeks to create new conditions for the development of the individual in the framework of the collective. One could claim, for instance, that because the State in Time is not limited to territory or national identity, it enables its passport holders to feel self-assertive as global citizens who can communicate with one another about important political issues and demands for flexible global citizenship. The state sees itself as a 'collective cultural work' and supporter of the various 'micronations' around the world, equally as unofficial as NSK State.[11] Through its website, readers' feedback, the citizens' congress and various artistic installations, NSK State in Time comes into being in the very act of interaction and exchange of experiences.

Since the state exists through such fertile moments of exchange, continual movement and temporary dwelling – for instance, NSK embassies inhabit their unusual residences only for the duration of official diplomatic events; NSK passports are only valid for a few days – I will briefly dwell on the NSK concepts of 'time' and the state as a 'suprematist body'. The NSK concept of time does not appear merely as an alternative to space, establishing an untenable conceptual binary, nor does it imply a teleology, development or quantifiable, measurable time. Anthony Gardner suggests that this seemingly formalised state is 'unworked through brevity and absurdity' because its official manifestations exist 'in a limited span of time' (2015: 134, 133).

However, the State in Time is also the state in flux, signalling that the state ideal is never quite equal to itself and that time is permanently 'out of joint', as its borders, citizens, statutes or any other ontological determinations are always-already temporary and malleable. The time in which citizens become the collective is not the empty historical time of the nation state but rather phenomenological time of experience, the unmooring of individuals from the soil to which they were born:

The role of art and artists in defining time which belongs to them individually is more effective than in defining territory. The real, not imaginary, 'fatherland' of the individual is limited to the circle of the house in which he was born, the classroom or the library in which he acquired knowledge, the landscapes in which he walked, the spaces to which he is oriented, to the circle of his own individual experience, to that which exists and not that he was born into. (NSK website: n.p.)

Such temporality implies the impossibility of creating a closed-off, organic community of the nation state, and gestures towards a transnational community of affinity rather than shared ethnic or racial identity. According to Johannes Birringer, the NSK concept of time invokes Russian mystical philosopher Peter Uspenskii's 'vision of time as the fourth dimension of space', a mystical intuitive ability which influenced Malevich, among other avant-garde artists, in articulating a Suprematist escape from representational, objective and panoramic painting (1996: 155). Malevich is NSK's favourite retro-garde inspiration, and NSK define the state as a 'suprematist body': abstract nodes of the state's articulation lodged 'in a real social and political space . . . comprising the concrete body warmth, spirit and work of its members. NSK confers the status of a state not to territory but to mind' (NSK website: n.p.). If, for Malevich, Suprematism is a push away from linear and objective representation, a pure 'supremacy' of feeling, the question arises where and when exactly does this state, then, exist? What is the *thing* that is the state and what sort of space does its represented world occupy?

One of the abstract spaces that the State in Time figures is that of the philosophical components of the state, the political utopias that deliver both threats and promises, that are continually desired and exorcised. This utopian component overtly permeates NSK's claim that the State in Time is based on the principles of 'non-alignment' and 'self-management', at once playfully replicating socialist Yugoslavia's official ideology and pointing to its promise of direct democracy and evasion of dominant world countries' power struggles. The utopian principles of NSK state have radically intervened in citizenship and loyalty restrictions underpinning 'real' states. Literally entering the space of political exchange, NSK state paraphernalia not only parallel and haunt 'real' states – much like the Centre for Political Beauty's actions mentioned earlier – but also rival them through the issuing of passports. In some cases, these passports have been confused with legitimate documents, helping, for instance, Sarajevo residents escape from the besieged city in the 1990s. More recently, large numbers of Nigerians applied for NSK passports, hoping to use them in lieu of Nigerian passports to enter the EU. Although crossing borders with an NSK passport is unsuccessful in most cases (both NSK and the Slovene government have issued official warnings against using these documents for travel), this tendency confirms that an artistic artefact has become a viable document. In this respect, the State in Time also renders EU borders porous and interrogates its exclusionary policies. Commenting on this development, NSK wonder:

> How can light be thrown on such a close encounter between two mutually exclusive worlds: the complex, highly sophisticated, and abstract sphere of contemporary art, and the politically, culturally, and economically profoundly destabilised Third World, where bare survival is frequently an issue and whence people decide to emigrate en masse to find a better life? (With Europe the coveted destination, the media report on worse shipwreck disasters every year and the growing numbers of casualties as people set off on expensive and dangerous illegal crossings.) (ibid.)

A utopian reading of the State in Time might argue that it stages the impossibility of an organic, enclosed state community by repeating the territorial project of the state but nodding to what lies beyond its borders: an open community defined by flexible citizenship, absence of teleological determination and constant exchange and communication among singular persons who are not sublated into a unified whole. This could be further traced through Jean-Luc Nancy's concept of community without 'organic communion'. According to Nancy, regardless of political differences among various states, we have only known one model of community: one that presupposes an 'immanent unity, intimacy, and autonomy'. From this perspective, 'community is not only intimate communication between its members, but also its organic communion with its own essence'. In this type of community, even the death of the other is not a singular event, but always absorbed into the destiny of the community, sublated into 'the life of the infinite'. But since the other's death is always singular – it can only take place before one as a witness but one cannot truly experience it – Nancy proposes that a true, inorganic community opens up in this realisation of the 'impossibility of community' where 'death loses the senseless meaning that it ought to have' (1991: 15, 14). For Nancy this re-visioning of community has implications for questioning the traditional concept of the subject, which, he argues, underwrites most states we have known: communist, capitalist and fascist.

If we adopt this perspective, then the State in Time represents what can be rescued from the historical and philosophical project of the state. In fact, scholars frequently interpret this project as an aesthetic idealisation of the state. Alexei Monroe argues that, despite NSK's ambiguous stance, NSK work and State in Time can seem 'romantic and escapist' and 'seductive and inspiring' even when they employ 'militant irony' (2005: 47). Later, Monroe implies that NSK's vision of the ideal state might 'strengthen civic society' and mobilise 'democratic participation' that will challenge pragmatic, corporate-minded global states, including independent Slovenia whose disenchanted secession was not characterised by romantic ideals of the nation employed in Serbia or Croatia (254). This utopian thrust 'frustrates the reproduction of cynical conformism and passivity' (254). Monroe sounds nostalgic for the democratic ideals of a liberal state, as well as, significantly, for a more romantic narrative of the state that would replace staid economic pragmatism.

Monroe, as well as Inke Arns (1996), another prominent NSK critic, resorts to Žižek's article 'Es gibt keinen Staat in Europa' to highlight the importance of the aforementioned aspects of the state. Following Yugoslavia's disintegration, Žižek virulently criticises both left- and right-wing positions that advocate abolishing the state. Unsupervised warlords have been able to kill and plunder in Bosnia and Serbia as 'the direct consequence of the disintegration of State authority or its submission to the power play between ethnic communities'. These situations, Žižek concludes, only prefigure future problems in the EU, which also erodes individual state control in favour of international economic interests. Therefore, 'the concept of utopia has made an about-face turn – utopian energy is no longer directed towards a stateless community, but towards a state without a nation', territory or ethnic ties. Though Žižek does not explicitly refer to the State in Time, he suggests that any subversive art today must be 'state art in the service of a still-non-existent country' (1993: n.p.). From this perspective, the NSK state could embody the best legacies of the Yugoslav state – including the principles of non-alignment and self-management which it overtly references – while simultaneously representing an alternative to the alleged state erosion and crude economic pragmatism of the EU. As we will see in the final chapter, Yugoslavia's dissolution is often used as an admonishment for the EU when it faces internal conflicts; however, the State in Time could be seen as resurrecting some of Yugoslavia's accomplishments so as to model the kind of state that the EU might be.

While this is a philosophically exciting and politically innovative line of thought, emphasising the utopian alternative that the State in Time represents downplays its parasitic relationship to key state signifiers, which enthral their audiences – including Žižek and Monroe – by serving them ambiguously idealised visions of state power. It is not so much that the State in Time is seductive and inspiring, as Monroe claims, because it innocently imagines a revaluation of traditional state models, but rather because it highlights the audience's own aesthetic and emotional experience of seduction and inspiration by state power. As Inke Arns observes, 'NSK's strategy does not aim at overcoming the power of ideological signs through irony, parody or satire, but it is rather about calling our attention to the power of these signs' (1996: n.p.). Similarly, the State in Time does not overcome the power of state signs, but rather draws attention to their deadly potential which cannot be clearly delineated from their mobilising promise or ability to foster a progressive community.

For example, the passport application website belies the utopian promise of the State in Time: citizenship is allegedly open to everyone, and yet NSK control the actions and political dispositions of their prospective citizens by insistently repeating that citizens must be prepared 'to identify with [the State's] founding principles' and that passports 'may not be misused for criminal, ideological, religious, or political purposes conflicting with the content and principles of NSK and/or those jeopardising the reputation and good name of NSK' (NSK website: n.p.). This is not an unreasonable request by any organisation in which one desires membership, and yet it signals that for such an organisation to exist, it must necessarily exert power and control over its subjects, moreover, demanding their complicity. In addition, the optimistic, inspiring proclamations about the new state are undercut by concluding statements such as 'We kill to survive. We shop to stay alive', which endow violent and mundane practices of corporate states with an aura of sloganeering romanticism.

Finally, the State in Time leadership tends to consolidate and defend state power against its citizens. For instance, the organisation of the First Citizens' Congress in 2010, which aimed 'to negotiate the shared and contradictory interpretations and visions of its citizens' was repeatedly criticised on the NSK website by the citizens themselves. The NSK Organising Committee invited all citizens to apply to attend the Congress and eventually selected thirty delegates, which provoked a flurry of citizen responses, questioning whether such a small number can represent the constituency of a state meaningfully and complaining about NSK not consulting the citizens in the selection process. This centralising, transcendent image of the state informs the related poster design competition, appropriately titled 'Volk art', where citizens are invited to submit art that celebrates the 'spirit and significance of the [NSK] state and the congress in a dynamic and memorable form' (ibid.).

What I hope to highlight here is that the State in Time is not only a haven of open, flexible citizenship, but is also absurd and impossible because it still depends on the 'emptiness' of the sign of citizenship. NSK strategy of overidentification reassembles the signs of the state which themselves act as manifestations of exclusion: as long as it traffics in citizenship, this citizenship will have defining content; as long as there are embassies, they will be defined in terms of what is outside; as long as there is a state, it has potential to become a 'Higher Order', or an 'Immanent Consistent Spirit' to which the citizens subject themselves much like the audience subject themselves to the rhythm of Laibach performances. Thus, the NSK state principle of 'collective absolutism' which informs the 'first global state of the universe' can signify Žižek's utopian state without territory or nation as much as the existing form of the European Union (ibid.). Even a global or universal state can, just like any nation state, represent an organic communion along Nancy's terms: a traditional tyranny of the community.[12]

Thus, we arrive at a much more ambivalent reading of the State in Time and its paraphernalia. For instance, how can one read as utopian the highly publicised issuing of the NSK diplomatic passport to the controversial Croatian and Kosovo Liberation Army General Agim Čeku? Would NSK, whose artistic practice both haunts and symbolises the proliferation of postcommunist disintegrations, endorse Kosovo's project of yet another drawing of clear national boundaries, which will only formally be dissolved once this new state joins the European

Union? Or would they hand the passport to Čeku to performatively remind him of his duty to be a tolerant diplomat, revelling in his acceptance speech full of utopian political clichés about multicultural coexistence and Kosovo as a hopeful new state?[13]

Perhaps the clearest warning against understanding the state as a utopian concept per se arrived at the moment that NSK staged their embassy in Sarajevo during the 'Occupied Europe NATO tour' in 1995. NSK's Peter Mlakar, dressed in a military uniform, delivered a lecture on the 'Apocalypse of Europe and Possible Deliverance' which critiqued the New World Order and Europe's racist attitude to the Balkans. The audience's shaken self-confidence in the face of a fratricidal war might have been strengthened by statements that 'the truth of Europe is evil itself' and that 'here European political history traumatically purged itself of its symptoms'. However, its message was complicated by hinting at Bosnians' own pretensions to theological and political legitimacy, especially the state embrace of self-victimisation in order to justify the purging of enemies:

> Death to criminals, that's OK. But it's only in forgiveness that you process criminals into sausages, only by forgiving the greatest evil that you will be forgiven and freed. Then the defeated will truly be defeated, God will stand on your side and the winner will bear your name. I myself guarantee you that. (*Laibach: A Film from Slovenia*)

The last sentence echoes wartime Serbian president Slobodan Milošević's promise to protect Kosovo Serbs against Albanians, on the eve of Yugoslavia's dissolution. Ironically, Mlakar uses Milošević's violent rhetoric to win the applause of Bosnian citizens who are themselves bombed thanks to its deadly potential.

Towards a new politics of community

In Michael Goddard's incisive Deleuzian reading of NSK strategy, Laibach's performances are 'hallucinatory collective psychosis' no longer 'operating on the level of representation but rather as a complex machine'. Like Artaud's theatre of cruelty, they are 'a convulsive experience of shock, rather than . . . an exercise in ideological recontextualisation or a psychoanalytic cure as Zizek suggested' (2006: 51). This observation applies to the NSK State in Time as well:

we should pay more attention to the ways in which it stages various manipulations of collective affect rather than to its alleged curative dimensions, as ways out of the shock and trauma of state power. NSK, like Černý and Schleuser, suggest that a supranational Europe restages twentieth-century traumas of totalitarian politics; NSK and Černý also invoke militant artistic avant-gardes who have helped popularise the nativist aesthetics of the state. Nonetheless, these artistic interventions embrace diasporic, displaced perspectives that not only interrupt an easy short circuit to nativism, but also confront Europe with its traumatic heritage. However, while Černý and Schleuser stage trauma as the content of various nativist fantasies which need to be exorcised, for NSK trauma is contained in the very mechanisms of the state for which there is no cure.

Ultimately, then, the NSK State in Time remains dependent on the logic of the spectacle that it *detourns*, in a Situationist fashion, but it cannot think the community outside of the *detourned* spectacle, even as it interrogates its guiding discourses through overidentification. The NSK state repeats what Jacques Derrida calls the hauntology that makes the res publica, any modern state, possible, by employing the media (news, tele-technologies, internet communication) which are inhabited by the phenomenality of the political – invested with the spectre of the nation, history and community [1993] (2006: 63). It points to the state's bankruptcy and deadly mythology even as it gestures to alternatives such as flexible citizenship, anti-nationalism and egalitarianism. Perhaps the most hopeful aspect of this artist collective is the absence of an enemy, of a political scapegoat that has, as Derrida suggests, characterised every traditional 'politics of friendship'. It is impossible to identify, with any certainty, a particular group that NSK performances target as their opponent. Rather than positing an oppressive state establishment or any other identifiable entity as a target, their spectacles involve exposing our shared contributions to the perpetuation of the 'Immanent Consistent Spirit': the myth of a closed-off state and organic community that leads us to war.

Keeping these traumatic aspects of the state in mind, we might ask how the artists discussed in this chapter devise aesthetic strategies that announce new political configurations for the EU, especially ones that might undermine the aforementioned myth of the organic community. *Entropa*'s fragmentation and interrogation of the politics of representation points to the necessity of Europe going beyond identity politics and static cultural 'essences' that, compiled, somehow make

Europe. Schleuser, on the other hand, focus not only on the 'essences' circumscribed by EU borders, but on the very ossified notion of the border that aids a socially reactionary, even if economically expedient, politics of mobility. If this is so, then we may ask what kinds of communities can emerge from the ramparts of old identity politics and national clichés? Do these artistic performances simply demonstrate that Europe has not caught up with itself, as it nostalgically looks back at the politics of identity and its visual, physical representation (official EU imagery abounds in objects and objectified identities, such as architecture, geographic spaces and maps, diverse bodies and faces)? Perhaps we should think of such new tendencies in European art as prefiguring the horizon of new political formations and conceptualisations to come – hopefully, those that would take into account the variously disenfranchised European multitudes that are unrepresentable by either national clichés or European civilisational ideals.

Both Černý and Schleuser stage their absence and silencing in the dominant 'distributions of the sensible', which Jacques Rancière defines as reigning regimes of aesthetic strategies which govern 'material rearrangements of signs and images, relationships between what is seen and what is said, between what is done and what can be done' (2000: 12, 39). Rancière argues that artistic challenges to reigning regimes of the sensible drive historical change because the emergence of innovative representational strategies and possibilities of thinking nurtures new political subjectivities and collectives. NSK, on the other hand, question such a glorification of aesthetics by highlighting how even an enchantment with 'signs and images' seen as progressive always-already contains potential for alienation of the social body, for violence and hegemony.

Dominant representations of the supranational community that is the EU enshrine national and/or (multi)cultural identity as an organising principle, which alienates the power of what Hardt and Negri describe as the 'multitude' in their eponymous book, or what, in the context of the EU, I have referred to as the possibility of subaltern transnationalism. This transnationalism of the disadvantaged would include, much like the concept of the multitude, the often invisible non-beneficiaries of EU enlargement such as the migrants, the impoverished, the workers who keep losing social and work benefits, the unemployed: a growing underclass that crosses European internal borders and shares common problems as well as goals. Hardt and Negri's multitude, as a swarming, diverse, fluid assemblage that acts in-common without having a predetermined, uniting, em-bodied identity presupposed in concepts such as the nation or ethnic group, reverses the illusion that humans are interchangeable – as members of the same cultural group, the same nation. So rather than delivering seemingly equal, objectified national clichés so satirised by Černý and easily interchangeable on the level of transcendental, sovereign signifiers, the multitude stresses singularity, which cannot be represented within the reigning regime of the sensible. Singularity is not a matter of mimetically depicting faces and bodies of different colours and sizes: multiculturalism appears insufficient in this case. Moreover, the multicultural, horizontal, non-agonistic representations of diversity also preclude the divided subaltern groups' creation of a transnational political ground over which to fight, as well as their understanding of their unequal, agonistic situatedness within the common European home.

The artistic strategies discussed in this chapter also call for an aesthetic which ventures into untapped potential beyond safe 'activist art'. However, representing some type of mobilisation from below does not suggest its immediate translation into an idealised politics of the multitude, recalling the historical subjection of art to prescriptive socialist-realist or populist clichés. My discussion does not advocate a rehashing of socialist-realist or national-socialist apotheoses of 'the hard-working', 'ordinary' people, even if this were to arrive in fashionably postmodern, multicultural avatars. In fact, one possible avenue to take in order to avoid such artistic apotheoses would be to assume a critical distance from dominant EU representational regimes which rely on objectified identities and bodies and currently act as the empty signifiers standing in for the broader European body politic.

This, broadly non-mimetic, aesthetics would not be easily conducive to promoting any type of founding myth of community, predicated upon the idea of unity, essence or transcendental ideal. Rather than offering representations of individual human or national bodies – visible and countable identities – such an aesthetic might highlight transindividual and transnational relations, dialogues, affects and historical ties, even allowing them to uncover uncomfortable and dangerous truths. If, for Hardt and Negri, multitude also means mobility, change and constant, active resistance, then an aesthetic of the multitude needs to give voice to its protean, dynamic nature within its groundless ground, rather than paralyse it within ossified representations that act as new founding myths of a group with an 'essence'. The artists discussed thus far overidentify with the ideology of founding myths to expose its inherent chauvinism. What this very overidentification gestures towards, instead, is an aesthetic akin to what Jean-Luc Nancy illustrates through the idea of a 'community of literature':[14] communication, cooperation and sociality in-common, an alternative to our default 'organic community', understood as a mythical fusion or an expression of identitarian 'essence'. In the coming chapters, I turn to literary and film figurations of such communities.

Chapter 2

Alternative Hospitalities on the Margins of Europe

Moisés Salama Benarroch's documentary *Melillenses* (2004) explores the political paradoxes of life in Melilla, which, along with Ceuta, has been a Spanish exclave in Africa since the fifteenth century. By virtue of being in Africa, Melilla explicitly participates in promoting the Spanish myth of *convivencia*, coexistence of multiple religions and ethnicities: its population is a thriving mix of Spaniards, Arabs, Berbers and Jews. However, *Melillenses* also documents the city's existence as a well-protected Spanish and European Union fortress on African soil. While its border fence and surveillance system fends off increasing numbers of migrants attempting to enter the EU, it walls are also temporarily porous to neighbouring Moroccans who pay daily visits to purchase its (cheaper) goods and make their living by selling them across the border in Morocco. The film highlights the following paradox: Melilla's diverse inhabitants speak of the necessity of hospitality to one another's cultural traditions, while the city effectively closes off its borders to non-European outsiders. And yet, while Melilla is politically controlled by Spaniards, it is economically dependent on surrounding Morocco.

This chapter will explore cultural narratives set in such exceptional spaces as Melilla, geographically and symbolically located in borderline Europe, where the boundaries between Europe and non-Europe blur and cross-hatch, resulting in crises of identity vis-à-vis 'proper' national and European homes. Mahi Binebine's novel *Welcome to Paradise* (1999; *Cannibales* in the French original) and Laila Lalami's collection *Hope and Other Dangerous Pursuits* (2005) portray African multitudes in waiting, reflecting on the history of European colonialism, as they hope to cross the Gibraltar into Spain. Emanuele

Crialese's film *Terraferma* (2011) and Theo Angelopoulos's film *Eternity and a Day* (1998) explore hospitality to African and Eastern European migrants, respectively, in the liminal spaces of Italy and Greece, while rewriting and questioning European identity.

In their insistence on the porousness of frontiers, such narratives challenge what, following Achille Mbembe, I call the necropolitics of the border: the European Union's insistence on violently protecting and fencing off its territory against any variety of 'illegal' migrant, including refugees and asylum seekers. According to Mbembe:

> The important feature of the age of global mobility is that military operations and the exercise of the right to kill are no longer the sole monopoly of states, and the 'regular army' is no longer the unique modality of carrying out these functions. The claim to ultimate or final authority in a particular political space is not easily made. (2003: 31)

Using the example of Palestine, Mbembe argues that late-modern colonial occupation is distinctive in that it combines 'vertical sovereignty' (aerial surveillance and control) with horizontal 'splintering occupation', which not only controls colonised populations but also secludes them, replicating the same logic behind late-modern 'suburban enclaves or gated communities' (28). Combined with the above-mentioned splintering of sovereign authority, this arrangement leads to the proliferation of sites of violence. While I by no means suggest that the situation at EU borders is the same as the settler colonial occupation of Palestine, I extend these concepts to discuss a similar employment of colonial tactics of surveillance, segregation and the right to kill. Both vertical and horizontal sovereignty are exercised, for instance, in controlling movement in the Mediterranean and policing the Schengen borders, while in borderline EU spaces which migrants manage to reach, the processing centres often carry out prison functions of seclusion from the local population, long-term detention and abuse of human rights. Simultaneously, the EU border in liminal Mediterranean spaces figures as ambivalently inclusive vis-à-vis culturally and economically 'backwards' regions that were viewed as internal colonies throughout history.

Within the EU, a symbolic politics of verticality is also exercised through top-down politics of identity that involves both national and EU definitions of 'ideal citizens', where the segregation of migrants in processing centres at the border is infinitely multiplied in urban seclusion and neglect of migrant communities of lower socio-economic status.[1] Subhabrata Bobby Banerjee extends Mbembe's concept by defining 'necrocapitalism', where capitalism becomes a crucial factor that leads to dispossession and creation of death worlds: 'If the symbol of past sovereignty was the sword, I want to examine the effects of the sword of commerce and its power to create life worlds and death worlds in the contemporary political economy' (2008: 1542). While economically dispossessed urban enclaves contribute to such 'death worlds', their extreme manifestation is at the EU borders where undocumented migrants are viewed as useless, dispensable and unemployable bodies from the perspective of neo-liberal capitalism. Gabriel Giorgi and Karen Pinkus employ the term biopolitics rather than necropolitics to analyse the symbolic operation of the border, but they make a similar point about delimiting sociopolitically valuable human life from 'bare life', in Agamben's terms, which can be sacrificed with impunity: the 'outside', of the EU border, 'although represented and "materialised" in spatial terms, seems to point toward to another dimension that is not exclusively territorial, geopolitical, or cultural, but fundamentally biopolitical' (Giorgi and Pinkus 2006: 99).

Marginalised within Europe, but within reach of migrants as major egresses into Europe, the borderland places portrayed in the novels and films I discuss in this chapter operate in what Giorgio Agamben terms a 'state of exception': the sovereign prerogative, on pretext of maintaining peace and security, to declare a war without end, a 'permanent state of emergency' thanks to borderline legal practices and exceptional bodies that enforce them [2003] (2005: 2). One such exceptional body, affirming Mbembe's point about the distribution of sovereign violence beyond the regular army, is Frontex, the EU agency for external border control. Frontex is meant to ensure justice and security by helping member states coordinate border enforcement. In practice, however, it has been criticised by human rights organisations for dramatically reducing the numbers of migrant boats that reach EU territories, also preventing asylum seekers from exercising their legal rights. It has also been charged with tacitly endorsing the abuses of migrants in reception centres, as well as contributing to increasing death tolls because migrants have to travel longer to avoid its elaborate surveillance systems. Frontex is the embodiment of a digitalised surveillance system, which further multiplies, as well as shifts, EU's virtual borders: 'as a result of the digital border, authority can be realised anywhere where the database systems can be accessed, even in countries that no longer have border controls' (Maurits 2015: 513). As a non-army that acts like an army, Frontex is constituted by several legal exceptions: its headquarters are within the EU but it operates outside of EU borders; the Frontex Regulation says that 'the responsibility for the control and surveillance of external borders lies with the Member States' and yet Frontex has 'full autonomy and independence', which problematises its accountability and transparency (Human Rights Watch 2011: n.p.).[2]

The war on migrants has thus become institutionalised and in fact, immanent to the EU construction of sovereignty, along with the concomitant state of legal exception. The late-modern colony and EU's (post)colonial frontier are both examples of zones of exception in so far as subjects of sovereign power have highly restricted agency and social death worlds are created in the name of reason and civilisation (Ahluwalia 2004: 637). In such frontier zones, not only can violence and death occur because there is no juridical intervention, but also because it is difficult for migrants to contest the EU military machine and the 'reasonable' discourse of EU security that justifies the violence.

The paradoxical distance between the official discourse of openness to diversity and practices of violence that circumscribe diversity structurally resembles Jacques Derrida's reflections on the conflict between conditional hospitality prescribed by law and unconditional hospitality that would exceed limitations, calculation and 'reasonable' generosity. The novels and films discussed in this chapter, however, gesture towards hospitality that exceeds legal norms, contests the national and EU monopoly on generosity to migrants, as well as map cross-cultural and cross-border solidarities that overshadow the importance of national (or other) roots and belonging. Such alternative states of exception also take place in the process of border crossing or near borders. The official 'politics of friendship' and the right to kill a 'public enemy' with impunity are contested through personal allegiances that complicate loyalty to one's culture or nation, asymmetrical relations of hospitality and gratitude and enclaves of intimate alliances that blur necropolitical boundaries which separate Europe from non-Europe. But hospitality in these narratives is neither unidirectional nor idealised. Engaging with Jacques Derrida's and Emmanuel Levinas's writings on hospitality and generosity, I will explore ways in which hospitality is also limited, or demanded, or not met with gratitude.

The settings of the films and novels are exceptional in their internal exclusion within the national and European imaginary as well: associated with Africa or Asia, seen as semi-European, their relationship to the phenomenon of migrancy is intimate in terms of their own history of emigration as well as a shared experience of subalternity. The narratives highlight the dual racism towards both migrants and internally colonised populations, where the latter occupy spaces associated with migrant deaths, infection and militant intervention in the European imaginary. Charges of 'backwardness', nationalism and inhospitality are projected onto such marginalised populations rather than seen as the result of larger EU geopolitical decisions. *Terraferma* and *Eternity and a Day* in particular challenge such projections by interrogating the discourses of protecting European borders – and identity – against invading 'others'. Finally, while the chapter focuses on these exceptional sites, it by no means argues that they are unique. Rather, such exceptional contact zones are increasingly typical of Europe in general.

Multitudes in waiting: passage to Europe in *Welcome to Paradise* and *Hope and Other Dangerous Pursuits*

In March 2011, a migrant boat set off from Tripoli to the Italian island of Lampedusa, carrying seventy-two migrants, mostly from Ethiopia, Eritrea, Ghana, Nigeria and the Sudan. Finding themselves stranded in the sea with dwindling fuel and food, they issued a number of distress calls, to both commercial and military vessels, the latter belonging primarily to Italian and Spanish NATO troops. While several helicopters dropped food and water and promised a swift rescue, nobody ended up evacuating the migrants over the next two weeks: they were left to die. Their boat never reached Lampedusa either, instead drifting back to the Libyan coast. Eventually, only nine migrants survived.[3] This harrowing incident, by no means unique in the year which saw 1,500 migrants die in the Mediterranean, was investigated by the Council of Europe, whose report concluded there 'was a collective failure by NATO, the United Nations and individual States in planning the Libyan military operations and preparing for an expected exodus by sea' (*Lives Lost* 2012: 20). The report's emphasis on the lack of clear jurisdiction and responsibility for maritime evacuations remains relevant in light of the sharp increase in Mediterranean crossings by migrants fleeing the continuing political turmoil in North Africa and the Middle East. Until recently, migrant deaths remained in the background of media attention; but increasing frequency of migrant boat disasters, resulting in almost 4,000 casualties in 2015, has made their invisibility in the media untenable.

Mahi Binebine's *Welcome to Paradise* and Laila Lalami's *Hope and Other Dangerous Pursuits* highlight this tragically differential visibility and importance ascribed to tourists' and migrants' deaths while rescuing the latter from invisibility and reduction to statistics in the European public imaginary.[4] These narratives suggest that the politics of travelling in the Mediterranean, the major entry point into the EU, challenges the myth of shifting, uncertain globalised identities since it is subjected to the strict EU rules of border policing: 'Either you are a tourist, or you are an immigrant; either you transport containers, or you use drag-nets; routes can cross, overlap, never blend. And when this occurs, it is only by accident' ('Solid Sea' 2002: n.p.).

Such persistent yet often futile attempts at stabilising and segregating identities also challenge traditionally benign perspectives on the Mediterranean as a fluid space of cross-cultural exchange and meeting of continents. Arguing that control over Mediterranean crossings exemplifies the EU's necropolitical regime of governance, I will consider these contemporary events in the context of the EU's neocolonial afterlife and transnational connections among former colonisers as well as the colonised. In 'Necropolitics', Mbembe suggests that sovereign power, exercised by the army as much as by 'repressed topographies of cruelty', is variously 'deployed in the interest of maximum destruction of persons and the creation of *death-worlds*, new and unique forms of social existence in which vast populations are subjected to conditions of life conferring upon them the status of *living dead*' (2003: 39–40).

Welcome to Paradise takes place in anticipation of the passage of clandestine migrants from former colonies to the former colonial empires – crossing the Gibraltar from Morocco to Spain – and downplays the importance of national origins and boundaries on either side of the strait. The migrants, both anxious and hopeful, are united in their shared goal regardless of their diverse backgrounds: they are from Algeria, Morocco, Mali and a number of other African coun-tries. The intended passage will take them through at least Spain and France and possibly other European countries, united by a single border. Binebine maps the new cartographies of contemporary neo-colonial relations, signalling that the EU as a whole should be con-sidered in light of the former colonial legacies of its most prominent member states.

Hope and Other Dangerous Pursuits also centres on crossing the short but deadly Gibraltar strait: the opening chapter builds around the common aspirations and apprehensions of prospective migrants as they cross illegally on a boat, but the narrative immediately moves into the 'Before' and 'After' sections to flesh out individual character backgrounds. The migrants are from Morocco, Guinea and other African countries; while many of them hope to remain in Spain, some see the trip as a ticket to the larger European home. Unlike Binebine, however, Lalami is interested in depicting a cross section of Moroccan society, in which the migrants are only one sample of unemployed, poor or otherwise trapped classes of people whose only 'hope' from the novel's title lies in the precarious future in Europe. The chapters that recount what happens to them before and after the crossing contextualise these characters in contrast to the more privi-leged sections of Moroccan society who live luxurious lifestyles and can look forward to a more dignified, education-based emigration to Canada and the United States. In *Hope*, Lalami triangulates the relationship between North Africa, the European Union and North America, highlighting how neocolonial structures of power intersect with the neo-liberal movement of labour.

The Gibraltar strait between Morocco and Spain represents mate-rial and symbolic divisions that exceed a mere border between two countries tied by mutually colonial relationships over the centuries and increasingly separated since the 1980s, following Spain's shift to democracy and ambitious pursuit of European standards of liv-ing. This border is the most unequal among the United Nations, effectively separating 'First' and 'Third' Worlds and representing a symbolic 'safeguard against the mixing of Africa and Europe, of Islam and Christianity' (Dotson-Renta 2012: 4). Crossing the Mediterranean in the direction of Europe, then, one not only tra-verses a material divide, but also breaks through the symbolic fron-tiers of Europe. While Spain can be seen as guarding Europe from Africa at the Gibraltar, this border also serves to consolidate its precariously European identity after its history of Arab rule placed it in an inferior position vis-à-vis 'properly' European countries to the north ('Africa starts at the Pyrenees' remains a popular saying in France and Spain). However, 'as Spain has become more "European" due to its participation in the EU and its more developed economy, its numbers of Muslim immigrants have increased dramatically' (Dotson-Renta 9). The more Spain desires Europeanness, the more it attracts migrants, just like other EU countries.

In *Welcome to Paradise* Binebine employs images of paralysis and listlessness to highlight common predicaments among the migrants as well as their fetishising of Europe as 'paradise', the excruciatingly elusive First World on the other side of the strait. At the beginning of the novel, the Moroccan narrator, Aziz, wonders if any of the gathered migrants could be in a 'deeper, blacker' hell than the one of poverty (3), in which they all languish. This question is addressed by individual background stories, which comprise many of the chapters in this novel of endless waiting to make the crossing into Europe. The narrative flow mimics the lethargy and idleness that the migrants desire to escape, lodging all the characters firmly in the past, or a suspended present, rather than the future. But neither the African past nor the European future is idealised. Individual characters' stories link their shared poverty to the repeated trope of circulating, like a commodity, in what Georges Bataille might call the restricted economy of monetary exchange that governs human relationships in the novel. This lack of agency, like the depthless nature of a commodity, 'cannibalises' human dignity by rendering their intimate, personal histories secondary virtually as soon as we are introduced to them.

Binebine builds the narrative around such stark disjunctions, suggesting that the protagonists live in what Pal Ahluwalia terms 'social death'. Building on Mbembe's discussion of necropolitics, Ahluwalia argues that in the contemporary death-worlds created in the name of reason and civilisation, there is no capacity for agency 'in living a life of unfreedom of being socially dead'. Sovereignty in such situations resides with what the subject perceives to be an 'illegitimate power – the master, the coloniser' who can arbitrate on 'who can live and who can die' (2004: 638). While Lalami suggests that both local and global 'illegitimate power' resides with specific, privileged social classes, in Binebine such power is diffused and drives every relation of social hierarchy on either side of the Gibraltar. Here the EU figures as a physically absent, yet pervasively involved neocolonial power.

As Chantal Mouffe observes, free trade policies promoting EU protectionism and neo-liberal hegemony force 'an increasing number of people to immigrate' to Europe, but they are perceived as a threat by 'Europeans who do not see that it is their own policies which are at the origin of the problem' (2013: 62).

On the Moroccan side of the strait, *Welcome to Paradise* depicts Marrakesh as a place where poor children and young people are forced into begging or prostitution for employers who exploit them. While generosity comes from those who have already left for Europe, it is often portrayed as self-congratulatory and the object of others' envy. Nuara, one of the Berber migrants who attempts the crossing with her baby hoping to join her husband Suleiman in France, recalls how Suleiman would return with bags 'crammed with presents' to show off in front of his village, bringing 'an infinite variety of objects no one knew how to use but that looked precious' (37). Meanwhile, Nuara has to pay for Suleiman's incoming calls in her village because the shopkeeper who had a phone was a 'real blood-sucker'. Similarly, the Malian Pafadnam receives the money necessary for the crossing from his cousin in France, but is warned not to be too happy too soon because 'there must be a snake in the grass' to guard against: if he shows off, he'll 'get it stolen' (63).

In virtually all interactions with Europeans, African migrants figure as cheap commodities, ready to perform services with minimum maintenance. Morad, one of the traffickers' aides who mesmerises prospective migrants with stories of life in the European 'paradise', fondly remembers his badly paid restaurant job and paltry dwelling, 'the space of six square meters' with 'cracked ceiling' and 'bare bulb by that small half-blocked-up basement window' (18). He recounts a nightmare in which his restaurant manager gradually cannibalises him while Morad acquiesces and keeps smiling, as he receives another benefit, including a residence permit, with each body part surrendered to the manager. This gruesome story points to the absurdity of a self-sacrificial, necropolitical economy which progressively destroys one's well-being even as one, paradoxically, pursues a 'better life' in Europe. The vampiric imagery of capitalism as cannibalism suggests that the waning European welfare state is no longer dedicated to 'the maximum of life but the minimum for living and sometimes not even this'. This new logic of the minimum organises the contemporary necropolitical social body (Gržinić 2008: n.p.).

In Lalami's *Hope*, prospective migrants also experience social deaths as their lives stagnate, their careers and personal relationships eternally suspended in the present. Everyone anticipates a liberating future across the strait, but with full awareness that it may never arrive. That this belief in a better future in Europe is a collective, rather than individual, fantasy is repeatedly emphasised in the novel. Seemingly every family has a member who supports them financially from Europe, and the community enthusiastically recount the stories of successful Mediterranean crossings, but keep at bay anxieties about the more numerous, unsuccessful ones (111). It is clear, however, that they are not welcome in Spain: in an attempt to deter migrants from crossing the Gibraltar, Spanish coastguards stack 'sunken fishing boats' on their side, 'plainly visible from the Moroccan side. They thought it would scare people. It didn't' (111).

Such potentially suicidal attempts at crossing are not a desperate escape from a life in death, but rather the only proactive decisions the characters can make. I propose reading them not as self-destructive denials of agency but precisely as a final, in multiple senses of this word, chance to reclaim one's life. Ahluwalia observes that, paradoxically, even the decision to take one's life is the only act of genuine agency in the situation of social death: 'Actual death as opposed to social death is the very instance where agency itself can be exercised' (2004: 638). In *Hope*, Morocco is awash in corruption, wasted possibilities and nepotism: the chapters in the 'Before' section establish the characters' shared social paralysis which also affects their most intimate relationships. Murad, the narrator of the opening chapter, is a university-educated English teacher who cannot find gainful employment and harasses tourists into hiring him as a guide; Aziz is an unemployed repairman who feels emasculated in his marriage; Halima is a working-class mother and wife fleeing an abusive marriage and an environment that blames her for the abuse. As in *Welcome to Paradise*, intimate relationships are mediated by money or lack thereof: either they are unable to sell their labour to support their families or, like Halima, they need money to bribe the authorities into granting them a release from an abusive relationship.

Perhaps the most intriguing character in this novel is the young university student with a religiously fuelled, anti-establishment anger, Faten. 'Before', Faten, who takes pride in her poverty, aligns herself with a radical underground mosque in Rabat which helps her expose to critique Morocco's authoritarianism, hypocrisy and obsession with emulating Western lifestyles. She pursues social mobility through higher education, but when caught cheating in an exam with the help of her friend Noura, Noura's father, employed in the Ministry of Education, pulls connections to have Faten expelled. The irony that Lalami highlights is that everyone cheats, and it is only Faten's poverty that strips her of any pretension to a charmed life enabled by connections. When Noura's father asks Faten if, like Noura, she would refuse the offer of free education at New York University, she replies, 'No one is offering me anything . . . No one gives anything for free. That is the trouble of some of our youths' (46). Faten is acutely aware of the system of exchange and indebtedness that marks everyday lives of the socially vulnerable. Noura, on the other hand, has the privilege to either turn down or accept the gift of 'free' education in the United States, funded by her father. Faten's expulsion irreversibly strips her of the possibility of social advance and pushes her towards a European 'paradise', where she becomes a prostitute.

Both *Hope* and *Welcome to Paradise* abound in exploitative sexual relations, including prostitution, to highlight the commodification of non-European bodies. In Binebine, cannibalistic commodity exchange underwrites sexual relations as well, where masculinity is repeatedly compromised in encounters with Europeans in positions of authority. For instance, Yarce is suspected of being a prostitute for the rich white people he massages in the exotic salons of Marrakesh. The European customers exude the 'bland, sickly odour of cadavers' (85), contributing to the image of such exchanges as lifeless and sterile, even when it comes to presumably passionate sexual contact. Aziz, who idealises his days at a French school run by nuns, allows himself to be 'swallowed up body and soul' by his teacher Mr Romanchef (162). The intimacy of his fascination with the European 'other' makes it difficult to differentiate between the repayment of debt – Aziz says he 'owes his new life and new world' to the teacher and has no way of 'refusing' him – and the lure of the forbidden, the 'pleasure in the sin' which suggests 'the glimpse of paradise' that is represented by the escape to Europe (161–2).

In *Hope*, Faten's downward slide from a devout woman to a prostitute is contrasted with the lost potential for upward mobility in Morocco, where she could speak and act freely until she was expelled from university and a careless remark about the king made her a police target. In Spain the only way out of her predicament is her client Martin who offers to get her immigration papers. Faten thus reverses Halima's fate, becoming a trapped patriarchal fetish only when she moves to the European 'paradise'. The narrator points out that, although Faten panders to Martin's Orientalist fantasies, her lack of education makes the language and critical thinking needed to identify this type of racism unavailable:

> Over the years that followed, she'd had time to hear all the fantasies, those that, had she finished her degree, she might have referred to disdainfully as odalisque dreams. Now they were just a part of the repertoire she'd learned by heart and had to put up with if she wanted to make a living. (148)

Faten is alternately treated as a fetishised commodity and an unacceptable 'other', from the moment she is raped by a Spanish border guard beyond the purview of law, to the realisation that she will never be accepted by Martin's Franco-supporting father. Significantly, she rejects Martin in the end, frustrated by his stereotypical thinking and confidence in '[knowing] her and her people' (149). She also concludes that Martin is more similar to his father than he would like to believe: fascism still lies at the heart of Europe, as Martin is just as racist as his father.

While the restricted economy in *Welcome to Paradise* is regulated through repayment of debt and turning oneself into a commodity, the inability to either produce or purchase – or circulate in the market at all – is what turns one into a barely living being. In France Morad meets Joel, a homeless man who, having lost his job and bourgeois lifestyle, complains that when people hit the bottom, the system only sees them as a 'stain' and waits for them to die. He continues, 'if it weren't for the fear of awaking old demons, they'd happily lock you up in a camp' (151). Binebine creates a resonance between the 'repressed topography of cruelty' in Mbembe's words – letting people die indifferently in French streets – and the organised system of exterminating socially undesirable 'others' that characterised World War II camps. Just as Faten remains off the radar in Madrid, so dying gradually in a French street remains invisible because it happens without direct targeting, often in spaces that are far from the purview of public opinion. This prerogative to kill with impunity and through indifference towards a failed commodity like Joel parallels the 'letting die' in the Mediterranean sea, in a neocolonial zone of legal exception.[5]

Nonetheless, Binebine offers an alternative to this pervasive sense of violence and commodified exchange in the shape of a general economy, which Bataille associates with sovereign expenditure and excess that are not predicated on exchange or profitability. This economy of help, nurturance and generosity without the expectation of return is notable in interactions among the migrants. Aziz feels compelled to take care of his cousin Reda, 'his blood', without expecting anything in return. He observes a similarly generous impulse in the Algerian Kacem Judi: he offers Aziz oranges after seeing that he is starving, without expecting anything in return, although at that point the oranges are 'worth their weight in gold' (25). Kacem, who has lost his family in a massacre at Blida, also gives money to a little boy selling cigarettes in Marrakesh, without helping himself to any goods, presumably because the boy reminds him of his own son (69). Finally, like many others who have received money from cousins, Aziz gets the money for the crossing from Sister Benedicte, who figures as his surrogate mother, leaving him her life savings so he can pay for university studies.

In the novel, therefore, family and other kinship structures, real or surrogate, complicate the restricted economy of capital, debt and repayment. Kinship terms such as 'mother', 'sister' or 'little brother' are used to foster an intimate sense of community with people who are either distant family relations or are excluded from the possibility of blood kinship through differences of race, class or gender. Binebine explores questions of responsibility and community through a Derridean politics of friendship that complicates traditional designation of public enemies and friends. Derrida proposes the possibility of friendship 'without a familial bond, without proximity' in order to challenge traditional Christian and Greek conceptualisations of friendship as affiliations based on a shared genealogy, culture, politics or interests. He asks, 'What truth is there for a friendship without proximity, without presence, therefore without resemblance, without attraction, perhaps even without significant or reasonable preference?' (2005a: 35).

In *Welcome to Paradise*, this 'truth' arrives through negative association, either affiliation by economic dispossession, loss of family or alienation from the familial ties to which one has been born. Reflecting on Kacef's loss of family in a massacre by Algerian fundamentalists, Aziz suggests that to live without a family is to be among the living dead, a ghost: 'To be a husband, a father, an uncle, a friend, and then an hour later – the time it takes for a stroll in the moonlight – to be nothing . . . Too weak to bury your family, or take your own life' (70). Loss marks his own family: Reda joins the French school Aziz attends because Reda's mother committed suicide. She felt guilty for having beaten Reda's twin brother so vigorously that he had to have his hands amputated and eventually had to turn to begging. Finally, Yussef also loses his entire family because he steals a bag of corn flour to feed them, unaware that it is to be used to poison rats. While I've only listed a few examples, such horrid family tragedies are repeated with symbolic regularity and are all linked to poverty.

The creation of a substitute family is not necessarily romanticised in the text, however. While examples of solidarity and alternative kinship structures are underscored even before the migrants arrive on the Moroccan coast – for instance, the unlikely bond that develops between Yussef's two wives and Nuara's treatment of Tamu, the family's poor, black servant, like a sister – they are set against a generally unsympathetic community that reinforces established hierarchies. Initially, the familiar attitude of suspicion and disapproval characterises the migrants' relationships. They are upset that Nuara's baby keeps crying and afraid he will give them away. However, they gradually become more protective of the mother and the baby, assuming responsibility for them collectively:

> We bent over to look at the baby, who had woken up. He had beautiful eyes, a turned-up nose and a full-lipped mouth which smiled at the circle of strange faces. We were suddenly captivated by this wriggling creature who had given us such a fright. Kacem Judi seemed so happy cradling the little mite that when Nuara returned she didn't dare take him again. (118)

This substitute family that includes multiple fathers stands in for the perpetually absent Suleiman; they begin to counsel Nuara about her husband, subverting her romanticised view of love and traditional marriage.

This vulnerability of the other and instinctive call to responsibility one cannot give up is dramatised in greatest detail in Aziz's relationship with his 'little brother'. Levinas describes this kind of encounter as an infinite responsibility in 'face' of the other, to the extent that one is 'obsessed by the other', restless and unhomed, and as a result 'no escaping is possible' [1974] (1998: 77). Aziz initially describes Reda as a sickly, dependent nuisance, an obstacle on their trip to Europe: it would be 'typical of him to go and let himself die in the most cowardly, squalid way possible' (173). But when he almost dies while launching the migrants' boat, Aziz stays behind the entire night and talks him back into regaining consciousness: 'I'll be your eyes and you'll be mine. We'll look after each other, we'll never split up, will we, little brother? But you've got to get up now. Do it for me' (175). Asserting their interdependence in this way, Aziz has relinquished his greatest obsession, his dream of escape to Europe, in order to take care of an injured other.

In *Hope*, the opening chapter 'The Trip' is the only shared locus of otherwise disparate life narratives of the prospective migrants. Rather than providing an external observation point, Lalami gives Murad the privileged first-person perspective in this chapter, which helps her highlight a sense of genuine curiosity and empathy in his attention to his fellow travellers. Murad ponders the ironies of the second North African 'invasion' of Spain, where 'instead of a fleet, here we are on an inflatable boat – not just Moors, but a motley mix of people from the ex-colonies, without guns or armour' (3). This observation also mocks the frequent emphasis on immigrating North Africans not as Spain's formerly colonised populations, but rather as its medieval colonisers,[6] which makes them seem more likely to dominate and 'contaminate' Spain. Murad's own apprehensiveness is slowly disarmed by the vulnerability he observes in other passengers, although he at first thinks of himself as better than others because of his university education in English and Spanish: 'he doesn't want to break his back for the *spagnol*' like everyone else (3). Murad is increasingly intrigued by Faten, frequently referencing her actions and emotions; he is also awed by Halima's 'aura of quiet determination' (6).

The passengers in the boat help one another – offering the last bits of food and water, and encouraging smiles, to those in need – and the narrative builds this sense of kinship not so much through conversation and exchange of ideas as by focusing on affect and body language. In the tight space of the boat, Faten retracts her leg so it doesn't brush against Murad's, her gesture suggesting reluctance and indecision; Aziz is 'tall and lanky and sits hunched over' (4) to make room for others; the Guinean woman is nervous as 'she cradles her body and rocks gently back and forth' (6). Despite the forced, even uncomfortable, sense of physical intimacy, the passengers communicate with one another through familiar physical reactions that unite them beyond cultural and linguistic barriers. It is the confrontation with the embodied presence of the other with an alien smell, feel and language that demands one's response and help. It divests one of identity boundaries, 'under the traumatic effect of persecution' by the suffering other to whom one becomes infinitely responsible (Levinas 1998: 112).

For instance, when the Guinean woman vomits on Faten and the stench is inescapable, Murad defends Faten after the trafficker Rahal yells at her to 'shut up'. In fact, Murad often defends other female passengers from Rahal's unscrupulous treatment of them as commodities to be delivered, while Rahal merely invokes his patriarchal authority to intimidate unaccompanied Muslim women. This earns Murad an appreciative smile from Halima, the only woman who does not let herself be scared into silence by Rahal's virtually limitless power in this imbalanced social dynamic. Murad's assumption of responsibility for others to whom he has become irretrievably united is dramatised in the final part of the chapter when Rahal makes the passengers swim the last bit of the trip. Murad is torn between helping Faten, who grips onto him fighting for her life and training her to swim so as to help them both survive (12). After making the difficult decision to free himself or else drown, 'a sob forms in his throat . . . He's already drifting away from her, but he keeps calling out, telling her to calm down . . . He closes his eyes, but the image of Faten is waiting for him behind the lids' (12).

This self-defensive decision means that Murad remains haunted by Faten's pleas for help. When he is arrested and taken to a detention centre, he vomits at the sight of body bags, recalling an earlier scene in the boat, as he imagines his own and other passengers' bodies in the bags (17). At this stage, his body has become interchangeable with others, only one variation on the collective migrant body, in the face of which former distinctions of education and plans to get a better job in Spain seem meaningless. Certainly, the border here works as a great equaliser, reducing the specificity of one's predicament to the label of illegal migrants, who are treated as if interchangeable. This resonates with European media discourses on migrant deaths and arrivals, most frequently expressed in terms of numbers and statistics. However, Murad's affect – nausea, caused by the migrants' shared anxiety – and tendency to empathetically align himself with people on the boat rather than a future community in

Spain suddenly ties him back to the African continent which he has decided to abandon.

In both novels, this unavoidable responsibility for the others with whom one has (unexpectedly) come into contact is also described as a function of one's fate, not only in the sense of passive, fatalistic reconciliation with a difficult situation but also as an act of agency, the need to deal with the here and now which cannot be wished away. In *Welcome to Paradise,* Aziz, though feeling like a 'stranger among his kin', believes he must make the best of his 'lot', a word which is often used to signify the inescapable circumstances of one's existential condition (166). The ethics of the here and now which creates unlikely affiliations among the migrants is only one manifestation of the unpredictability of social relations and refusal of hegemonic cause and effect narratives. It is expressed through a frequent use of words such as lot, fate and luck, as well as references to looking to the stars for guidance or ascribing turbulent emotions to *djinn* possession. These references also articulate a religious world view, although the very belief in God's providence is subverted at the end, when most of the migrants drown at sea, despite Aziz's conviction that God would not create such a beautiful creature like Pafadnam only to kill him. But frequent invocations of the mystical ways of the universe also implies that, in *Welcome to Paradise*, the social circumstances into which one is born are like fate in that they largely exceed individual control and agency.

Reflecting on European hippies who visit Morocco, unaware of their accidental privilege of birth, Aziz says:

> What did they want from us, these people who taunted us with their freedom to come and go as they pleased? . . . Just think! To be able to leave, leave and forget this devouring sun, this lethargy and idleness, this corruption and filth, this cowardice and deceit that are our lot here. (47)

The hippies' careless attitude to being born into a European nationality is all the more insulting to Moroccans who can hardly hope to acquire the prized European citizenship and for whom even the prospect of arriving in Europe appears just as distant and magical. Binebine suggests that Europe is either one's birthplace by sheer luck or an elusive Neverland beyond the reach of migrants. Such a dialectic challenges meritocratic assumptions about existing opportunities to earn a European work visa by being a model hardworking immigrant.[7] For migrants, Europe becomes an elusive chimera, the Real, disaster or success, dream fulfilment or perpetual nightmare. Given the trafficker Morad's stories of Europe as paradise, the thought of leaving for this 'elsewhere' that provides a solution to all earthly worries is described as a 'virus' that cannot be overcome.

While all the characters have pragmatic plans for their lives in Europe, it is this mythical image of Europe as a dubious paradise that trumps any portrayals of Europe as an actual geographic space of increased employment opportunity. The characters themselves barely come across as actual people with vibrant lives, languishing, instead, in a social death. Both in their countries of origin and in their crossing over to Europe, they already are, or must become, invisible. As they wait for their trip on a lifeless beach away from the bustling city, they are depicted as shadows and ghosts, their boat resembling a 'sea coffin'. Aziz observes that a life of hardship tamed Pafadnam's 'wild, virile beauty' into a small, 'humble and fearful' creature that already slipped 'into the skin of a refugee' (66). This humility prepares them for their European future, where they will have to practise disappearing into the crowd, avoiding eye contact and being 'another shadow, a stray dog, a lowly earthworm, or even a cockroach' (66). This association of illegal migrants with scorned animals and vermin is telling, given direct references to Nazi extermination camps in other parts of the novel. Undertaking a risky crossing that often results in death, paradoxically, highlights their only, rebellious, act of agency, but the narrative cannot imagine a substantial improvement over the past life of social death, even if they were to survive the crossing. Binebine forecloses the image of Europe as a safe haven – they can never truly arrive in Europe – and instead, locates the essence of this act of agency in the creation of an empathetic community among the migrants.

When most of the characters drown in the crossing, their disaster is only mediated as a real event via a television programme that Reda and Aziz watch; they are momentarily evacuated from invisibility even as they are reduced to a statistic. Not only are their individual backgrounds obliterated and meaningless in the media report, they are additionally 'unreal' in the eyes of international law because they have become the 'harragas', those who join the ranks of the stateless by burning one's identity papers – people without a past or a future, perfect necropolitical subjects.[8] From this perspective, paradise is not just the European utopia where every need has been met; it is also the place to which one goes upon death, a final dissolution of identity. In Binebine, paradise is a place of anticipated, forbidden pleasures, as well as a place of respite from earthly worries.

Going back to the pervasive tropes of luck and fate, in Lalami's *Hope*, the sheer luck of birth differentiates between migrants who have a choice to study in North America and those who are forced to undertake an illegal crossing of the Gibraltar Strait. Interestingly, the stereotype of religiosity as a ubiquitous, fatalistic Arab mindset is mocked here by tying religious devotion to the accidental birth into a specific social class in Morocco. For instance, the wealthy Nuara can choose whether she wants to wear modest Islamic dress or not; poor women like Faten only have access to Islamic dress or other traditional clothes, so their choices are severely limited. The underground mosque Faten joins gives her not only a sense of dignity and community to sustain her in the face of taunts over her poverty, but also the language with which to criticise rampant social inequalities.

A sense of fatalism pervades this novel, exemplified by social paralysis, constant mourning of missed opportunities and obsession with an unattainable future. Given limited possibilities, the decision to cross the Gibraltar Strait, while an act of radical agency, is interpreted as a dangerous gamble: tempting one's luck, as it were. The characters see the crossing as an event that disturbs the established order of things, as if their very act of asserting independence from the circumstances of birth is an unthinkable betrayal. The narrative suggests that they merely substitute one type of prison for another: their destinies, even at this moment, are not their own. They are in the hands of 'the captain, the coast guards, God'. The Mediterranean is unpredictable, Murad ponders, and so is their boat, breaking down in the middle of the sea. Faten sees this incident as a confirmation that this 'unnatural' trip is cursed; while other passengers do not share her religious interpretation and pragmatically focus on the engine problem, 'her hysteria is contagious' (8).

In *Hope*, some characters make it beyond European borders, but as in *Welcome to Paradise*, most do not. For survivors of the trip, whether they stay in Europe or are deported back to Morocco, daily subsistence is all they can hope for. Living with low or non-existent income in Morocco suggests a social death in the face of which even a suicidal, 'blasphemous' crossing of the Mediterranean becomes an act of agency, a potential line of flight, as in *Welcome to Paradise*.

Repeated crossings, while economically disastrous, imply a refusal of life in death and of bare survival, which comes across as even more unbearable.

Tracing Morocco's migrant flows to both Europe and North America, Lalami's novel also muses on the advantages of education as a path to upward mobility. For upper-class Moroccans, being educated in private French *lycées*, a leftover from colonial times, makes them competitive candidates for North American universities, which enable a neocolonial brain drain. If they were to remain in Morocco, the novel implies, their economic status would be far from certain, not least because of unemployment and endemic corruption.[9] For instance, Murad prides himself on his Bachelor's degree in English and his love of British literature, but his education is virtually useless in Morocco. Also, his upward mobility is severely limited by his class status; his family can neither afford to send him abroad nor do they have connections to find him professional employment at home.

Lalami implies that Murad could make more money smuggling goods from Melilla than using his English degree; ironically, his survival would again be dependent on the existence of a Spanish 'beyond'. He can only use his degree as a freelance tourist guide for Americans who visit Morocco on a pilgrimage to cultural sites related to Paul Bowles and William S. Burroughs. Such tourists are consistently portrayed as benevolent but oblivious to the social dynamics they enter. For instance, Murad witnesses a haggling over a 'vintage' Moroccan Quranic schoolboy's tablet which the tourists treat as a quaint commodity they can turn into a decoration on the other side of the world, disengaging it from its historical and cultural context. Murad slowly awakens to this problematic dynamic, even though it is described indirectly: he imagines the schoolboy's life, his history and community, which includes another reflection on the lost potential of Moroccan children's education. Murad reads the inscription the boy made, 'a verse from Sura 96 . . . "Read, in the name of thy Lord, who created"'. While the inscription reflects the hope and promise of education, Murad cannot know if the boy 'finished Quranic school and went on to public school or whether he'd been sent into apprenticeship' (179). He then reflects on his own generation's forgetting of their cultural heritage, deciding that it was wrong of him to be so focused on his future in Spain: 'when he thought of the future, he saw himself in front of his children, as mute as if his tongue had been cut off, unable to recount for them the stories he'd heard as a child' (186).

The novel ends on a hopeful note: in the final section, 'Storytelling', Murad reclaims the past, thinking of the oral stories and songs that had been forgotten and regaling American tourists with a Moroccan fairy tale rather than his usual, tourist-adapted spiel on Paul Bowles. As the Americans haggle over a Moroccan rug, Murad tells the story of love between a poor muezzin's daughter and a rug maker, which triumphs over various obstacles presented by those in power. Like many fairy tales, this one too is a narrative in which injustice is redressed and the poor and the scorned end up victorious, mirroring Murad's own development as an empowered subject who has found an independent, albeit unprofitable, voice. Ahmed Alami observes that Murad's transformation 'from a reader, a consumer of translated Moroccan oral tales written into English by Bowles, into a storyteller, a producer of tales in their original oral form' is 'an act of postcolonial resistance and personal cultural triumph' (2012: 151).

This event spurs a profound change of heart: Murad develops a new sense of self, abandoning his lifestyle of begging Western tourists for work. While this denouement by no means suggests a radical or even comprehensive political change, the novel's refusal to fetishise Europe as the only possible future for desperate Moroccans is significant. It is through this and other small, however isolated, gestures of hospitality to the history which has become foreign, and to foreign people who share one's own predicament, that Lalami's *Hope and Other Dangerous Pursuits* suggests possible modes of connecting.

In Binebine's novel, the migrants' quest to reach Europe, if not entirely self-destructive, is more Sisyphean than Odyssean, as their repeated failed attempts far outnumber successful arrivals and those who eventually arrive in the European 'paradise' encounter the eponymous 'cannibals' who will ingest them economically and culturally. Simultaneously, however, the novel imagines hopeful transnational connections among aspiring migrants, highlights points of contact, mutual aid and compassion and complicating identity politics that isolates rather than connects both at home and abroad. Despite the grim ending, the migrants could perhaps be seen as communities prefiguring the multitudes who will someday appear en masse in European streets as political subjects demanding recognition, being and acting in-common, despite not having common ethnic or cultural backgrounds.

On the other hand, this impetus for empathy and social levelling results from an extreme, deadly situation, and we might ask where it might lead, beyond a momentary connection, after the migrants disperse into their individual predicaments. This problem is especially highlighted through Lalami's narrative structure, which hinders the alternative mapping of solidarity and community since individual narratives remain solipsistic both 'before' and 'after' the Gibraltar crossing. In contrast to *Welcome to Paradise*, however, *Hope*'s main focus is not so much the tragedy of social death through emigration; rather, its main concern is the future of Morocco as a postcolonial state that drives away the educated cadres it needs. This brain drain is aided by Moroccans' self-denigration, active obliteration of the country's educational and cultural heritage in favour of Western standards of intellectual advancement. As the ending of the novel suggests, then, agency can be asserted not only by rejecting life in Morocco altogether, but also by remaining in the country and acquiring a new sense of identity through anticolonial resistance.

Terraferma and solidarity in a state of exception

Emanuele Crialese's film *Terraferma* shifts the focus from the experiences and relationships among migrants who jointly undertake Mediterranean crossings to borderline zones of legal and cultural exception where necropolitical EU sovereignty overlaps with controversial acts of hospitality and generosity between EU citizens and prospective immigrants. Like Crialese's *Respiro* (2002) and *Nuovomondo* (translated as *Golden Door*, 2006), *Terraferma* centres on isolated, economically marginalised and culturally idiosyncratic islands off the coast of Sicily. But rather than exploiting stereotypes of 'backwards' islanders entrenched in their ways and rejecting outsiders, *Terraferma* places the state and EU border laws under scrutiny, as the islanders' private gestures of hospitality contest legal prohibitions against hospitality to undocumented migrants. Here, hospitality is alternately offered or demanded, creating precarious but hopeful forms of non-filial community between citizens and migrants.

Terraferma won the special jury prize at the Venice film festival and went on to become Italy's entry for Best Foreign Language Film at the 2012 Academy Awards. It also received a warm applause from the residents of Lampedusa, Italy's biggest landing point for illegal migrants arriving from Africa and a major entry point into the EU. While *Terraferma* was filmed on Linosa, Lampedusa's smaller neighbour, which has also become a migrant destination since the 2011 Arab Spring, the film's unnamed setting invokes the more familiar Lampedusa because of its proximity to Africa, economic marginalisation and long-standing conflicts with the Italian coastguards over the treatment of illegal migrants. Certainly, Crialese's dignified and complex treatment of the issue that is often sensationalised in the media, along with his decision to cast a former migrant who herself crossed the Mediterranean illegally, attests to his concern about the treatment of African migrants at the hands of coastguards.[10] Significantly, Crialese's feature joined more than ten other films depicting immigration and racism at the 2011 Venice film festival. According to Annamaria Rivera, this suggests that Italian cinema has finally become a space for meaningful discussions of 'issues of racism and of the general living conditions of immigrants', a remarkable development in a climate where a deconstruction of stigmatising, anti-immigrant rhetoric is limited to 'a minority consisting of a few scholars, some excellent journalists . . . a certain number of anti-racist activists and some specialised media outlets' (2011: 8). Like 'illiterature' which opens up new political discourses by tackling taboo topics, film here assumes the role of critiquing Italy's encounters with non-European others.

Like Spain, Italy too attracted greater immigration only since the 1980s; in that respect, it is a latecomer among European nations whose immigrant populations began to arrive in greater numbers after World War II, often as a result of decolonisation. The relatively recent phenomenon of immigration, along with the abovementioned scarcity of anti-racist discourses, makes it possible to relegate to public oblivion Italy's own participation in European colonialism and history of racism towards non-European others. Italy's profound internal divisions, history of invasion and subaltern status within Europe and massive emigration to North America have led to a situation in which 'despite its aggressive past, Italy still perceives itself more as a colonised country than as a coloniser' (Ponzanesi 2004: 105). Because of their own marginalised status, Italian colonisers in Africa perceived themselves as 'good brothers of the African people (*italiani brava gente*)', selfless, sensitive civilisers who brought progress without engaging in calculated economic exploitation (Ponzanesi 109).

Italy's self-marginalisation even within European colonial discourses and claims of kinship with the colonised peoples are mirrored in internal divisions, where the North is perceived as more
European and developed and the South as more African, a virtual
internal colony associated with laziness, poverty and disorganisation.
If, in Spain, Africa begins south of the Pyrenees, in Italy, according
to a popular saying, it begins south of Rome. Today, the assumption
of these various subaltern positions leads to the rejection of responsibility for (neo)colonialism and the downplaying of racism through
the myth of Italians as 'good brothers' to immigrants. On the other
hand, this affiliation with the marginalised, along with traditional distrust of central government and the privileging of solidarity as a core
Christian value, often inspire Italians to embrace their lack of clear
European 'roots' by taking to the streets to protest anti-immigrant
sentiment and race crimes. Sabrina Brancato argues that this sense of
kinship and empathy, especially towards southern Italians, pervades
African-Italian literature as well, resulting in a 'much more concilia-
tory and reassuring tone' than their counterparts in English or French
(2009: 52, 56).

Since the Italian South is a European border within reach of
Africa, the relationship between local southern and central Italian
authorities has become strained over the treatment of undocumented
migrants. *Terraferma* explores issues of hospitality to strangers, especially the conflict between private modes of island hospitality (the
law of the sea) and the government laws of hospitality which guard
the Schengen border against illegal migrants even at the cost of letting
them drown. Italian laws on intercepting migrants in the sea became
even more stringent than EU laws in 2009, when Italy negotiated
the so-called 'pushback policy' with Libya. Because of this policy,
Italian military vessels stopped migrant boats and returned 'nearly
1000 migrants – mostly asylum seekers from Eritrea, Somalia, Ethiopia and Sudan – to Libya, a country that has not signed the Geneva
Convention and doesn't recognise the right of asylum' ('Solid Sea'
2002: n.p.). The policy has since been suspended and condemned
by the European Court of Human Rights, but *Terraferma*, filmed in
2011, responds to this absolute denial of the right to a safe landing.
Currently Italy has to allow undocumented migrants to land and
accept asylum requests, but it can repatriate migrants who do not
receive asylum. In late 2013, after 366 migrants perished a mile away
from Lampedusa, prompting Pope Francis to call for a more humane

treatment of migrants, Italy also launched the 'Mare Nostrum' military operation, which actively scouted the sea for migrant boats in need of help and rescue. But Italy's policy to prevent further deaths in the Mediterranean remained isolated in the EU, which provided very limited financial and logistical support.[11] In 2014 this operation came to an end and was replaced by the much more limited operation 'Triton', in cooperation with Frontex, which consists in boats patrolling close to the Italian coast.

In *Terraferma*, shipwrecked migrants are invariably rescued by fishermen, while Italian coastguards remain an absent presence. Nonetheless, Italian fishermen assisting illegal migrants who are stranded at sea – according to a longstanding code of compassion and aid which ensures that nobody will be left to drown – are in danger of being declared smugglers and arrested. The act of helping a person in distress effectively criminalises Italian citizens by associating them with the maligned profession of human trafficking.[12] Significantly, it also negates the possibility of help and hospitality that is not economically interested, since, from a necropolitical perspective, unsolicited migrants are economically useless and superfluous. The island portrayed in *Terraferma* struggles with the arrival of illegal migrants after Ernesto and his grandson Filippo, members of the fishing family on which the narrative centres, rescue four African migrants from certain death. Sara, a pregnant Ethiopian woman, and her son are hidden from the authorities in the family garage, where the family reside over the summer, having decided to rent their house to tourists. Consequently, the various family members have to make difficult decisions which put them in conflict with one another, the authorities and tourists from the mainland.

The family conflicts over aiding and abetting migrants are contextualised within the larger island community debates over their economic impoverishment and insignificance. At the meeting of the island elders, ageing fishermen say that the sea used to be so full of fish that families could feed many children, whereas now they only fish 'live and dead bodies'. Moreover, they were taught to save people, and now they have to teach their children to change course when they encounter 'black skin'. These shifting social and economic trends resonate with Lampedusa's current travails due to the depletion of resources through overfishing and the inability of local fishermen to compete with large corporations and Tunisian fishermen in the neoliberal economy.[13] The islanders' response in *Terraferma*, as in the case of Lampedusa, has been to supplement income in the summer by attracting mainland tourists to the island. Lampedusa itself was 'discovered' by Italian media only after a Libyan ship crashed against its coast in the 1980s, and ever since, it has struggled to market itself as a pristine tourist resort and overcome the stigma of being an immigrant detention centre. But Lampedusans are still anxious that they are seen 'as just a pinprick on the map' (Van't Klooster 2012: 1). In the film, this sense of geographic and symbolic marginalisation informs the scene in which Giulietta, Filippo's mother, is unable to find their island on the globe to show Sara her current location. 'We're not on the globe. Our island is too small', she explains.

Dreaming of a more economically secure life, Giulietta advocates selling the family fishing boat and moving with her son to the mainland (the eponymous *terraferma*) which lures her with the promise of a full-time job for herself and increased educational opportunities for Filippo. The family is torn by both generational and gender gaps: Ernesto wants to preserve the old tradition of fishing and clashes with his daughter-in-law Giulietta, whose husband died at sea and whose sense of youthful, stifled energy pervades the film. Giulietta's decision to rent out the family house to tourists alarms both Ernesto and Filippo because of her new-found initiative and freedom. Crialese often accentuates the pent-up sexual energy for both mother and son, who have no outlet that would place them beyond the Oedipal dynamic. Filippo is ridiculed by their three tourist-lodgers, who are his age, for living a sheltered life with his mother (for instance, he doesn't know what 'topless' sunbathing means), while Giulietta cannot demonstrate her affection for Filippo in public without making him uncomfortable.

While Giulietta sees *terraferma* as an escape into modernity and increased opportunity, her brother-in-law Nino clashes with Ernesto because he wants to make the island part of the modern economy by attracting tourist investment and complying with the law in surrendering illegals to coastguards. At the meeting of the elders he argues that half-dead migrants washing up on their beaches are bad for 'publicity', prompting Ernesto to mock his son's calculated pragmatism and ask 'Mr. Publicity', 'Do you want us to let them drown so we have good publicity?' This foreshadows the larger clash between the local ethics of personal help and necropolitical disposability of unprofitable lives in the interest of economic prosperity. The film's central question about who has the right to offer or curtail hospitality to strangers results in alternating assertions of authority by the islanders, the local police and the coastguards, without any group claiming ultimate power. As Mbembe notes of the colonial logic of domination:

> The claim to ultimate or final authority in a particular political space is not easily made. Instead, a patchwork of overlapping and incomplete rights to rule emerges, inextricably superimposed and tangled, in which different de facto juridical instances are geographically interwoven and plural allegiances, asymmetrical suzerainties, and enclaves abound. (2003: 31)

In the film, the incongruity as well as the blurring of limits between private and public, informal and formal, modes of hospitality, which Derrida discusses in *Of Hospitality* [1997] (2000), metonymically invoke the South's subaltern status and resentment against being controlled by the more affluent North. Derrida writes, 'from the moment when a public authority, a State . . . gives itself or is recognised as having the right to control, monitor, ban exchanges that those doing the exchanging deem private . . . then every element of hospitality gets disrupted'. This disruption of privacy by the State 'becomes a violation of the inviolable, in the place where inviolable immunity remains the condition of hospitality' (2000: 51).

Lampedusa's history is marked by such agonistic interactions with external authorities, which has affected the island's approach to offering shelter and hospitality. An exceptional, intercultural space at the crossroads of trade routes between Africa, Europe and Asia, it developed well-established practices of hospitality to pirates, runaway slaves and other subjects outside the law (Friese 2008: 6). After Italian unification, its renegade status was neutralised by both physical and symbolic assertion of national authority: it became one of the penal colonies where anti-unification southern insurgents, already seen as racially inferior to northerners, could be sent into internal exile (*domicilio coatto*). According to Joseph Pugliese, 'the arbitrary and abusive exercise of discretionary police power' that characterised this nineteenth-century policy is a blueprint for Lampedusa's current 'state of exception' where similar violations of human rights occur in the treatment of migrants in refugee camps and detention centres (2010: 111). Lampedusa's state of borderline exception, like that on the island in *Terraferma*, is thus twofold: island practices are extrajuridical in

disobeying national policies, whereas such policies are in turn controversial both because the law itself issues 'exceptional laws' to deal with
undocumented migrants and because its enforcers arbitrarily suspend
existing rights and duties (Agamben 2005: 21).

Lampedusans' offer of hospitality to the first migrant arrivals
was informal: people cooked for them, accommodated them in
their homes and gave them clothes (Friese 2012: 72–3). As more
migrants kept arriving, hospitality became institutionalised, leading to a split between informal and professional modes of hospitality and a physical segregation between migrants and residents. As
in *Terraferma*, Lampedusans also became torn between demands
for hospitality by two groups of visitors whose life worlds are not
meant to meet: migrants and tourists. Indeed, their reactions have
ranged from blatantly disregarding official warnings against aiding migrants; feeling compassion for migrants due to their own
history of emigration and scarcity; profiting from the 'migrant
industry'; condemning those who do; to annoyance that migrant
arrivals and protests interfere with tourists' relaxation on their
island.[14] On this previously isolated island, far-reaching economic
and political events are displacing local control in a culmination of
extremes that encapsulate the global North-South divide. To maintain this divide, the authorities must ensure a separate existence of
overlapping, yet exclusive geographies (Mbembe 2003: 28): the
two groups must 'unsee' each other, like in Mieville's *The City
and the City*.[15] Pugliese observes, 'These two incompatible orders
of space-time fold silently, invisibly, one into the other yet never
breach their respective borders. The presence of the immigration
detention prisons' is 'unspeakable' (2010: 119). *Terraferma* demonstrates that unseeing becomes increasingly impossible because
of inescapable proximity to the other's vulnerability and evolving
relations of intimacy in a restricted space.

The film repeatedly highlights the unseen economy of death that
haunts and, literally, underlies oblivious tourist enjoyment of the Mediterranean. The three camera shots filmed from under the sea surface
and directed upward, towards 'normal' life taking place above the sea,
ominously invoke the graveyard in the sea that remains physically and
symbolically submerged, making above-surface lives possible. The film
opens with the shot of Ernesto's boat from below the sea surface, with
fishing nets being lowered menacingly, spreading into a cage across the
screen. Elena Past argues that:

The image of the net becomes a poetic sign for Crialese, a visually overdetermined symbol that evokes human dependence on the sea, human entanglement with marine life, and the intensity of relationship for any life – human or nonhuman – so closely bound to another. Both porous and perilous, livelihood and instrument of death, the net encompasses the paradoxes of island existence. (2013: 57)

While the lives above and below sea are thus paradoxically intertwined, they are juxtaposed and contrasted, almost as a play between what is consciously visible or admissible versus what remains repressed in the collective subconscious. When the camera moves beyond the sea surface, the contrast surprises the viewer as the noise of seagulls and the hustle and bustle on the fishing boat come rushing in. Initially, Ernesto and Filippo float by the debris of a boat with Arabic script but ignore it (though it breaks their propeller), just as, in a later scene, the tourists on a boat which Nino operates for entertainment remain blind to the fact that they share the Mediterranean with illegal migrants. In this scene, Nino leads tourists in a fun dance to loud music; the tourists wave their arms and sway their hips before jumping off the boat in unison. Crialese divests this event from its carefree atmosphere as the viewers are reminded of an earlier, almost identically constructed scene, in which illegal migrants packed on a boat wave their arms calling for help and then jump into the sea to swim to Ernesto's boat. After the tourists have jumped off the boat in the latter scene, the camera moves below sea surface, distorting the sound of the music completely and transforming the swimming tourists into mere bodies floating in the sea, eerily indistinguishable from drowned migrants.

The final below-sea-surface shot follows the scene in which shipwrecked migrants wash ashore on a popular beach in broad daylight, ruining Nino's carefully constructed tourist utopia. The camera moves from the few survivors to scan the seabed, recording such mundane belongings as lost shoes, toothpaste and combs. While the far more numerous dead bodies are made invisible here through the metonymy of personal items, these intimate, everyday objects seem effective in contesting ubiquitous media representations of migrants as indistinguishable, countable, dead bodies. Such objects attest to the once living, desiring beings, silenced and inaccessible, but, again, no different than the tourists with their mundane routines.

From the very beginning, the underwater scenes suggest that the sea is already full of dead human bodies. The invariably gloomy, horror-film tone and camera angle of the scenes make this truth seem almost obscene, rewriting typical images of the sea as either a peaceful, if mysterious, dwelling of life-sustaining wildlife or as paradisiacal, temporary summer respite for deserving tourists. The real horror is not that clandestine migrants might harm the islanders – in *Terraferma*, their actions are exceptionally benign – but that they will not remain clandestine. They repeatedly address islanders for help, and it is just a matter of time before it becomes impossible to feign indifference and maintain the lines of segregation that dooms them to invisibility. Regardless of how assiduously the islanders try to promote the image of a Mediterranean paradise, the reality of migrancy ultimately makes this vision impossible, as illegals arrive with increasing ethical urgency and at most inopportune moments. As in Lalami and Binebine, it becomes impossible to control access to the Mediterranean; the disruptive arrivals in *Terraferma* parallel recent trends of migrants landing on Lampedusa (and more recently Linosa) vastly outnumbering the residents. With residents, tourists and migrants all laying claim to the Mediterranean, Crialese blurs the boundaries of nationhood and selfhood.

In *Terraferma*, the islanders are alternately resentful of mainland laws and concerned about their negative image as an Italian frontier outpost 'infected' by migrancy and death. Their preoccupation with their marginal status, along with the seemingly more urbane tourists' mockery of their 'backwardness', places them in another state of exception in terms of being both connected to and divorced from the larger national body. The provincialised islanders see *terraferma* as a Big Other whose approval they desire but whose control they fear. Nonetheless, the film never actually takes us to the mainland, suggesting that the island is a world unto itself, where community ties and established forms of sociality take precedence. As one of the fishermen says, in defence of assisting illegals, 'we live on a reef in the middle of the sea and we have to respect the law of the sea'.

On the other hand, this reef, rather than mainland, becomes a provisional *terraferma* for the migrants, who re-inscribe it as Italy. Crialese suggests that the island's shifting geo-graphing, along with its ultimate absence on the map, makes it possible for the islanders to help and connect with the migrants, as both groups have historically been cast as colonial subjects vis-à-vis the mainland. As an unrelenting critic of economic 'progress' and contemporary policies on deporting migrants and denying them assistance in the sea, Ernesto is unsurprisingly the most selfless among the family members when it comes to hiding the migrants in his garage. Of failing health, Ernesto risks his life when he jumps into the sea and rescues the migrants; he helps to deliver Sara's baby; he loses his boat, his means of livelihood, when it's seized by the coastguards for allegations of sheltering illegals; and finally, he tries to smuggle Sara and her children in his car onto a ferry destined to the mainland before turning back to avoid police checkpoints. While the film focuses on conflicts within a single family to explore intimate spaces of private hospitality, they are not alone in their fight against the authorities. At their meeting, the elders pledge solidarity in standing up to the authorities, which results in the subversive act of unloading truckloads of fish in front the police station after the police impound Ernesto's boat. However, not everyone demonstrates the same level of hospitality; while private modes of hospitality certainly contest official modes, they are still botched, usurped, alternately demanded and refused.

As Mireille Rosello points out, the 'chain of hospitality has to be contested, alternatively usurped and ceded, to make hospitality less of a power issue' (2002: 17). Rosello imagines the guest's agency while building on Derrida's observation that both conditional and unconditional hospitality place the host, however precariously, in a position of power. The gesture of offering hospitality, according to Derrida, is characterised by an irresolvable aporia – the fact that one can generously or without reserve offer hospitality to some other is already predicated upon an existence of a home, one's dwelling over which he or she rules supreme and from which others can be shut out (2000: 51–5). The film develops several interactions between Giulietta and Sara, where the guest refuses to play by the host's rules, makes demands, and places more responsibility on the host than she wants to accept. In one of the early scenes, Giulietta says that Sara can eat and then has to leave, to which Sara, whose Italian is limited, responds, 'eat', without agreeing to the demand to leave. This power dynamic slowly shifts as Giulietta finds a new source of confidence and utility in tending to Sara's newborn and to Sara herself as a recuperating mother. In one scene, Guilietta has taken the crying baby in her arms and almost instantly calmed her down. She is visibly uneasy when Sara tells her, the baby 'was born with your hands', so Giulietta's smell soothes her. Giulietta is overwhelmed by this demand for intimacy and responsibility which comes with saving someone's life and delivering her child, and it is difficult for her to remain in a position of distance and power when Sara decides that these life experiences have made them 'sisters', placing them on an equal footing. In this state of exception, the two women slowly negotiate a community that is not based on ethnic or racial belonging, but rather on one's ability to care for the other. As in *Welcome to Paradise* and *Hope and Other Dangerous Pursuits*, such community is not necessarily negotiated through language, but rather through affect, instinctive physical reactions and acknowledgement of the other's pain.

Giulietta's full change of heart never takes place, however, and would appear sentimental and unconvincing in a film that highlights imperfect hospitality and fear of authorities that criminalise private initiatives to help migrants. Likewise, it would strengthen the colonial myth of good-hearted Italians who selflessly help the less fortunate 'others'. Sara says the newborn will be given the name of her saviour, asking Giulietta, 'What is your name?' to which Giulietta doesn't respond, equally refusing to ask Sara *her* name. This refusal to exchange names suggests another denial of intimacy; nonetheless, by the end, before attempting to cross to the mainland, Sara apologises to Giulietta, as if to acknowledge the risk the family have willingly entered for her sake, and it is only at that point that Giulietta embraces her, crying. This recognition of mutual vulnerability[16] in the act of illegal hospitality is compounded by their shared problems of motherhood, as Sara's difficult relationship with her elder son reminds Giulietta of her own problems with Filippo. Sara's son is angry with his mother for caring for his baby sister who is the result of war rape. Sara's sexuality, like Giulietta's, is a site where patriarchal control must be asserted: because she has been dishonoured by rape, the son is afraid that his father, when they reach him, might reject both her and the baby.

Filippo similarly goes through a transformation in his attitude to the migrants, which the film, as in the case of Giulietta, expresses through changing facial expressions, affect and instinctive actions rather than through dialogue. He is haunted by the faces of shipwrecked migrants who wash up on the beach packed with tourists and even more so by the migrants who cling to his boat when he takes Maura, one of their tourist-lodgers, for a romantic night ride. In the latter scene, he beats the migrants' hands with an oar until they finally let go of his boat, the darkness of their hands blending with the colour of the sea, black in the moonlight. However, Filippo becomes a 'hostage' to this trauma, in Levinas's terms, a self obsessed and persecuted by alterity, '"in myself" through the others' (1998: 112). He is no longer capable of unseeing the migrants, and, for that matter, neither can Maura; this scene has momentarily united them in their shared privilege vis-à-vis the pleading migrants. Crialese inserts affect as if to remedy increasingly frequent, real-life situations in which tourists on a beach react to arriving migrants with inactivity and indifference.[17]

By the end of the film, Filippo disobeys his family by spontaneously whisking off Sara and her children to their boat and heading to the mainland. In the final scene, the lone boat is rushing to the mainland, and the camera zooms out, so that the boat is ultimately seen gliding across the globe, finally placing the islanders on the map. The boat has now become a lone reef in the middle of a vast sea, which suggests that their journey to *terraferma*, both physical and figurative, is as far from certain as in *Welcome to Paradise* and *Hope and Other Dangerous Pursuits*. The scene can be interpreted as either optimistic or rashly utopian due to this nearly fantastic setting, in which a lone boat (impossibly) sails across a vast sea in defiance of everyone. Past observes that as the 'rhythmic waves fill the screen and gradually erase all signs of forward progress' Crialese highlights the 'collective, liquid movement' of the Mediterranean that overwhelms individual human agency (2013: 63). Despite this diminution of individual agency, the importance of this scene lies in its impulsively compassionate gesture, the independent decision made by Filippo: he has finally come of age by breaking with the authorities, aligning himself with his grandfather Ernesto's, rather than his uncle Nino's, sense of ethics. *Terraferma*'s closing scene, without regard of the outcome, then, affirms the (im)possible island ethics of hospitality to strangers, embodied in the intense entanglements of neighbourliness and a shared condition of subalternity. Filippo's and Sara's family's breach becomes a line of flight from the necropolitical mechanisms of policing the EU border, and preserving the global North-South divide, by ensuring that residents remain segregated from and in control of migrants.

Strange encounters and multicultural love in *Eternity and A Day*

In the final section, I will focus on another film of border crossing in liminal zones of Europe to think about the interplay between official policies of multicultural hospitality and embodied everyday encounters between 'others' separated by the aforementioned dichotomies that inform the EU's political imaginary. Theo Angelopoulos's *Eternity and a Day* thematises Greece's struggle with revising national spaces into multicultural spaces in the1990s, both in the context of a rising number of postcommunist migrants and the country's position as an EU frontier outpost in the Balkans, symbolically and physically severed from the rest of the Schengen single-border zone.[18] *Eternity and a Day* gestures towards an ethics of unconditional welcome and responsibility for another, outside of and prior to discourses on national (or other) identity, historiography, or a remembered ill for which one must offer reparation. However, the film does not offer a facile vision of multicultural coexistence which would obscure or dismiss the history of antagonism. Instead, it takes stock of history – of the conditions of possibility for encounters between citizens and migrants – while seeking an opening onto a different type of history: history as an event engendered by such encounters.

Angelopoulos attempts to rethink Greece's contemporary position in the EU, historically defined by a periodic resurgence of Hellenism, at once nationalist and Eurocentric, and geographically representing a porous frontier to Europe, surrounded as it is by the Mediterranean sea and bordering 'unstable' countries such as Albania and Turkey.[19] Greece's 'vulnerable' borders have made its islands and remote mountain regions popular entry points for migrants to the EU, much like the liminal spaces of Lampedusa and the Gibraltar Strait.[20] Like Spain and Italy, Greece began attracting migrants relatively recently – since the downfall of communism – due to its history of civil war (1946–9), US-backed military dictatorship (1967–74) and gradual economic development. The popular image of Greece as the cradle of European democracy has, thus, been offset by its long-standing marginalised cultural and economic position regarding Europe 'proper', which has assumed the role and discourse of a colonial master in much of Greece's recent history.[21]

Greece's 'belated modernisation' has made it both defensive against European prejudice as well as self-conscious about its peripheral position: its 'lack of modernity is seen as a flaw' (Jusdanis 1991: xiii). This ambivalent image has been projected onto migrants in contrasting ways. On the one hand, its long history of marginalisation has, like in Italy, solidified the discourse of Greeks as nurturing the Hellenic tradition of instinctive *philoxenia*, according to which Greeks are 'both culturally and biologically predisposed to oppose' racism (Cheliotis 2013: 726). On the other hand, defensive isolationism and ethnocentrism have resulted in popular and official xenophobia reflected in subjecting migrants to violence, long and inefficient asylum process, disproportionate imprisonment, labour exploitation and physical attacks by both police and members of the neo-fascist Golden Dawn party (727–8).

Like *Terraferma*, Angelopoulos's film challenges xenophobia through its utopian open-endedness and absence of a limiting political horizon in a cinematic gesture which contemplates the politics of friendship towards migrants in a reluctantly diversifying Greece, and by extension, Europe. I will show how this open-endedness not only resurfaces through the film's title – eternity and a day – and repeated reflections on temporality, but is also embodied by the narrative structure, which meanders and changes unexpectedly, precluding any certain denouement for either of its protagonists, the distinguished Greek writer Alexander or the homeless (and nameless) migrant from Albania. The film centres on ageing Alexander who, after being diagnosed with a terminal illness, wanders around Thessaloniki trying to decide, over the course of a single day, whether to enter a hospital. We witness the unfolding of his identity, his attempt to take stock of his life's achievements, through scattered, recurring flashbacks of apparently frustrated relationships with his wife Anna and other family members. Such memories are embedded in implicit reflections on Greece's past, present and future, exploring the relationship between literary creation, meditative freedom and personal and political responsibility. Describing the narrative staging of Alexander's identity in the film, Julian Wolfreys observes that the 'many phantasmic projections [are] momentarily brought to light in the place of a singular identity', which becomes a 'place of witness and relay, a momentary locus from where the overflow of memory exceeds all ontological determination' (2004: 121).

As he sets out to put his affairs in order, Alexander encounters a young Albanian migrant who earns his living by cleaning car windshields at busy intersections. In a scene that highlights the necropolitical incongruity of power between towering, well-equipped policemen and underage illegal migrants, Alexander rescues the boy from imminent arrest by spontaneously and without much premeditation offering him a ride in his car. This is a significant ethical decision (if ethics is understood as being in excess of conventional rules of morality or 'rational' thought) because Alexander is preoccupied with taking care of personal business before he enters the hospital and is thus chronically short of time. At this instance, a predictable narrative trajectory is interrupted through an exposure to the vulnerability of another, in spontaneous, face-to-face proximity, where one is 'put in question by the alterity of the other, before the intervention of a cause, before the appearing of the other' (Levinas 1998: 75). As in *Terraferma*, this unintentional welcoming of the other into one's space, which instantly calls the ownership of that space into question, unfolds through what Levinas terms a 'non-thematised proximity' of contact: Alexander's exposure to the infinitely other for whom he is always-already ethically responsible, prior to language, political discourse or historical guilt. Chased by the police and short of time for himself, Alexander reaches towards an Albanian migrant 'against all logic' (87). Levinas describes this as obligation to a neighbour who does not belong to the same 'genus', and this is precisely why 'he concerns me . . . The neighbour is a brother' (87).

The power dynamic that underlies the offer of hospitality is highlighted in juxtapositions between spaces of intimacy and dwelling, on the one hand, and destitution and insecurity, on the other. Alexander's car, family house on the beach and meditative strolls through peaceful Thessaloniki are manifestation of a secure life to which the boy has no access. He crops up in transitional situations and provisional spaces: hiding from police, warming up by street fires with other homeless Albanian migrants and trekking to desolate country borders (he's even banned from a morgue where his friend Selim lies dead). But the film also undermines Alexander's expected generosity which affirms the host in control and entitles him to ask questions of his guest. For instance, Alexander's initial, insistent questions to the boy about his background, family and fluency in Greek – 'Where are you from? Do you speak Greek? Can I take you somewhere?' – remain largely unanswered. After the first encounter in the street, the boy disappears and reappears without Alexander's control, even as Alexander assumes responsibility for him, at one point attempting to take him 'home' to Albania and at another saving him from an illegal child trafficking ring catering to wealthy British and American couples.

Withholding answers about one's identity or background speaks to the right of marginalised others to remained unidentified and therefore escape symbolic control. This is different from Giulietta's refusal to reveal her name in *Terraferma*, which enacts a denial of intimacy with a vulnerable other. *Eternity and a Day* offers glimpses of what Derrida sees as unconditional hospitality to foreigners whom one should not interrogate upon arrival, not even asking their names, which would allow one to know the others' background, legally categorise them and register them with the authorities, making the other safe by making him or her familiar. The boy, thus, remains unnamed, and indeed, unnamable, his intimacy with Alexander unfolding without the honouring of this condition. This is a hospitality of 'unconditional welcome, in a double effacement, the effacement of the question *and* the name' (2000: 29).

Moreover, it is the boy rather than Alexander who speaks, sings songs about exile and separation, or in other ways directs the development of their encounter. But also, as Sarah Ahmed shows, this effacement of the name as an ethical gesture could signal a blindness to the larger power dynamics on the political and economic level that govern the arrival of migrants. Ahmed believes that the refusal to control the other through discourse and knowledge should only come after we have asked them for their name:

> What is required is a hospitality that *remembers* the encounters that are already implicated in such names (including the name of 'the stranger'), and how they affect the movement and 'arrival' of others, in a way which opens out the possibility of those names being moved *from*. (2000: 151)

After Alexander travels with the boy to the Albanian border, he asks, again: 'How did you come to Greece?' The boy's account of his escape from a village attacked by armed bands and of crossing the border while evading landmines is given full emphasis in a surreally sombre scene at the Greek-Albanian border. In one of the several suspensions of narrative time, prolonging the camera shot, Angelopoulos evokes both the absurdity and impassability of EU borders, where we, together with the protagonists, bear witness to the emaciated faces of prospective Albanian migrants dotting the barbed-wire fence, as if foreshadowing the barbed-wire fence at Evros.[22] The film reflects on the conditions that enable Alexander to encounter the boy in the first place, underscoring the responsibility of knowing how and why 'the stranger' arrives.

In this instance, strangeness, rather than being a fetishised site of phenomenological difference, visible on the body of the other or a facet of another's 'identity', becomes an immanent characteristic of an encounter between two people. What is strange is Alexander's confrontation with the haunting memories of migrant life: they exceed the naming and fixing of others as refugees, illegal immigrants or 'shifty' Albanians. The latter is precisely the type of ontological violence of identifying 'strangers' and their behaviours that many xenophobic Greeks who surround Alexander voice. When the boy runs off, yet again, at the Greek-Albanian border, this can only be interpreted as 'typical' behaviour: 'That's what they do', a man says to Alexander, the police round 'them' up and then 'they' just cross the border again. Instead, Alexander and the boy's bond forms according to no pre-established hierarchy between a citizen and non-citizen. Throughout the movie, their leisurely strolls and conversations take place without either of them attempting to know or assimilate the other entirely. Earlier in the film, we witness such an ethical relation with a neighbour whom Alexander can encounter through the sound of music but never know. Meditating on their non-linguistic communication, which consists in them alternately playing the same music for each other, Alexander initially desires to know who the neighbour is, but later decides it is better to 'just imagine'. One can only keep imagining an identity that articulates itself as absence, while remaining exposed to what the other communicates; what is imagined anew is always different, fluid and conceptually insufficient.

On the one hand, Alexander's treatment of the boy as a neighbour who occupies the same physical and symbolic space could be interpreted as egalitarian hospitality of a Greek man who sees no distinction between non-citizens and citizens. However, this reading is complicated by repeated references to Alexander himself as an exile in 'his' country, an unhomed Greek citizen who is a bystander in both his family life and his country's history. The Greek word *xenitis*, at once signifying a foreigner, outsider and stranger, reappears and haunts the narrative after it is first used by the boy. Alexander's position as both a *xenitis* and bystander belies the frequent trope of the loss of agency in Greek film productions which predates 'the emergence of immigration as a national issue' (Lykidis 2009: 93). This absence of agency stems from the perception of Greece's twentieth-century political upheavals and economic policies – from the civil war to neo-liberal restructuring under the auspices of the EU – as colonial manipulations beyond local control. Importantly, however, Angelopoulos does not imagine a hermetic Greek national body, united by familiarity and a shared genealogy (the traditional politics of friendship), which would label illegal immigrants from Albania as 'strangers'. He instead calls attention to strangeness within one's own home, not just in relation to identifiable 'strangers'. As Sara Ahmed notes, 'if we think of "home" purely as proximity and familiarity, then we fail to recognise the relationships of estrangement and distance within the home' (2000: 139).

Alexander's estrangement within his own home is manifested in frustrated communication with his closest family members. For instance, at a hospital where his mother lies mute and can no longer answer him, he asks, 'Why have I lived my life in exile?' and 'Why didn't we know how to love?' The question of responsibility and love as a mindful concern for others' well-being looms large in the film. In flashbacks to his family gatherings at the beach house, Alexander is chided for always being away on 'one of his trips' when something important happens; his wife Anna complains, 'You live beside us, but not with us.' There is a sense of continual displacement, of the present being out of joint with itself, which on the narrative level surprises the audience through frequent, disjointed flashbacks and unanswered questions, unheard answers and desire for intimacy that never takes place. Alexander's life is written for us as something interminable and fragmented – where, as he says, his 'mind is elsewhere' – precluding the ontological illusion of a coherent, complete identity.

Additionally, time is permanently out of joint and in fact cannot be put 'right' because Alexander only feels at home when he 'can speak his language, retrieve lost words from silence'. Paolo Virno suggests that any thinker who questions 'public life [and] . . . the political-social community' is always-already a stranger: to think means to enter the existential condition of 'not-feeling-at-home' (2004: 38–9). One of the crucial problems that Angelopoulos attempts to tackle, perhaps, is this continual oscillation between, on the one hand, meditative and artistic freedom, existential anxiety about one's 'home' that allows for its interrogation, and on the other hand, responsibility for the environment into which one has been thrown, a 'home' with which one must build a relationship.

Such an oscillation is couched within the larger anxiety of revisiting Greek identity and history in the context of the European Union. Fredric Jameson notes that Angelopoulos's films have shifted location from small towns to places of 'waiting and refuge', and accordingly, from Greek national history to some 'transnational situation they cannot properly fix or identify' (1997: 91–2). While the supposed 'end of history' – Greece's parliamentary democracy in the context of the EU – makes it impossible or ultimately unnecessary to either 'mourn or forget' Greece's difficult past, Angelopoulos still 'posits the possibility of some new narrative of regional mapping . . . reaching out beyond the older national allegory in order to invent a cultural politics commensurable with the world system' (94). For Jameson it is imperative to think new global subalternities in the face of universal Americanisation, 'inventing a new politics beyond the current "end of history," that paralysis of action in submission to the world market' (ibid.). This 'end of history' becomes a screen behind which Greek historical traumas are obscured, but old colonial relations are nonetheless re-articulated as a seemingly neutral rhetoric of EU economic adjustment. Negative perceptions of Greece's economic performance in the 1990s, common among EU officials,[23] have resurfaced through 'good white Europeans" patronising stereotypes about Greeks' alleged laziness, corruption and inability to control their urges, blamed for the country's economic breakdown in 2010 (Bratsis 2010: 302). Criticising EU colonial attitudes, Étienne Balibar concludes, 'Europe did not display any real solidarity towards one of its member-states, but imposed on it the coercive rules of the IMF, which protect not the nations, but the banks, and promise deep and endless recession' (2010: n.p.).

Perhaps Alexander's melancholy, then, serves as a displaced expression of this borderline, paralysing transnational situation where the (defensively nationalist and confidently Eurocentric) Hellenic narrative of Greek identity is being undermined and where it is unclear how to 'retrieve from silence' a new identity to deal with the larger context of EU and global capitalism, with both external and internal 'strangers'. From this perspective, for a film that deals with a country whose discourses on national identity and history are in flux, both Albanian migrants and Greek citizens are necessarily *xenitis* in Greece, Europe

and the global arena. This sense of a common history of marginalisation and subaltern status has, as in Italian cultural narratives,
inspired empathy and affiliations across the xenophobic divides in
recent Greek cinema.[24] In opposition to social vilification and invisibility, 'immigrant characters function as catalysts for renewal of a
Greek society debilitated by social anomie and institutional failure'
and 'their narrative centrality in these films attempts to resituate
immigrants at the heart of Greek social practice' (Lykidis 2009: 85).
From this perspective, highlighting Alexander's lifelong reluctance
to re-connect with the community to which he is bound by a common genealogy (family, nation) signals less a nostalgic return to one's
imaginary roots and more a need to rethink one's relationship with
one's immediate neighbours, citizens or not. Angelopoulos describes
community as:

> A number of people who are on the same wavelength in a number of
> ways that they can recognise immediately in each other. Thus a com-
> munity is not defined by nationality or boundaries and can be a kind
> of communication that coexists in different parts of the world, as
> various people 'find' each other voluntarily or by accident. (Horton
> 1997b: 109)

Given his environment, however, Alexander's intimate communication with the boy marks him as a 'strange' man, just as it creates the
possibility of a new type of history and a politics of friendship not
based on familial or national belonging. What Jean-Luc Nancy terms
a community without 'organic communion' – communication as an
'unworking' of the 'production' of community that is 'social, economic,
technical and institutional' – arrives through the sharing of language
(1991: 9, 31). Having decided to complete an unfinished poem by
nineteenth-century Greek poet Dyonisios Solomos, who lived in exile
from his country and language in Zakynthos at the time of Italian occupation, Alexander finds himself depending on the boy for 'his own'
language, for the very possibility of Greek literature.[25] In a symbolic
repetition of the nineteenth-century poet's gesture, the boy picks up
Greek words from passers-by and 'sells' them to Alexander in an effort
to help him speak to his own people. Here an outsider, an unwelcomed
guest becomes a transmitter of language and creator of meaning. In
contrast, Alexander has trouble speaking and completing sentences.
This scene emphasises the unruly, unpredictable dissemination of

language, which both hosts and guests can appropriate without, none-theless, becoming its proprietors. If language travels, and if anyone can use it, what does it mean for it to be possessed, legally owned – or as in Angelopoulos, purchased or stolen? Perhaps this is the ultimate gesture of hospitality: one can only learn a language by listening and talking to an-other, by recognising that anything that makes one secure in one's dwelling – language, land, home – is never an exclusive posses-sion immune to sharing.

Significantly, the scenes where Alexander accepts Greek words from the boy stretch out alongside rivers and the sea, highlighting a similar porosity and vulnerability of European territorial borders, where water precludes the drawing of stable property boundaries. The film places migration in a broader European perspective in a scene in which the boy mourns Selim's death. During his solitary eulogy, the boy identifies Selim as a figure that has haunted all major European ports, including Marseilles and Naples, which are as vul-nerable to an influx of immigrants as Thessaloniki. In Angelopoulos's customary preoccupation with the problem of European borders, Greece is thus disenchanted as a fetishised site of Europe's begin-nings, whose borders and prosperity must be protected, claimed for the West and rescued from its 'unruly', Orientalised neighbours in the Balkans and Asia Minor.

Eternity and a Day, much like Angelopoulos's *Ulysses' Gaze*, proposes an alternative, regional geo-graphing of Greece as inextri-cably connected to the rest of its Balkan neighbours, with whom it shares the Ottoman legacy, history of multiculturalism and a tradi-tion of radical leftism, all of which have been suppressed in modern Greek society at one time or another. In the post-war period, right-wing parties portrayed 'Greeks as racially superior progenitors of European civilisation to label left-wing democratic forces as foreign agents (typically, Slavic), whose actions and principles are incom-mensurate with ancient Greek ideals' (Lykidis 2009: 128). Their spirit of freedom and individualism was seen as incompatible with 'collectivism of "Slavo-Communism"' (Hamilakis 2002: 318). After 1974, prime minister Konstantinos Karamanlis, founder of the right-wing New Democracy Party, used the same rhetoric to steer Greece towards Europe's Common Market, saying that 'Greece belongs to the West' (Markakis 2012: 35). *Eternity and a Day* fearlessly links Greece to its non-EU(ropean) neighbours through a 'contagion' with 'Slavo-Communism'. It recalls the history of dictatorship, war and carnage, without projecting these on Greece's Balkan fringes, where Yugoslav civil wars were raging at the time.

This is encapsulated by the film's invocation of the pre-empted 1967 election, which, under another pretext of battling the threat of communism, resulted in a military coup and seven-year dictatorship, crowning the violent suppression of leftist politics in Greece since World War II. In a flashback scene, the question of political responsibility and care for the community is made conspicuously urgent in the context of Alexander's disinterest and sense of displacement. Commenting on the upcoming election, a family member asks, 'What does the left have to say?' to which Alexander can only reply with a clueless 'About what?' While the film criticises 'organic communion' with the national body as one of the traditional community models, it still suggests the need to explore the ways of living-with based on concern, surpassing the indifference of living-beside.

Haunted by what he believes is a failure to live-with his family and friends, Alexander is always portrayed as arriving 'too late'. *Argathini*, meaning 'too late', resounds throughout the film, as one of the Greek words the boy sells him. At the end of the film, it is 'too late' for Alexander and the boy to establish a firm bond as they are both leaving; it is also 'too late' for Alexander to correct the mistakes of the past as his wife is dead and he is not close to his daughter. But this temporal disjunction, the non-contemporaneity of the past or the present with 'itself', and the existence of multiple, singular times is necessary to undermine the univocal narrative time of the film, which, I argue, also makes it impossible to re-present a community to which we're bearing witness as a completed, homogeneous totality. Perhaps, then, this communication that engenders community has to take place in an indirect, displaced and continually deferred manner: Alexander heeds the voices of the past, even though they arrive 'too late'.

This opening towards the understanding of history as an event that ruptures univocal temporality – a timeline delineating past, present and future – arrives through the suspension of the normal film tempo during the bus ride sequence. Alexander and the boy's final passage through Thessaloniki takes place in a transitory space full of potential, where the assemblages of passengers combine and break up unpredictably, communities coming together only in the here and now. Traces of the past thus enter and disembark: Dionysios Solomos, who finally can't finalise his poem except for repeating the last line

('Life is Sweet and . . . Life is Sweet'), a string quartet whose music tenuously unites Alexander and the boy in mute admiration and a student from an unseen, but overheard left-wing demonstration carrying a bright red banner.

This temporal suspension announces the worlding of new possibilities through continual reaching out to the incalculable, the possible. Like the 1967 election remark, the seemingly casual reference to student demonstrations repeat the fraught, suppressed history of leftist movements. This gesture is especially significant in light of Greek 2008 government protests and 2010–12 anti-austerity protests, which also invoked historical precedents and symbols[26] while worlding new assemblages of European protest culture. Perhaps one of the most significant achievements of the protests was the 'uninvited', unanticipated entrance of migrants into public space as political actors. Echoing their contestation of the necropolitical regime of EU borders, migrants have also effected a 'real rupture' in the public realm as newly politicised *'rebellious immigrant*[s]' (Kalyvas 2010: 356). Commonly invisible and excluded from institutionalised politics, they became part of the protest community that was 'formed between the current, largely immigrant and very urban, proletariat in Greece and the student, anarchist and other autonomous leftist movements' (Bratsis 194). *Eternity and a Day*'s bus ride sequence prefigures this, perhaps fragile and transitory, community; however, its traces, as already noted, persistently haunt recent Greek films that thematise hospitality to migrants.

As Derrida writes:

> This encounter of the unforeseeable itself is the only possible opening of time, the only pure future, the only pure expenditure beyond history as economy. But this future, this beyond, is not another time, a day after history. It is present at the heart of experience. Present not as a total presence but as a trace. (1990: 95)

When, in a subsequent flashback sequence, Alexander asks Anna how long tomorrow lasts, she replies 'eternity and a day'. This non-duration of time, not a 'day after history' but rather a trace at the 'heart of experience' is what has made Alexander realise that potential is both always-already there (eternal) and forever unpredictable (in the excessive day 'beyond' eternity). From this perspective, his relationship with the Albanian boy was never 'too late'. If, for Levinas, history is blindness to the other, and thus any ethical encounter with the other is anarchic, Derrida proposes a different approach to history: 'One wonders whether history itself does not begin with this relationship to the other which Levinas places beyond history' (1990: 94). As the boy stows away on a ship bound for the US, Alexander concludes he will not enter the hospital because 'the neighbour will answer him with always the same music, and there will always be someone to sell him words' – a relationship that lasts 'an eternity and a day', consummated in mutual exchanges of words and sounds, but not aiming for any clear denouement.

Eternity and a Day expresses the urgency of unworking the dead weight of traditional community, a political gesture imperative in a Europe that feels like a hostage in its own 'home'. Hospitality as suspension of identity politics has the potential to be radically transformative in envisioning a community 'against all logic', but this is contingent on the confrontation with history. Despite this hopefulness, however, the loving encounter between Alexander and the boy is consistently framed as physically isolated in the sea of communal politics of friendship based on familial and/or national resemblance. This reflects the situation in which European citizens are increasingly contesting the state monopoly on hospitality by becoming unofficial 'hosts' to migrants, although each effort, thus far, remains isolated from others.[27] While *Terraferma* imagines imperfect, yet collective solidarity with migrants, *Eternity and a Day* undermines the discourse of *philoxenia*, making it unthinkable on the level of community.

Chapter 3

Colonial Spectres in Europe's Historiography

In *The European Tribe* [1987] (2000), Caryl Phillips describes his interactions with students of various European backgrounds after moving from the Caribbean to Great Britain for study: 'They all seemed to share a common and mutually inclusive, but culturally exclusive culture. Reorienting myself in Britain seemed spurious; the problem was a European one, as exemplified by the shared, twisted, intertwined histories of European countries' (9). As each essay records Phillips's impressions of various European locales, the common thread of the 'European tribe' is its conflicted historical relationship to otherness. Phillips reflects on anti-African racism in Western and Eastern Europe alike, resentment towards Europe's peripheries and the history of anti-Semitism. His observation that Europe is threatened by a 'continued toleration of racism in her belly' is only partly tempered in the 1999 afterward to the book, where he contends that Europe has become more multicultural, but it still mistrusts the 'other', whether 'it is a former colonial subject, a "guest worker," a political or economic refugee or an "illegal" migrant'. Phillips doesn't blame racism on extreme right-wing parties which attract 'swastika-brandishing youths and ugly skinheads'; instead, he says that they are merely '"shock troops" for a blazer-clad middle class' (2000: 133).

The European Tribe suggests that Europe's reluctance to offer hospitality to non-European or peripherally European 'others' is a supranational phenomenon which cannot be extricated from the continent's intertwined histories. Moreover, it argues that discrimination cuts across social classes and discourses, rather than being an extreme viewpoint of an alienated, disenfranchised minority, as it is so often portrayed. In this chapter, I explore three literary texts – Leila Sebbar's *The Seine Was Red* (1999), Bernardine Evaristo's *Soul Tourists* (2005) and Jamal Mahjoub's *Travelling with Djinns* (2003) – which make a case for a similarly supranational focus on Europe's historical hospitality to 'others', especially the hospitality of official historical narratives to the existence and contributions of 'others' to the imagined communities of both the nation and Europe. Whether these alternate histories have been suppressed to disavow the legacies of racist violence, or to delegitimise the right of others to belong in the common European 'home', these imaginative texts not only uncover buried histories but also explore the political consequences of this gesture for Europe's conception of community. It seems that hospitality to uncomfortable histories might be a prerequisite for a multicultural, postcommunist as well as postcolonial, ethics of reconciliation – understood not as an end of history or political antagonism, but as a move towards recognising discrimination and working towards egalitarian mutuality. And yet, what might constitute such hospitality? Are such histories to be sublated within the narrative of a unified European history? Or does the fragmentariness and incommensurability of competing historical accounts challenge the concept of univocal history? Is historical closure to be desired if it leads to the conceptual closure of the community – if it elides its immanent discontinuity, heterogeneity and dissensus?

The European Community (EC), which set the blueprint for the EU, was founded in response to the shared historical trauma of world wars: its goal was to prevent future European wars by fostering cooperation and mutual dependence. EU political discourses frequently invoke the Holocaust as a founding event of contemporary Europe, as the burden of responsibility that European nations share and an ethical injunction intended to prevent future genocides.[1] Acute awareness of the history of anti-Semitism becomes a negative ground over which Europe asserts its dedication to individual freedom, respect for human rights and democratic diversity. As Lothar Probst argues, however, official commemorations of the Holocaust and frequent references to the Holocaust in EU political statements only became prominent after the downfall of the Berlin wall, with greater awareness of the contribution of all European nations to anti-Semitism. Initially the European Community was dedicated to 'Anti-nazism and Antifascism' and the 'eradication of the European Jewry was scarcely a point of reference at all' (2003: 54).[2] Nonetheless, it is significant that Europe began to unify not only around its victory over fascism, but precisely at the moment when its historically most numerous internal 'other' had been erased, even if the continent-wide (rather than individual national) discourses of mourning provided a belated acknowledgement of shared guilt.

Although it might appear that the myth of unifying Europe stands as 'a convenient suppressor of the widespread collaboration with Nazi crimes', it is also, as Talal Asad claims, 'the resurrection of those memories' that solidifies the myth. Far from being threatened by internal, violent self-purging, Europe's 'solidarity is strengthened' by it (2000: 212). This narrative of mourning and ethical reparation at the heart of Europe's community of compassion both reveals and hides a fundamental wound: the Holocaust is at once intimate and distant, both a central event and a dark continent of pathological racism that is decidedly un-European. Paradoxically, Europe recognises its anti-Semitism by disavowing it as something alien to European values. This disavowal echoes the current projection of Islamophobia, for instance, onto undemocratic, aberrational elements such as extreme far-right parties and their supporters.[3]

Much like the Holocaust is 'the "Other" of European values,' the history of fascism itself is disavowed as un-European: a tradition radically alien to the democratic heritage, a deviant exception to European politics rather than its constitutive part (Rigney 2012: 612). The current European project is invariably presented as having overcome the troubled past, but simultaneously as being ontologically distinct from it. In 2009, the European Parliament passed a resolution on 'European Conscience and Totalitarianism', controversially equating communism and fascism under the umbrella term totalitarianism. The resolution condemned 'strongly and unequivocally all crimes against humanity and the massive human rights violations committed by all totalitarian and authoritarian regimes', declaring that the 'European Union has a particular responsibility to promote and safeguard democracy, respect for human rights and the rule of law' ('European Conscience' 2009: n.p.). While the resolution condemns the massive casualties of various fascist and communist regimes, its language suggests that these are past aberrations of which current European democracies are fundamentally incapable. The awarding of the 2012 Nobel Peace Prize to the EU affirmed this 'enduring mythology of an ethical European project established in the service of peace' (Bhambra 2016: 198).

Building on these insights, this chapter analyses ways in which the history of violence to Europe's 'others' perceived as external – primarily colonial violence – remains insufficiently acknowledged in public discourses and divorced from analyses of contemporary violence to non-European migrant populations. This paradoxical erasure of enormous acts of violence similarly dates back to the beginnings of Europe's unification: as the post-war EC proclaimed opposition to tyranny and totalitarianism, its member states carried on extensive military campaigns and committed numerous atrocities in their colonial empires. Peo Hansen argues that European integration is rarely brought into connection with colonialism and decolonisation, resulting in an undiluted view of unifying Europe as an agent of peace at the very moment that it was, for instance, waging a war in Algeria which killed over a million civilians and engaged half a million French troops (2002: 487). This invisibility is aided by the failure of most former colonial powers to condemn, both individually and on the European level, colonial atrocities in no uncertain terms and by their refusal to address requests for compensation. At the time of writing, some former European colonisers have issued apologies and/or offered compensation for specific colonial atrocities, but none have condemned colonialism as a system, in the way that they have condemned fascism and communism.[4]

Even with the recent surge in postcolonial scholarship on contemporary institutionalised racism in the EU, 'its relationship to scholarship on colonialism remains severed from an analysis of a contemporary racial state' (Stoler 2011: 153). Because of this reluctance to draw connections between intertwined historical events, the situation that Étienne Balibar describes as the urban 'apartheid' (2003a: 39) forming in the wake of postcolonial and postcommunist migrations to Europe continues to be seen as a phenomenon dissociated from the history of Europe's colonial past. Non-European and peripherally European minorities are in Europe, but not of it; their sense of belonging is precluded by the perception that they have only just arrived, as opposed to having been part of Europe's socioeconomic structure and cultural imaginary all along, whether through their literal presence in Europe over the centuries or as Europe's colonial subjects in the peripheries and non-European locales. As El-Tayeb argues, 'Europeans possessing the (visual) markers of otherness' are 'forever suspended in time, forever "just arriving," defined by a static foreignness overcoming both individual experience and historical facts' (2011: 228).

This sense of always having just arrived blocks both established and recent migrant populations from inclusion in Europe's contemporary social imaginary and the historical accounts of the 'idea' of Europe. Public debates which focus on the supposedly ahistorical presence of 'foreigners' in 'our' midst and their rights and obligations vis-à-vis the common European project, fail to ask, as Aamir Mufti suggests, 'What did we do to their countries in the past? What are we doing to them now? What does that have to do with who they are, who we are, and why they are here?' (2007: 19). In recent years, there has been greater acknowledgement that Europe's historical narratives have to address diversity in a more substantive way. For instance, the EU Commission funded the 2005–10 CLIHORES historical research project, which aimed at 'achieving and disseminating greater understanding of both the actual histories and the self-representations of the past current in Europe today, highlighting both diversities and connections and explaining the context of their development'. This interdisciplinary project, bringing together researchers from European universities, developed six thematic groups, including 'Frontiers and Identities' and 'Europe and the World', and centred on historical inquiry into patterns of migrancy, discrimination and identity.[5]

In different ways, Sebbar's, Mahjoub's and Evaristo's novels address Europe's self-fashioning by re-narrating distant and recent histories of the continent as always-already creolised, to use Françoise Lionnet and Shu-Mei Shih's (2011) term, where cultural and ethnic groups are never separate or distinct to begin with, but instead evolve through hybridisation. Accounting for 'others' at the heart of Europe does not lead to imagining community as founded on the erasure or sublation of its negative remainder, in order to achieve unity. The novels develop contested histories as a site of dissensus (Rancière), which negotiates rather than blocks European unity, resulting in fragmented but relational histories that take non-European perspectives to bear upon European history. What Édouard Glissant [1990] (1997) calls 'poetics of relation' contests the possession of history as an exclusive property of any one group since they necessarily affect one another's development, often violently; simultaneously, these narratives move beyond the binary conception of European history, as non-European legacies are not treated as either a potential replacement of or supplement to the idea of Europe.

Doing away with the centre-periphery model and critiquing the vertical politics of group identity, these narratives move towards connections among subaltern communities which offer a bottom-up, agonistic and often melancholy view of Europe's history rather than a triumphant narrative of overcoming violence and racism. This is akin to Lionnet and Shih's praxis of 'minor transnationalism', as a 'less scripted' and 'more scattered' process of hybridisation, where it is possible for the transnational to be seen as a 'space of exchange and participation' without mediation by the centre (2005: 5). All three novels imagine and advocate belonging in this alternative conception of Europe, which, however, does not result in an optimistic celebration of European diversity or slip into the vertical politics of recognition by the centre. I will explore this gesture as a political attitude of claiming one's rightful ground, which was denied in the past and continues to be denied to minor (non)citizens who are perceived to have 'only just arrived'.

Colonial aphasia in *The Seine Was Red*

On 17 October 1961, Parisian police drowned, according to varying accounts, several dozen to several hundred peaceful pro-FLN (Algerian National Liberation Front) demonstrators by throwing them in the Seine. Over 11,000 were arrested and many were deported to Algeria, after being judged undesirable and too dangerous to remain on French soil.[6] Glossing over the 17 October bloodshed echoes the long-standing attitude to this event in the French public sphere. Examining Leila Sebbar's novel *The Seine Was Red*, I argue that this event, while by no means exceptional in the context of the Algerian War which resulted in over a million casualties (or the long history of French colonial abuses in North Africa), metonymically captures the structural silencing and inadmissibility of (post)colonial violence against 'others' in the French, as well as European, imaginary. In attempting to piece together the narrative of this massacre as its central elusive object, the novel makes visible not so much a definitive account – instead opting for fragmented and contradictory personal experiences – but rather the layers of both voluntary and official silencing that prevent it from entering public consciousness. What distinguishes the erasure of this event from other attempts to downplay colonial violence against Algerians is the fact that it takes place on French soil, where its initial denial and perceived insignificance, and subsequently slow and insufficiently transparent official recognition, parallels the exclusion of (post)colonial migrant groups from the heart of national historical concerns and imagined community of belonging.

El-Tayeb argues that in mainstream narratives of European identity, related historical events, such as colonialism, World War II, the Cold War and migration, are rarely considered together since colonialism is perceived as having taken place 'outside' of Europe. As I have argued, this contributes to the foregrounding of only selected events as foundational and the failure to come to terms with colonial abuses. As an alternative, El-Tayeb proposes linking these events around key years in which they converge; one of them, in fact, is 1961, the year 'of the Eichmann trial in Jerusalem', the intensification of the Cold War 'marked by the building of the Berlin Wall and the failed Bay of Pigs invasion', 'a year also in which more than a hundred Algerians were murdered by French police in the streets of Paris, a largely uncommemorated event exemplifying the repression of European colonial history', and, finally, a year in which the 'West German government signed a "guest worker" treaty with Turkey that brought to Europe what is now its largest ethnic and religious minority community' (2008: 659).

Building on El-Tayeb's act of tracing connections between these epistemologically isolated historical events and my discussion of Europe's self-image as an agent of peace in the midst of the Algerian War, I wish to foreground 17 October as an event whose recognition and commemoration are not only of French but also broadly European significance. 17 October also brings together supranational events such as World War II, the Holocaust and colonial wars, in so far as Maurice Papon, the prefect of French police who was responsible for the massacre, was found guilty in 1998 of 'illegal arrest' and 'arbitrary detainment' (but not of 'complicity in the murder') of Jews in Paris during World War II (House and MacMaster 2006: 312). However, the broader narratives of anti-Semitism and colonial racism were not brought into meaningful conversation, given that his role in 17 October remained overshadowed by his role in the Holocaust: the former remained a 'trial within a trial', for which there was no verdict or assumption of responsibility.

Nonetheless, this trial highly publicised the event, leading to a gradual opening of state archives on the Algerian War in general. The archives on 17 October only became accessible to the public in 2011,[7] the fiftieth anniversary of the event, which also saw François Hollande commemorating the victims by throwing a rose into the Seine and, after he was elected president, calling for state recognition of the violence. Nonetheless, as Jonathan Lewis notes, 'the official historical narrative continues to deny the state's responsibility in the violence' (2012: 321). This pattern of partial admission and silencing characterises the treatment of the massacre over the decades: from denial and disbelief that it happened in the immediate aftermath; to burying it among broader 'anti-fascist' struggles against Gaullist France in the 1960s; to commemorating the event in Algeria and among diasporic Algerian communities in the 1970s; to literary accounts which describe it, directly or indirectly, in the 1980s; and finally, to increasing numbers of historical and cultural narratives in the 1990s and onwards.[8] However, in the 1980s when the literary texts came out, they were sometimes quietly removed from prominent bookstores or had to 'prove' that the event had actually happened, since they produced knowledge about it in the absence of official archives.[9] In parallel, while 1991 saw the publication of Jean-Luc Einaudi's *La Bataille de Paris: 17 octobre 1961*, the first comprehensive historical study that documented the police atrocities, in 1996 former president Jacques Chirac unveiled a monument to military and civilian victims of the war in North Africa while praising 'the colonial enterprise as a national accomplishment' distinguished by '"peacekeeping, uplifting territories, spreading education, founding a modern medicine"' (Amine 2012: 186). Despite increasing attempts at recognition, then, the French state and public are invested in relegating this event to (partial) invisibility, which is emblematic of France's ambivalent attitude to its colonial violence.

In *The Seine*, the protagonists re-inscribe the unsettling history of 17 October onto Parisian walls and sidewalks from which it has been erased. This event is contextualised within a number of inquiries into the importance of colonial history in France, specifically, the incipient colonisation of Egypt that resulted in the conquest of Algeria and the impact of postcolonial Algerian history on diasporic communities living in France. The narrative, while combining these disparate but connected threads, centres on Amel, a teenage girl of Algerian descent who grew up in the Parisian *bidonville* of Nanterre, densely populated by immigrants. She is frustrated by the silence she faces from her family, especially its matrilineal side, on the events surrounding the 17 October protest. Amel's grandmother, *lalla*, took her mother Noria, then a little girl, to the protest, but she refuses to tell Amel the story of the 'day of woe', assuring Amel that these are 'secrets' which will be told 'when the time is right' (1–2). Amel runs away from home, and, together with Omer, a young Algerian journalist in exile in Paris, sprays political graffiti in an act of peripatetic rewriting of celebrated Parisian landmarks which were, unbeknownst to most of its residents, marked by the 17 October protest. Their French friend Louis, a young man who is filming a documentary about the event, tries to locate Amel by following – and filming – the written traces they leave. In the absence of Amel's and Omer's physical presence, what makes Louis's tracing possible are these commonly shared spaces in Paris and the historical messages they carry.

Amel decides to run away only after watching Louis's documentary, which, to her surprise, features her staunchly silent mother's eyewitness account. It is this account that spurs her to spray graffiti, which, as an unofficial, anonymous and transgressive mode of writing, revises official captions on monuments and plaques, supplementing and demoting official historiography. The first revision refers broadly to the Algerian war of independence. At the Sante prison, which bears a plaque commemorating the arrest of Parisian students who opposed the Nazi occupation, Amel emphasises the brutal treatment of Algerian resisters, who were 'guillotined' for rising up 'against French occupation' during the war (15). On the facade of Hotel Crillon, at the famous Place de la Concorde graced by an Egyptian obelisk, symbol of French colonial power, Amel writes 'On this spot Algerians were savagely beaten by Prefect Papon's police on October 17 1961' (67). Finally, by Saint Michel bridge from which police threw protesters into the Seine, Amel writes 'On this spot Algerians fell for the independence of Algeria October 17, 1961' (93).

In 1999, when *The Seine* came out,[10] and even more so in 1996, when the events of the novel are taking place, this gesture of physically making visible the erased violence carried even more weight than it does today, after an official plaque commemorating 17 October victims was dedicated by Saint Michel bridge in 2001. Nonetheless, Sebbar's larger point that only unofficial, even illegal, practices were necessary to mark this event at all is confirmed by the French authorities' persistent refusal to place permanent plaques or erect monuments before 2001. In 1985, only a temporary plaque was placed at Saint Michel by SOS-Racisme, while in 1991, a commemorative stele placed downstream at suburban Bezons, where Algerians were also drowned, was removed by the local prefect. Even the decision on the 2001 plaque was made, and its dedication marked, only on the local (rather than national) level, thanks to initiatives by Socialist mayor Bertrand Delanoe and local Algerian councillors (House and MacMaster 2006: 317).

This circumspection of the 'proper' space for the history of Algerians in France is twofold – famous Parisian landmarks which metonymically evoke the nation implicitly exclude Algerian presence, and even when their presence is admitted in the heart of the capital, it is seen as purely local, accidental and dehistoricised from the larger concerns of the nation. Subverting such exclusions, Amel's graffiti claim central Paris, the heart of the nation, as a legitimate political space for Algerians, who are also physically distant from it by being segregated into shanty town *bidonvilles* and more recently, *banlieues*. Even their attempt to gather in central Paris for the 17 October protest is understood as illegitimate movement: in the novel, eyewitness accounts repeatedly highlight the theme of being blocked from entering the city proper after arriving from suburban metro stations.

Sebbar does not develop a chronological, cause-and-effect sequence of events, which remains elusive, and instead highlights the seemingly absurd, inexplicable and highly affective aspects of the protest, which would be beyond be the purview of an official historical account. A prominent theme in the novel is the fact that civilian protesters were thrown in the Seine despite being peaceful and unarmed, dressed in their Sunday best, and accompanied by their families, as if they needed to earn legitimate entry into the political space of central Paris. Noria recalls the air of celebration with which her family prepared for the protest: 'The tub was ready for the children's bath . . . We dressed up in our best clothes', while her father 'had put on a tie, a lovely shirt, a velvet jacket' (42). This sense of confidence and joyful anticipation of the protest sharply contrasts with another protester's description of the ensuing violence against Algerians:

> The Seine spit them back out. Even the Seine didn't want Algerians . . . And what about those killed during the peaceful demonstration? I know it was peaceful. No knives, no sticks, no weapons; those were the orders of the French Federation of FLN. I know. They marched with their families – wives and children, even elderly

women – and they shouted and chanted the national anthem. They were clapping. The men did not defend themselves, they did not respond with violence. (46)

Such impulsive violence towards defenceless civilians of a different culture and religion is often compared to the Holocaust, which had ended a mere sixteen years before this incident. In this way, *The Seine* brings into conversation the chronologically close but discursively separated histories of Europe's anti-Semitism and racist Orientalism. Predictably, the novel links them through the figure of Prefect Papon, 'the same civil servant who signed the deportation order for the Jews arrested in the Gironde region, the same one sent on a special mission to Constantine during the Algerian war' (78). The French police refer to the protesters as 'rats, they keep coming out . . . They are vermin' (79), echoing the rhetoric of infestation in anti-Semitic propaganda. In the novel, French icon Brigitte Bardot is criticised for denouncing Muslims as 'barbarians' for their halal slaughtering practices; her gesture evokes Nazi propaganda against Jews for their 'abuse' of animals through kosher slaughtering methods (48).

By drawing these parallels, Sebbar focuses on the structures of thought and feeling that have made it difficult for the French nation to register these events as crimes against fellow human beings, worthy of public empathy, discussion or commemoration. After scores of peaceful protesters are drowned in the Seine, there is no significant public outrage beyond the Algerian community, either immediately or decades after the event. This is partly due to the media blackout that made this event invisible (reflected in aforementioned 'disbelief' that it happened), but more significantly, to what Ann Stoler describes as 'colonial aphasia', the systemic occlusion of knowledge through 'racialised regimes of truth', not because of deliberate ignorance or malicious intent, but because of disassociated affective practices and the unavailability of conceptual tools to speak of such events *as* crimes. Stoler observes that in French academic and public discourse, 'the very nature of political thinking . . . valorises only some formats for considering questions of human dignity' (2011: 129, 128). Until recently, this 'racialised regime of truth' has contributed to 17 October being seen as important only to the Algerian diaspora rather than to French national – and colonial – history. The impossibility of affective investment in violence against Algerians, beyond the anti-war activist minority, was aided by widespread stereotypes of Algerians and

FLN as aggressive terrorists, making the police 'retribution' justified. Choosing complicity and affiliation with state power, therefore, Parisian 'bystanders helped police to hunt down Algerians attempting to escape' instead of identifying with the protesters' cause (House and MacMaster 2006: 222).

This affective and conceptual aphasia on the French side is complemented, as Sebbar's novel suggests, by layers of silence and repression of the event among Algerian protest participants, which renders the knowledge of the event inaccessible to the next generation to which Amel belongs. The novel's structure as a series of discontinuous trajectories of remembrance travelled by Amel, Louis, Omer, Noria and others illustrates, both through content and frequent blank spaces in narration, the dislocation from family and collective memory that Amel sees as a profound loss. The denial of entry into personal, familial archive of experiences further cements Amel's dislocation from the culture of her parents insofar as she doesn't speak Arabic, but is fluent in French, Latin and Greek.

This self-imposed silence has been variously interpreted by literary critics: as a culturally inflected protection of intimate, female space, from the public, male space of politics;[11] as the inadmissibility of female roles and experiences of the protest and war as significant;[12] and as a collective impossibility of recounting a traumatic experience and reluctance to 'transmit a legacy of pain and suffering to the next generation' (Mortimer 2010: 1250). In terms of remedying the exclusion of female protagonists from the theatre of war, *The Seine* centres on a number of French and Algerian women's accounts. Notable among these is Louis's mother Flora's experience of imprisonment as a 'suitcase carrier' who aided the Algerian cause by transporting money and papers. Also, Noria explains how *lalla*, who was a dressmaker, 'hid political tracts in fabric, in wedding dresses; the women distributed them. Women musicians would spread the news from wedding to wedding' (27). But Noria's delivery of her eyewitness account undermines the interpretation of women's silence before Amel as a withdrawal from the public world of men and retreat into a feminine space whose intimacy is enhanced by the use of Arabic. In fact, Noria recounts her memories in French, methodically and persistently, as if it is an urgent task for her to have her story recorded. As Amel watches Louis's documentary, she notes, 'her mother talks and talks and talks. She doesn't stop and she looks straight at Louis while he films her' (17).

This mode of delivery suggests not only that Noria can confidently enter the public world allegedly reserved for men, but also that it may be easier or more acceptable for her to recount the story in an impersonal manner, rather than directly to her daughter.[13] In *The Seine*, this silence includes men as well as women – Noria cannot persuade her father to talk about her uncle's murder or the fact that he was punished for belonging to MNA, a rival Algerian faction (28). Indeed, this could be symptomatic of the reluctance to transmit the traumatic memory of anger and discrimination to the next generation, who might have a chance at fuller acceptance in France, or of a fundamental rift in the experiences of different generations of Algerians living in France, which cannot be bridged by narrative.

Instead, however, I wish to highlight external circumstances, beyond psychological coping mechanisms of the Algerian community, which concern the structural conditions in which Algerians cannot recount such memories because their audiences are not receptive to the truths they carry. As House and MacMaster explain, being forthright in the conditions of media blackout could have cost Algerians arrest, loss of employment and even deportation (2006: 274). Also, since, officially, no massacre had happened, 'Who would have believed Algerians' testimonies?'; for a long time the public memory discourse was occupied by *pied-noirs*, *harkis* and other former military personnel who 'produced a highly charged politics of memory from which most Algerian economic migrants were absent' (ibid.). Even decades later, at the time of Papon's trial, when the media 'rediscovered' 17 October, they tried to document the violence by publishing 'a flurry of interviews – a remarkable number of which turned out to feature perpetrators rather than victims' (Graebner 2005: 173).

Taking these important factors into account, Sebbar perhaps implies that *lalla* and Noria revisiting their memories with Amel in private may be profoundly insufficient. The protest can only be understood as a communal experience, a historical phenomenon affecting all of Algeria and France, which must be jointly narrated, rather than kept under wraps among family members. After all, the promise of revealing suppressed memories is built into the very beginning of the novel. *Lalla* doesn't say that Amel will never find out 'secrets . . . that must be kept hidden'; instead, she says, 'The day will come, don't worry; it will come and it won't be a happy one for you' (1). It seems that the day arrives when Louis's documentary promises to find larger audiences for such memories. The framing of the documentary makes Noria's testimony doubly public, in that it becomes contextualised by other testimonies featured in the film as well as available for public viewing. The camera becomes an indirect tool of communication, substituting for the broken link between mother and daughter; also, it fosters a conversation between personal memory and public history as it has the potential to uncover events that have remained buried in official narratives.

The resulting story of 17 October is told from a host of perspectives, creating a polyphonic historiographical document, which, like the frame narrative of the novel itself, includes interrelated but ultimately mutually exclusive and radically different experiences. Alongside anti-colonial protesters, Louis's documentary features Algerian *harkis*, FLN supporters, French police and civilians who aided Algerians secretly or joined them in the protest openly. Noria's own tale is mostly stripped of political analysis because she experienced it as a child, so she describes her dislike of the shanty town in which she grew up in a blue-collar family, the preparation for the protest and the immediate experience of violence – seeing people beaten, killed and rounded up. Her narrative frequently switches from past to present, and she returns to gaps in earlier parts of the story to fill them out. As she says of the process of remembering, 'when you tell a story, you forget, everything comes back pell-mell' (89).

Her perspective is supplemented by the experiences of other military and civilian actors, which attest to different political attitudes to the protest. For instance, an Algerian bar owner denies that FLN are 'brothers' as they disapprove of his business, but, under pressure, closes his bar on 17 October (23). An Algerian prostitute who runs a 'café-cabaret' establishment denies allegiance to Algeria because 'They don't like women over there, and not women like me' (52). An Algerian *harki* is an impoverished young man drawn by the urban world of police officer salary and privilege, one that readily obeys command and takes pride in a job well done. Even his narrative, callous as it is, ends with a surprising confession to crime which changes the haughty tone of his earlier description of shanty town Algerian dwellers as 'rats': 'We fired on demonstrators. We threw demonstrators into the Seine' (32). On the other hand, this dispassionate, matter-of-fact description contrasts with other narratives which highlight the horror of wounding and drowning. French narratives abound in examples of mutual aid and compassion, one of them featuring a French student taking care of a wounded man who 'was disoriented . . . I took the metro with him. He didn't want to go to the hospital . . . He had worn his Sunday clothes, a tie, a vest under his suit jacket. His white shirt was spattered with blood' (82). In another account, a French man explains his decision to respect the secrets of his Algerian girlfriend who had probably taken part in the protest and been tortured by police.

Louis incorporates a medley of perspectives without providing an overarching commentary: the participants speak into the seemingly indifferent eye of the camera. This silent neutrality might imply the undecidability of any historical event, with each perspective being relative to the narrator's sociopolitical positioning and nobody having the final word. Nonetheless, the frame narrative privileges Algerian and French youth whose families were subjected to state terror, which precludes giving equal ethical weight to all the narratives. Moreover, Sebbar's dedication of the novel to 'the Algerian victims of October 1961 in Paris' and to the authors, scholars and photographers who rescued it from oblivion, including Didier Daninckx, Jean-Luc Einaudi, Elie Kagan and François Maspero, privileges this tradition of alternative historiography. While the novel's structure highlights the different actors' shared vulnerabilities in the face of historical events, it complicates both moral relativism and unambiguous designations of victims and heroes. French accounts evince a broad spectrum of empathetic and ambivalent attitudes to the war, while Algerian accounts fail to idealise FLN or other militant groups that seemingly deserve accolade in the face of French oppression.

The absence of a unified narrative perspective in the documentary is mimicked by Sebbar's non-linear structure, which emphasises unruly dissonance and fragmentation of responsibility for the events of 17 October. But this does not create a sense of postmodern celebration of the slipperiness of historical grounding, but rather a mimetic invocation of the absence – and perhaps impossibility – of reconciliation of the former colonisers and colonised in light of such an agonistic cacophony of voices. The interviews are presented in isolation rather than dialogue, as conflicting rather than complementary. As Laila Amine remarks, '*The Seine* questions the possibility and desirability of a French or Algerian national consensus around the Algerian war, for such consensus is produced through exclusion' (2012: 191). However, although these perspectives' divergent content precludes the formation of consensus, they are still unified via the medium that brings them all together in a single forum for discussion – visual and textual narrative – highlighting their common exclusion from the official narrative of the French state. These perspectives provide a sense of complex (dis)identifications from the hierarchical politics of group identity, be it the French military or FLN. A common thread among them, even in the absence of dialogic format or thematic overlap, is their shared victimisation at the hands of dominant group narratives and the potential for transcultural solidarity. By including excluded perspectives – like those of militant women – the novel also hints at the possibility of a transnational community among marginalised and subaltern subjects, which could narrate its own competing history.

The Seine thus imagines alternative communities of remembrance in addition to highlighting a common exclusion of politically incorrect perspectives from official historiography. Jane Hiddleston observes that in Sebbar's work, memories of the war are testimonies of 'individuals whose stories are difficult to insert into any imaginary communal narrative . . . perplexing the idea of a collective consciousness' (2005: 169). She argues that Sebbar never chooses between the singular and the collective, but the 'provisional and incomplete form' of her literary texts 'demonstrates the necessary ambivalence of collective formations' (173). While group identity in Sebbar is radically provisional, it is difficult to claim that any communal narrative is impossible given the multitude of temporary, minor communities throughout the narrative. Not only do eyewitness accounts abound in examples of French passers-by spontaneously aiding Algerians, but it is the friendship between French and Algerian women who collectively exposed their lives to danger during the war that makes future relationships – and desire to learn about 17 October – possible for their children. *The Seine*, addressing both Algerians and the French, implies that 17 October is a shared historical trauma, and the only way to process it is to cross the lines of segregated group identity and history. After all, Louis learns more about 17 October by interviewing Noria; and, as Robyn Banton observes, if it hadn't been for her friendship with Louis and Omer, Amel would not have learned of the historical events that affected her parents (2014: 363). The necessity of tracing alternative histories across national lines is also confirmed by the fact that in 'over 300 histories of the war published in Algeria and throughout the Arab world, in both Arabic and French', there is 'no hint of coverage of the events in

Paris, before the appearance in Paris of the stream of works' from the mid-1980s onwards (Graebner 2005: 174).

More significantly, *The Seine* suggests the necessity of connecting segregated historical concerns to understand the broader colonial context of any historical event, similar to the way in which it considers 17 October in the context of the Holocaust. Amel's mission to unearth the events surrounding 17 October is in conversation with Omer's research on postcolonial Algeria and violence caused by its contemporary political factions. The narrative highlights a continuity between FLN violence towards Algerians during the war of independence and the fratricidal wars in postcolonial Algeria which repeat the logic of sacrifice: to purify the social body they believe 'they are destroying all bad souls who are unworthy of God' (49). For Omer, accepting this history and interrogating the need for continuous bloodletting is necessary if things are to heal: 'We have to live with that, you understand, with this act of death, the knife. Not only do we have to live with it, but we have to think about it, so that some day the things will change' (49). In turn, Louis obsessively compiles library resources on Napoleon's invasion of Egypt, the defining moment in French colonial expansion. In the novel, the three young people continually clash over the relative importance of their chosen research topic, but the narrative framing highlights their unavoidable interconnectedness.[14]

This triangulation of events suggests that they need to be explored jointly: Louis, Amel and Omer accidentally ending up in Alexandria together at the end of the novel is indicative of this unity of purpose. Napoleon's invasion of Egypt is thus invisibly, yet indissolubly entangled with the history of Algerian presence in post-war France. Also, just as a historical documentary creates an indirect bridge between Amel and Noria, so Louis can only declare his love for Amel by writing to her of Napoleon in Egypt: 'He doesn't tell he loves her. He writes to her about Egypt in 1798, the Orient that Europe dreams of conquering, discovering it to civilise, instruct and occupy it. The cruel colonial myth' (74). Intimacy in private relationships is so inextricably linked with political events in this novel that it takes place primarily through discourses of politics and history. Common ground and reconciliation among the French and Algerians may be imagined exclusively in this private arena of familial and romantic relationships, but these are always-already implicated in the broader process of anamnesis, invoking and then exorcising the ghosts of colonialism. In short-circuiting the discourses of love with those of history, Sebbar metaphorically suggests that such a politically over-determined relationship is the only possible kind of intimacy in post-colonial France.

Haunted European homes in *Soul Tourists*

Bernardine Evaristo's *Soul Tourists* counteracts the whitewashing of European history as its protagonists, Stanley and Jesse, attempt to come to terms with their postcolonial backgrounds and sense of (un)belonging in Great Britain. While the novel addresses the intricacies of British postcolonial heritage and race relations, it places these issues in the larger context of European history, which, Evaristo suggests, is haunted by non-white ghosts that pop up in official accounts, rumours, literary texts and lineages from England to Russia. In a magical realist fashion, these ghosts confront Stanley and Jesse during their travels around Europe, on which they embark as a way of escaping the ennui of Stanley's nine-to-five job and after initiating a passionate love affair. Evaristo's preoccupation with exploding the founding myth of white Europe is foreshadowed in an earlier novel, *The Emperor's Babe* (2001), where Roman Britain is 'globalised' through the presence of Africans and Asians in Londinium. While *Soul Tourists* imagines all of Europe as a multicultural melting pot to help the protagonists negotiate a sense of belonging on this continent, *The Emperor's Babe* casts London as a place settled by non-white subjects from the vast Roman empire, which is as multicultural as Rome.

Evaristo wrote *The Emperor's Babe* while she was a poet in residence at the Museum of London,[15] which nonetheless didn't provide her with much scholarship on multicultural Londinium. The construction of this history, therefore, has been partly speculative and partly inspired by available historical knowledge, which suggests that 'there were black soldiers in the Roman army at Hadrian's wall in the early third century' and that thanks to good roads, Romans frequently travelled across vast distances of the empire, including from Africa to Europe (qtd in Hooper 2006: 6). The historical basis of this book was made possible by Peter Fryer's account of early African presence in Britain in *Staying Power* (1984), as well as by a subsequent surge in publications, journals and conferences dedicated to understanding the overlooked contributions of Africans to European history.[16] However, despite this renewed interest in exploring the non-white presence in Great Britain preceding post-World War II waves of immigration, we do not yet, and may never have, reliable information about multicultural Londinium. While Evaristo's historical specula-tions in *The Emperor's Babe* and *Soul Tourists* are probable, they address this impossibility of ever knowing the firm line between fact and fiction, which is reflected in her playful mixing of magical and realist elements, humour and seriousness. More important than cor-roborating historical events is allowing for the possibility of imagin-ing a different history than the one that has become dominant, even if its unpacking is permanently frustrated by the limitations of available archival data. The impact of Evaristo's strategy has been quite pow-erful in that the Museum of London integrated her work into their displays (Muñoz-Valdivieso 2009: 169), including quotes from *The Emperor's Babe* and a 'black Roman character played by an actor who guides people around the Roman part of the Museum' (Hooper 2006: 6). This revision of historical information available to the broader public following the novel's publication is one of the hopeful, tangible results that such cultural narratives can have for reimagining European belonging.

Soul Tourists, which addresses broader questions of European multiculturalism, was published in 2005, after much of post-Cold War Europe had already been absorbed into the European Union. However, Evaristo sets this contemporary picaresque novel in 1980s Europe, which Stanley describes as 'not safe' for people of Jamaican origin like himself (51). Europe is placed in the larger context of concurrent (post)colonial racisms: 'Aborigines dying in police cus-tody . . . Fascist thugs all over Europe . . . apartheid in South Africa' (51). The kinds of discrimination that Stanley observes both in his adopted country, Great Britain and across Europe seem predictable in the aforementioned context. I propose reading them as Evaristo's take on European attitudes to immigrants immediately preceding the political unification of Europe in the 1990s and the growing popular-ity of multicultural models and discourses that accompanied it. The novel, thus, operates, on several historiographic levels. First, it looks back to the 1980s from the perspective of a consolidated Europe, mapping European unity that will culminate in common statehood via a history of shared, postcolonial discrimination towards always-already existing racial and religious 'others'. Additionally, it staggers the accounts of different generations of postcolonial migrants, who evaluate their relative integration and acceptance in Great Britain in the decades following World War II, from the perspective of the 1980s. And finally, it revisits the erased traces of non-white Europe over the centuries from the perspective of the dominant assumption that non-European immigration is a twentieth-century phenomenon.

The novel opens with the description of Stanley's difficult relationship with his father, a Jamaican immigrant who arrived in England in 1965, barricaded behind the bitterness of not belonging and reduced 'from fully qualified chemist in his home country to ill-paid postman in his adopted one' (19). Stanley grows up believing he doesn't belong either, although his father Clasford forces him to assimilate through learning 'proper' English, attending good schools, becoming a well-paid banker and dating exclusively white women. Despite his best efforts to assimilate, Stanley is forever inscribed through his colonial heritage: even his face is a veritable history book of the Caribbean, combining an 'archetypal Caribbean face', 'bright slanting eyes' inherited from an indentured labourer from Macao, a 'broad, shining forehead' from African slaves and the 'thin mouth of an aristocratic Scottish planter' (29). From the outset, *Soul Tourists* undermines the possibility of monocultural, assimilated and even hyphenated, diasporic identities, envisioning, instead, the variegated offspring of intersecting European colonialisms, which implicated all of the world's continents.

The insufficiency of cultural and financial capital in overcoming the trauma of displacement is evident in Stanley's ambivalent mourning of his father's death and his enchantment with Jessie, his opposite in terms of social position, except that she is also non-white. Jessie, a juggernaut of sensuality, rich life experience and vibrant personality, also has the advantage of being a decade older than Stanley; while Clasford obsessively returns to his experiences from the 1960s, Jesse recounts the difficulty of being black in Britain in the 1970s, which ushered in rising unemployment, the right-wing National Front and the ideology of Thatcherism which has evolved into twenty-first century neo-liberalism across Europe.

Of partial Ghanaian parentage, Jesse feels damaged by not having any familial connection at all; she grew up in the destitution of an orphanage and, unlike Stanley, never had a shot at upward mobility or solid education. From her perspective, the 1980s are a marked improvement over the 1970s, and her insistence that they are both privileged, well-assimilated Britons, rather than illegal migrants, is a constant warning against Stanley's tendency towards self-victimisation and *ressentiment*. As a stand-up comedian, she has faced both gender and racial discrimination: 'Do you think it was easy getting up on stage and telling gags in 1970? I was shot down on account of my colour or gender or the size of my protuberances or usually all three by those bastards' (33). She accentuates the problems migrants faced in Britain before immigration took place en masse, which later framed Stanley's adolescence and career success:

> we were few in number
> and often outnumbered – by thugs.
> Got no back-up then, no fancy
> Race Relations Department at Council. (34)

Evaristo therefore chooses to tell the history of post-war Europe from the perspective of first- and second-generation immigrants, whose experiences span three decades. In contrast to *The Seine*, whose protagonists are third-generation immigrants uninitiated into the history of their parents' unbelonging, *Soul Tourists* offers a more direct engagement with the history of racism, of confronting the 'pre-Race-Relations-Department', pre-multicultural imaginaries of European nations. The problems of negotiating identity are also different: in Sebbar, the third generation cannot integrate their roots because they have limited access to their parents' experiences of racist violence, whereas in Evaristo, Stanley has full access to his father's stories, but chooses to leave them behind through endless attempts at assimilation. Stanley's assimilation is never secure, however, suspended as he is between his parents' Jamaican identity which he doesn't quite understand and eager attempts to make his roots invisible, or pass for white. His affluent lifestyle shelters him from the need to confront the history of racism, but, as the narrative suggests, it is also like an anaesthetic that prevents him from living a full life and taking risks.

Stanley's apartment externalises this sense of an impoverished life, as there are no ornaments, photos, nor 'sentimental mementoes'; instead, there are only different shades of white: 'ivory painted walls . . . squares of snow-white floorboards, pearl-white skirting and an eggshell sofa throw, with flake-white cushions on it' (11). When Jesse waltzes into his life, she criticises him for leading such a mundane existence and presents herself as a bohemian, who, despite financial poverty, leads a much richer life. Even though, by her own account, Jesse is more victimised by racism than Stanley, she is more confident in acknowledging and inhabiting her black body. She is unapologetic and 'fascinated with her own reflection' as much as Stanley, who finds her 'extraordinarily dramatic-looking' and 'sexily fleshy' (29). Jesse's racial and cultural hybridity seems natural; she is a 'black woman with the novelty of a Northern accent', owning her British identity as a matter of fact rather than as an act of defensive insecurity (32). Their magnetic attraction implies that Stanley's obliviousness to the issues of race and colonialism is impossible: as she unmoors him from all of his life's coordinates, he becomes ready to revise his attitude towards his (post)colonial roots.

As the first important non-white person in Stanley's life following his father's death, Jesse undertakes the task of shaking him out of his complacency by driving him across Europe and Asia and ending the journey in Australia, where she plans to reunite with her estranged son. Embarking on this adventure, Stanley and Jesse drive across much of Western Europe and eventually end up in Turkey and the Middle East; though much of Eastern Europe remains omitted from the novel's peripatetic descriptions, Russia is obliquely included in the common signifier 'Europe' during one of the exits into Turkey's history. The novel is conceptualised as a sentimental journey which details various trials and tribulations in Jesse and Stanley's unravelling relationship. From the beginning they are established as opposites, but during the trip Stanley complains that Jesse exploits him financially and suffocates him with her possessiveness, while Jesse feels insufficiently loved and frustrated by what she sees as Stanley's petty shopkeeper mind.

For my purposes, however, the most significant source of incompatibility is their differing degree of openness to the ghosts of European history. Evaristo bequeaths the voices of erased history to various non-European residents of Europe, from Roman times to the eighteenth century, who stop Stanley in his tracks at each leg of his trip and, in Ancient-Mariner fashion, urge him to hear their stories. Unlike Jesse, who is uninterested in 'dead things or touristic things like great big fuck-off Rococo palaces', Stanley is, predictably, fascinated by Europe's star tourist attractions and 'civilisational' accomplishments. But the ghosts who address him at tourist haunts sense that he is also more 'susceptible' (94) than Jesse and has a 'sympathetic pair of ears' (288), a quality inherited from his Jamaican mother who also communed with ghosts. While Stanley comes to eagerly anticipate the voices of the past that eventually help him unlearn the Eurocentric history of his education, Jesse deems this both impossible and uninteresting: she remains impenetrable to the voices of history.

The first instance of haunting begins with his incipient amorous encounter with Jesse in London. In this scene, Evaristo blurs the distinction between Stanley and Jesse, the contemporary couple, and William Shakespeare and so-called Lucy Negro, the imagined sixteenth-century couple. The character of Lucy Negro, or Black Luce, is based on a madam of a brothel in Renaissance London, and while there is scholarly disagreement on whether she was 'black' morally or racially, her imagined fate of being brought from a 'village on the Guinea coast', then purchased and freed, would not have been exceptional or unbelievable at the time (62). Placing current fears of immigrant invasion in historical contexts, Evaristo includes Queen Elizabeth's announcement that 'blackamoores brought into this realme . . . should be sent forth of the lande' (63). The narrative imagines the encounter between Shakespeare and Lucy as that between a poet and his muse – the rumoured inspiration for the 'dark lady' of his sonnets, though a cause of much disagreement among scholars[17] – but mocks the poetic reification of ideal womanhood when Lucy doesn't respond, since she is preoccupied with being 'Damned / by the colour of my skin, hounded. As I speak, / they are rounding us up.' Shakespeare replies with 'I will hound thee too, because of thy skin', followed by more metaphor and symbolism, while Lucy brings him to the literal here-and-now, crying 'stop the drivel and help me out, goddamit!' (65–6).

In response, Shakespeare requests sex, deeming her a playful vixen, and Lucy relents in desperation: he is impenetrable to her needs as a subject rather than a mere object of fantasy. Their exchange parallels the contemporary relationship, not least in terms of Stanley's fascination with Jesse's beauty. Jesse is as anxious to escape her life as Lucy, while Stanley is a man in a position of gender and class power, one who also wields cultural capital, including familiarity with the Bard's opus. While Lucy is portrayed as bearing tribal markings – 'a circle of cicatrice dots stamped betwixt shoulder blades' (62) – Stanley thinks he can see 'a rash of mosquito bites between [Jesse's] shoulder blades' (68). Beyond this direct analogy, Jesse is portrayed as another muse, a woman that can link Stanley to the lost heritage of colonial history, recalling the symbolic roles women have historically been given as 'vessels' preserving cultural or national heritage. Jesse's indifference to either official or ghostly histories, then, should also be read in this context: if history is an idealist discourse of high seriousness, which objectifies classed and gendered 'others', her dismissiveness mocks its methods and goals.

As we shall see, Evaristo often uses humour so as not to idealise either officially important or unimportant historical characters. Shakespeare's exchange with Lucy, while humorously depicting the Bard's self-absorption in what is today deemed high culture, highlights ways in which privileging the figurative language of poetry can gloss over immediate violence against 'others' perpetrated by quite straightforward royal pronouncements. Moreover, this kind of encounter can only be imagined since it would not have been recorded as significant even had it happened – it constitutes the magical register of history which Evaristo chooses to supplement the language of realism. Marginalised characters like Lucy and Jesse help the readers recognise the rhetorical strategies of their objectification and silencing by diverting their attention away from 'drivel' and 'fuck-off Rococo palaces' that aestheticise the past. Instead, they approach history as lived experience: with a sense of urgency and the possibility of intervention in the here and now. Despite Jesse's disinterest in the ghosts of history, then, she provides a conceptual opening to the possibility of an alternative past, although the narrative stresses the problematic gendering of this role, as I note above. Without meeting her, Stanley would not have been privy to his sense of privilege nor his immersion in Eurocentric modes of thinking. Following this episode, Stanley imagines other omissions in British history, which he studied at school: 'no one resembled me – until now . . . This history, this country – could it really be mine?' (69).

Following this instance of haunting, at each leg of Stanley and Jesse's trip, the history of Europe is rewritten to include people who resembled them. Like Sebbar, Evaristo takes her protagonists on a tour of famous landmarks which become resignified through the presence of 'otherness' that has been erased. In Florence, Stanley is exposed to a tirade full of historical *ressentiment* by Alessandro de Medici, Duke of Florence, offended at the slur 'muulaatooo bastardooo' (188). In the novel, Alessandro's historically documented cruelty is ascribed to being an outcast – he was nicknamed 'The Moor' – and to his ambivalent status of being a Medici, on the one hand, and an illegitimate son of the pope and a 'slave girl from Africa'

(188), on the other. When Stanley draws parallels between Alessandro's and Clasford's immigrant bitterness, he realises that the anger and self-pity that repels him in Alessandro in fact reminds him of his father. Stanley therefore places the ghosts he meets in the context of both personal and social history, and they help him to deal with his parents' entrenched beliefs about not belonging:

> You belonged because you made a decision to and if you truly believed it no one could knock it out of you. These visitations came from inside the body of history, turning its skin inside out and writing a new history upon it with a bone shaved down to a quill dripped in the ink of blood. (189)

This lesson is even more forceful when Stanley meets the ghost of Mary Jane Seacole, fellow Jamaican, on the bus to Istanbul. While Stanley uncertainly wavers between Jamaican and European identities, Seacole is proud of her father's 'Scotch blood' and of her 'Creole mother' who 'passed on the science of herbs and midwifery that had been handed down by the slaves' (223). This hybridity characterises her approach to medicine: she supplements her mother's expertise with European medical knowledge, becoming one of the most venerated nurses during the Crimean war (223). Seacole's services were initially rejected by Florence Nightingale because of her race; nonetheless, she 'stood her ground' and eventually went on to oversee the building of a hotel for the war wounded (227). Thus, Seacole is the polar opposite of Alessandro: comfortable with her split identity, undeterred by racism and proud of her service to the British army. When Stanley asks how she could help those who profited from slavery, she replies in a religiously inflected register that is incomprehensible to him since it cannot translate into Stanley's secular worldview. Seacole says 'it was my duty as a healer to help those who needed me' and 'I was following the Good Lord's calling' (227), suggesting a Christian ethics of compassion and forgiveness. This would undermine attempts to portray her as a rebel fighting for racial equality, which might be the interpretation offered by a secular discourse of multiculturalism, for example. Through her religion, calling and bravery, Seacole decides to belong.

While earlier Evaristo uses humour to illustrate the distance between the lofty discourse of history and the vernacular voices it erases, here an absurd discrepancy between Stanley's impassioned indictment of racial oppression and Seacole's humble insistence on duty emphasises the ultimate untranslatability of history. From Stanley's perspective, Seacole could be a former slave brainwashed by the master through Christianity. And yet, she unnerves him with her persistence and accomplishments; her life experience cannot be reduced simply to misguided religiosity. Evaristo introduces historical figures with all the limitations and value systems believable in the context of the era in which they lived. Also, while Europe is always-already black, 'others' are either admitted as outstanding specimens of their race or reluctantly acknowledged as surreptitious interlopers in noble lineages. This is the case not only with Alessandro the Duke of Florence, but also with Chevalier de Saint George, an accomplished musician known as 'black Mozart' and the 'first black colonel in the French army' (119). Stanley meets him in Paris, where the Chevalier recounts the bitter history of slavery in his native Saint-Domingue and his admission to European society: 'I am of a rare breed/for whom society opened their doors/ even as they despised my people' (119). This parallels Stanley in the sense that he is accepted into middle-class society in London due to his educational and financial capital, but at the cost of disregarding his history and racial difference.

In contrast to opening doors to exceptional individuals who could demonstrate the level of accomplishment equal to those of Europeans, historiography has virtually excluded or glossed over 'illegitimate' interlopers into European noble lineages on which *Soul Tourists* particularly focuses, perhaps for the lack of historical information regarding classes other than nobility. Also, the presence of racial difference that dilutes blue blood suggests that the dreaded spectre of miscegenation has struck at the very heart of Europe's most powerful elites. At the end of the novel, after we have come full circle and returned, albeit sans protagonists, to Great Britain, Queen Charlotte Sophia, wife of George III, playfully examines the roots behind her 'swarthy complexion' and her 'true mulatto face', suggesting she could be descended from an Iberian Moor or a West Indian washerwoman (287). Undermining the myth of origins, Evaristo suggests that some part of history is undecidable, just as it is impossible to maintain the racial purity of any familial or national lineage: '*Mutti? Papi?* Infidelities and embarrassments swept under the carpet, as usual?' (287).

Like Sebbar, Evaristo also rewrites famous European landmarks through such historical embarrassments swept under carpets for the sake of preserving uninterrupted, embellished histories of Europe's noble families. When Stanley visits Versailles, he is accosted by Louise-Marie, the 'black nun of Moret', appropriately, in the hall of mirrors. Louise-Marie was hidden away in a convent following rumours that Queen Marie-Therese gave birth to her after an affair with a black dwarf. While this rumour has not been confirmed by historical research, that Louise-Marie's ghost presents this as true in the novel and that people of her time believed it, demonstrates the vulnerability and dread that pervades any attempt to fortify one's identity against 'otherness'. Stanley can only see Louise-Marie in the mirror, when he also sees his own reflection. Their destinies thus intertwined, he wishes he can retroactively rescue her from her fate of being taken to a convent: he wants to 'pull this woman through the mirror, into the twentieth century . . . to initiate her into a world where she would have choices' (96). This encounter opens up the comparison between black women's choices or lack thereof throughout the centuries and suggests that, while Jesse has faced the same orphaned childhood in a convent, history has repeated with a difference, in the sense that she can still find a way to support herself and live independently, despite the racism she continues to battle. Moreover, this encounter helps Stanley realise that he has been comparatively lucky compared to both women: Louise-Marie 'made him realise how grateful he was to have had parents who made sure he was given opportunities that their own immigrant selves were not' (96).

Through these encounters Stanley fills in the gaps in the collective history of non-European Europe, which simultaneously helps him to mourn his father's death while processing their difficult relationship full of distance and resentment. Personal history is indelibly linked with the broader history of colonialism and migrant displacement, which Stanley was forced to ignore until his adult years: 'my people come from a straggly, disgruntled queue / of slaves, masters and indentured servants, / of whom I was never allowed to speak' (122). Although his parents never considered Great Britain their home, their shame and humiliation silenced their discussion of colonial history, and Stanley grew up disconnected from past generations 'stuffed anonymously into an airless attic trunk' (122). He connects to the past not through familial history, forever inaccessible to him, but through learning about common historical exclusions of non-white Europeans. Claiming a collective past not only allows him to let go of his resentment of his father but also completes his entry into adulthood because he can confidently leave the manipulative relationship with Jesse. Here Evaristo again privileges the imagined, even if incomplete, shared histories of the 'other' Europe rather than reducing the narrative of healing to relationships within a single family.

Stanley's new coordinates of belonging transcend Britain to claim a broader European home, suggesting that, as John McLeod observes, Evaristo's goal is '*not* to reanimate the retrieval of Black British history' but 'to expand the horizon of this kind of work in a European context as a way of reframing the nation beyond the parochial parameters of Black Britain' (2010: 49). The international framing of the 1980s in *Soul Tourists* prefaces the debates regarding multiracial imaginings of community on the European Union level in the decades to come, implying that the erased histories of 'imperfect' Europeans are of crucial concern not only to diasporic or migrant populations but to Europeans in general.[18] Given Evaristo's insistence on complicating national as well as hybrid identities in her novels, her dedication to expanding the parameters of topics and geographic limits expected of black British writers is not a surprising move. Evaristo rejects the label of a black British writer as limiting; she argues that black Europeans need to claim their rightful place in Europe rather than align themselves with Africa, the US or the Caribbean alone. She notes that her own journeys across Europe 'demystified and familiarised' the continent, which most other black Britons spurned, expecting hostility (2008: 5). This decision to engage with a space that represents an alien, uncertain home echoes Stanley's difficult but bold venturing out of the comfort zone of insecure belonging. Seeing Europe for Evaristo translates into registering the ineluctable traces of interracial mixing across the continent rather than disavowing the obvious to affirm conservative myths of racial purity: 'How could it be otherwise when the lips of the Mediterranean coasts of Europe and Africa are practically kissing?' (2008: 3).

In *Soul Tourists* Europe is described as merely a crossroads of trade and conquest routes originating in Africa and Asia. Stanley and Jesse 'camped next to the ruins of fortresses and monasteries; *han*-caravanserais', as 'Stanley willed Alexander the Great to saunter out of the ruins, to regale him with tales of travel and conquest, or Tamerlane, and why not Genghis Khan or Marco Polo' (205). The constant nomadic flow negates the idea of firm roots and plenitude of self-contained identity, subverting Europe's presumed centrality.

While it is tempting to read this couple's tourist travel through Europe as reflecting the kind of privilege wielded by European colonial travellers who chronicled non-European 'others', *Soul Tourists* displaces the conceptual and rhetorical strategies associated with colonial travel narratives. Evaristo explains that her goal is not to 'write back' to this genre,[19] and indeed, she proceeds in a virtually opposite way, not least because the novel heavily focuses on internal rather than external journeys. Travel leads to demystification in Evaristo, rather than affirming timeless, internalised assumptions about a place which would lodge it in the realm of myth. Her irreverent and comical treatment of European history precludes the idealism associated with any mythification of the past, whether positive or negative. In this way, Stanley and Jesse's journey is more picaresque than epic, and while Evaristo employs epic conventions such as encountering obstacles on the voyage of discovery, accomplishment and character growth, they are delivered in anti-heroic, satirical form characteristic of postcolonial narratives that engage with classical Western genres.[20]

It would appear that Jesse's initial and Stanley's eventual sense of belonging, overcoming resentment and completion of the melancholy cycle gives Evaristo's novel a rather optimistic edge. Nonetheless, Evaristo treats many narrative and generic features as malleable and loaded with potential for ironic subversion. If we read Stanley's shifting attitude to his father and his heritage via Freud, we might conclude that he has moved from melancholy, understood as an unhealthy inability to come to terms with the past, to mourning, successful integration of the past and completed identity formation. At the end, however, the novel resists closure in that Stanley's next move is uncertain: we take leave of him feeling 'very passionate about life', on a beach somewhere in the Middle East (288). He does not return to Great Britain to re-enter either his erstwhile bourgeois lifestyle or the multicultural fabric of its society: 'I cannot return home. Perhaps not ever' (282).

Stanley's return to Britain would not only narrow down the European-scale inquiry into postcolonial race relations to national coordinates, but might also suggest an affirmation of Great Britain as a home that he can finally embrace. But neither does he return to Europe. His journey does not alter his reluctance to adapt to his place of birth; rather, in inspires him to negotiate a way of adapting beyond assimilation. Thus, the novel does not end in a reconciliation or resignation to one's home which may be imperfect though familiar, but, instead, poses an open-ended question about negotiating belonging in a Europe that has been creolised through an alternative history. In this sense, rather than concluding that Stanley has overcome melancholy, it is perhaps more fitting to see this figure as oscillating between movement and paralysis, optimism and melancholy. On the one hand, Evaristo articulates a broad historical discourse that affords an alternative sense of affiliation for non-white Europeans, suggesting that they can – and should – claim their rightful place in Europe, beyond insecurity and melancholy. At the same time, she cautions against a hasty celebration and embrace of Europe as always-already multicultural, as an increasingly hospitable home.

To draw on Vedrana Veličković's innovative reading of the significations of melancholy in *Soul Tourists,* at stake here is an attempt to negotiate modes of belonging that are not predictable or hegemonic (for example, based on 'visible' differences in multicultural discourse), as well as resist the drive to integration – and narrative resolution – by affirming the complex afterlives of Europe's colonial past. Bypassing Freud, Veličković privileges the definition of melancholy as an active engagement with loss and pain, rather than a 'pathological and passive condition' (2012a: 66). Evaristo's narratives, Veličković asserts, insist on the 'melancholic obligation' to resist 'neat resolutions' of identity formation, highlighting ways in which the protagonists are 'marked by the remains and residues of unresolved histories of nation, "race" and empire' (67). In this way, melancholic attachment, as a potentially productive tension point of acknowledging and processing loss, becomes a political statement in favour of revising hegemonic ideas about European memory.

In *The Promise of Happiness* (2010), Sara Ahmed analyses the negative stereotypes of 'melancholy migrants' in contemporary cultural discourses, noting that they are seen as obstacles to multiculturalism and reconciliation due to their inability to 'let go' of resentment and admit to any progress in racial relations. Ahmed notes that such a depiction both stems from and serves the ideology of happiness which downplays actual conflict in favour of a positive attitude to official discourses of multicultural love. Because melancholy is also denounced by a hegemonic cultural discourse that downplays the history of colonial racism, it becomes all the more important for literary narratives to refuse to let go of the attachment to uncomfortable truths. In Evaristo's novel, Stanley's increased confidence and optimism allows him to accept his belonging in Europe as a matter of fact, approximating Jesse's attitude; on a more personal level, it also results in a hedonistic ethics of enjoying life without guilt over his father's unhappiness. But this is not to be done at the expense of finally mourning the past, of letting go the memory of racism that includes his father as much as all the spectres of non-white Europeans. The novel's final narrative suspension – Stanley feels the lust for life yet is unsure how to proceed living it – perhaps reflects the difficulty of imagining how, precisely, this newly carved out space in social history can change the insistence on sweeping history under the carpet in a postcolonial Europe which has a melancholy attachment to its own colonial grandeur.

Melancholy nomadism in *Travelling with Djinns*

Jamal Mahjoub's novel *Travelling with Djinns* opens a peripatetic window into Europe's repressed histories so as to creolise Europe's heritage and revise the view that the arrival of non-European migrants is a recent phenomenon. As in *Soul Tourists*, the frame narrative is that of a road trip: after deciding to separate from his wife Ellen, the protagonist Yasin takes his young son Leo on a road trip from Denmark to Spain, with famed European landmarks inspiring pedagogical reflections on history and conversations with Leo. Through a non-linear narrative, which, much like *The Seine*, relates historical events through constellations of shared themes and actors rather than chronology, this exit into the European heritage of otherness alternates with Yasin's memory trip into the relationship between his Sudanese childhood and his adult life as an immigrant in Great Britain. The central mystery of the novel – reasons behind Yasin's breakup with Ellen that prompts the trip – is only slowly and intermittently revealed to readers, stylistically evoking Yasin's search for meaning and cohesion in a life made up of 'juxtaposed opposites, fragments, flinty chips'. Marrying and clinging to Ellen, who is of British and Danish background, is described as an attempt to absorb Europe; in the wake of losing his mooring point, Yasin fears, 'I shall make no sense – I will have lost all coherence' (228).

Travelling with Djinns further refines customary tropes in Mahjoub's writing,[21] such as the desire to 'make sense' and develop a community, as well as travel and incessant motion, which suggest the open-ended process of identity formation and constant interactions between Europe and its 'others'. In an earlier novel,

The Carrier (1998), Mahjoub similarly juxtaposes travelling stories set in the past and present, bringing into conversation the story of an African man arriving in Denmark during the Renaissance and collaborating with a local astronomer on developing an observatory with the contemporary narrative of an Arab scholar trying to decipher the repressed history of their collaboration, while being subjected to similar prejudice as his migrant predecessor. *The Carrier* highlights not only the cross-cultural, hybridised nature of allegedly European scientific achievements, but also racism to non-Europeans and violent religious opposition to science that, in the end, trumps the worldview espoused by the Danish astronomer, who is killed as a result. *Travelling with Djinns*'s excursions into history bring into sharp focus similar stains of intolerance and violence that bind Europe together, presenting a counter-narrative to the popular conviction that there was a long-standing tradition of racial and religious homogeneity in Europe before the twentieth-century arrival of immigrant communities.

In Mahjoub, travel, even when undertaken voluntarily, comes across as an unavoidable, unsettling and psychologically gruelling experience. In an interview, Mahjoub has expressed regret that there 'is a lot of romanticism involved with the idea about being nomadic, whereas, in fact, nomadic people live at home, they just have a large radius, when they move, it is to the same places, circular' (Sévry 2001: 91). Travel suggests the impossibility of fixing one's personal and social coordinates, because one has been forever put 'out of joint' through the material and cultural displacements of colonialism, or more recently, global capitalism. At the same time, reaching a different physical destination does not entail leaving the vicious circle of one's existential condition, and in *Travelling with Djinns*, this is not merely metaphysical posturing by an emigrant intellectual, but also the burden of various migrant lives in the novel, circumscribed by poverty and alienation. According to Yasin's Danish father-in-law Claus, travel is 'a way of evading the world', but 'you can never get away from the things that are troubling you. No matter how far you go, they go along with you.' That both Danish and Arabic languages share this assumption is confirmed by similar cultural expressions describing 'troubles' as nuisance travelling companions, *nisse* (an 'imp-like creature') and *djinn*, respectively (179).

In the novel, Yasin is an (un)comfortable citizen of Europe, acutely aware of the nuances of prejudices he faces, but at the same time, his exceptional erudition and modest and undistinguished, but nonetheless middle-class existence set him apart from the other 'nomads' traversing Europe in search of existential comfort. He describes Europe as always-already constituted by difference and the process of creolisation, made invisible through sacrifice:

> The face of this continent is scarred by the passage of people . . . From the earliest neolithic wanderers to the Mongol hordes, from the Huguenots to the Calvinists, pilgrims, refugees, gypsies . . . A history of transgression, of frontiers and border lines being crossed and recrossed. The Romans, the Visigoths, the Jews, Bosnians, Albanians, Kosovans, the blind, the sick, the old, the crippled. These are the people upon whose sacrifice the history of Europe is written, and our collective destiny is written in the course of these migrations. (173)

Despite his obvious class privilege in relation to the various disenfranchised migrants he enumerates, Yasin writes himself into the history of those who have been sacrificed to the idea of Europe: 'We are part of that vast, nameless body of mongrel humanity with nothing to claim as their own, not even the road they are on' (173). Throughout the novel, Yasin does not shy away from highlighting disparities of power and class as he attempts to find a common ground with 'mongrel humanity' through a shared history of displacement and the necessity of claiming their road collectively.

Travelling through Great Britain, Denmark, France, Germany and Spain, the narrative addresses not only the countries' histories of violence, carnage and racism, but also their joint participation in the unifying EU project, reflected in the supposed erasure of internal borders. Europe as a project and idea is invoked exclusively through its constituent nations' negative legacies, inverting contemporary European discourses about overcoming the histories of war and totalitarianism. Europe is represented through the notion of borders, which traverse the novel like a motif from beginning to end, in contrapuntal reflections on the politics of frontiers in the past and present. Early on in the novel, Yasin and Leo arrive at the German border, and as border guards 'with eagles on their tunics' check his name in the database of internationally wanted suspects, Yasin muses, 'Is it the car, I wonder, or my face? The borders are now open, but these guards haven't heard of the Schengen Agreement, or didn't care either way what those clever gentlemen in Brussels and Strasburg decide' (10).

The continuing presence of invisible borders, evoking the legacy of World War II, is underscored again at the end of the journey, as they wait in a bus at Port Bou to cross into Spain. At this point, Yasin again assures the reader that the border 'is supposed to be open', but the police, flashing torches in the faces of sleepy passengers, look for 'strays who should not be flitting about the continent' (304). Yasin is the only passenger whose passport is examined, his skin colour associating him with illegally moving 'mongrel humanity'.

This event occasions the conjuring of Walter Benjamin, 'another illegal immigrant' who was detained by Spanish border guards as he tried to cross at Port Bou and committed suicide in the face of 'the cruel prospect of a train journey back to Germany, to Buchenwald, or Auschwitz' (305). Yasin feels an affinity with Benjamin because they are both collectors and lovers of books, possessed by the *djinn* of knowledge and language, building an intellectual labyrinth in which they can disappear (305). But none of their erudition or creativity matters in the face of extreme identity politics that reduces both to illegal 'strays' who can be erased from European soil.

While the ghosts of history in Evaristo appear in a magical realist manner, in Mahjoub they are conjured by Yasin's reflections on the interconnectedness of Europe's past and present. In uncovering the historically marginalised presence of migrant and diasporic communities in Europe, Yasin addresses not only the relationship between Great Britain and the Sudan, but more broadly, the inextricable intertwining of the histories of Asia, Africa and the Caribbean with that of Europe. Because Mahjoub's object of study in *Travelling with Djinns* is a creolised Europe,[22] María Carbacos Traseira argues that reading Mahjoub in the context of 'Black British' writing is limiting and instead proposes that Mahjoub be read as an 'Afro-European' writer, since his novels trace the contributions of Africans in Europe and examine the intersections between the two continents' colonial and diasporic histories (2012: 191). While I agree with this broadening of the critical lens, I argue that even this framework overflows with a variety of diasporic examples that are not limited to African presence, as the Benjamin fragment demonstrates.

In teaching Leo about European history, Yasin creates constellations from various traditions which demonstrate the kaleidoscopic mixing of cultures built into the fabric of European societies. For instance, as they enter Rhineland, Yasin reflects on Roman presence in Germany, at whose time the country was covered in endless forests;

this leads him to trace the word for the tree neem, found in both the Sudan and Europe, to the Latin word *nemus*. Next, observations on the ancient worship of trees reminds him of mystics and visionaries such as Hildegard von Bingen who lived in twelfth-century Rhine-land. Finally, her opposition to the Second Crusade because 'she knew what the Church was up to' after the First Crusade which began 'with a massacre of Jews' leads him to explain to Leo that the Crusades were to continue with massacres of Saracens in the Holy Land (57–8). When Leo asks, 'Who were the Saracens?' Yasin responds, 'Well . . . they were us' (58), reminding him of their uneasy belonging in Europe and uncovering the forgotten labels of otherness.

Later on, their trip to visit Yasin's brother Muk in Tossa del Mar, Spain, allows Yasin to reflect on the surreal combination of cultural inscriptions that are all but untranslatable to a contemporary visitor. While Tossa is an old Moorish town with a tenth-century fortress, 'most visitors scratch their heads' when encountering the lines from Omar Khayyam's *Rubaiyat* carved into a clifftop overlooking the town (308). But this poetry has to do less with Arab presence and more with a monument commemorating the filming of *Pandora and the Flying Dutchman* in Tossa, the story of which originates around a Dutch East India captain and is related to the European colonial tradition. Unlike *The Seine*, where the traces of undesirable history are silenced by their inadmissibility into official discourses on the past, *Travelling with Djinns* suggests that such traces already exist in linguistic and cultural heritage but they need to be translated and contextualised. The history of Moorish Spain needs to be brought into meaningful conversation with European colonialism in Asia because they are both reduced to exotic, depthless consumer objects – a picturesque fortress, a romantic film – separated from contemporary racism towards 'Moors' and 'Saracens'.

Yasin says, 'Europe is my dark continent, and I'm searching for the heart of it' (59). This statement inverts Joseph Conrad's search for the heart of darkness in Africa, but the element of escape to an exotic location in *The Heart of Darkness*, which one views from a safe distance and recounts to an empathetic audience at home, is crucially missing. Yasin does not have 'an Africa to run to when . . . life turns sour': there is no elsewhere for him, outside of the influence of European colonialism, and he must claim his own space within it (59). If Europe, then, is inescapable, he rewrites its history not only to trace its indebtedness to distant 'others' it has sought to consume, but also to underscore that its violence to itself, its intimate cleaving, is at its heart of darkness before the onset of colonialism. Yasin makes numerous references to intra-European wars and persecutions, beyond the aforementioned instances of historical anti-Semitism: he reflects on Brecht writing *Mother Courage* after taking refuge from Hitler and Stalin in Jutland and empathises with Joseph Roth, who, fleeing Hitler's Germany, 'remained on the move . . . in solitary exile' for the rest of his life (30, 302). In the pastoral hills of Moselle, Yasin recalls the history of World War I carnage, saying, 'If we had X-ray vision we would see through the placid surface of these dewy fields . . . Terrified men huddled shivering in waterlogged trenches' (80). That the idea of Europe is built upon such graveyards of invisible sacrifices is important to understand the contemporary instances of racism, ubiquitous swastikas painted on British housing-estate walls and simplistic reporting on the Iraq-Kuwaiti war where Saddam Hussein is vilified as the 'Baghdad Butcher' (92, 99).

Yasin turns to art and literature to examine this continuous history of erasures as well as borrowings, of the presence of external influences as well as their marginalisation. Like Benjamin, he is a collector of books: he travels with 'Dorothy Parker, Faulkner's *Sanctuary*, Blaise Cendrars, Kenzaburo Oe and Homer' (117). But this is more than a paean to Western literary influences: travelling with books is like travelling with *djinns*, who can take the form of both noble and mischievous spirits, but whom one cannot escape. For Yasin, they are both a burden imposed by the history of Western colonialism and a discursive space that allows him to 'make sense' of displacement as he imagines other writers' similar destinies. Combining observations on Benjamin, Rimbaud, Roth and Orwell, among others, around their joint alienation from hegemonic European ideals, Yasin comes to the conclusion that everything is 'intricately connected. I occupy the centre of a complex maze', and his familiarity with this literary history allows him to find clues everywhere (302).

This maze is also the one of translating borrowings and mutual influences,[23] creolising the narrative of European accomplishments by bringing up a fourteenth-century Danish church that was inspired by Arab architecture (53), or describing the ways in which Sufi poetry led Goethe to believe in the possibility of 'universal literature' and to produce a series of poems paying homage to Hafiz's *ghazal* (178). Yasin acknowledges Goethe's Romanticist Orientalism, but he underscores the element of aesthetic enjoyment, curiosity and appreciation in such literary contact zones that exceeds the mere exoticisation of cultural difference. The sheer serendipity of finding 'others'' stories in 'our' midst affirms to him the impossibility of cultural and national isolationism – after all, the travel of stories cannot be controlled or policed.

For Yasin, the familiarity with written literature and history is not necessarily a way to distance himself from the less educated migrants or compatriots, but rather an argument for its promotion as a necessary tool to overcome one's subaltern status of silence and marginalisation. Reflecting on his schooling in the Sudan, Yasin notes that history and other humanities were not a priority and were downplayed in favour of developing 'concrete' scientific and technical skills in the future builders of a postcolonial society. He insists on making intricate and roundabout historical connections for Leo because in the Sudan 'our history was never going to be a straightforward, linear narrative, but rather a series of contortions, disjointed incidents, haphazard circumstances' for which his own teacher had no time (63). If traces of historically shared references, meanings and ideas are inherent in cultural narratives, which one must rescue from oblivion and 'translate' assiduously, then their erasure becomes a tragedy. Thus, Yasin notes of his childhood, 'we had stories, but we didn't really have museums or books to put them in' and, significantly, relates this to the colonial destruction of written records that did exist, such as the French 1912 burning of the 'legendary library' of Samara in Western Sahara (62, 186).

In this respect, *Travelling with Djinns* itself, in the sheer abundance of literary and historical references, resembles an encyclopaedic attempt at recreating or preserving a written record of erased transcultural connections, demonstrating the advantages of meaningful education which Yasin advocates. And yet, as he and Leo move between spaces and narratives, trying to link interpretation and understanding with lived experience, Yasin continually runs up against the abyssal rift between educated, middle-class migrants and economic underclasses. As he ponders visiting the exhibition at the Louvre on 'The Lost Art of Memory', his attention turns to 'a row of young men . . . from places like Dakar and Conakrt, from Lome, Abidjan and Bamako. Each has a square of cloth spread out before him on which there are arrayed a selection of compact discs and sunglasses' (105). Realising none of them could ever afford to visit the museum, he is incensed at the exhibition fee and steps out of the ticket line, since culture has become 'a fashion accoutrement' for the financially privileged, rather than a universal human right, as Yasin would wish (106).

The foregrounded rift in this scene reflects both the (im)possibility of and desire for community and compassion expressed through the narrative perspective. Structurally similar to Yasin's tendency to create labyrinthine connections among sundry cultural narratives, which are asymmetrical in terms of the political power they wield, the meanings of migrancy and travel are re-signified by bringing into conversation their singular manifestations, revealing disjointed levels of social class and status. Carbacos Traseira argues that the novel engages with questions of distance and privilege in an account of journey with an 'uncertain destination', attempting to reconcile tensions between 'the political and the personal, between academic erudition and memoir of exile' (2012: 194). Instead of thinking of these in terms of opposition or tension, though, I propose interpreting them as always-already manifesting together, as being singular-plural, to borrow Nancy's concept: Yasin's insights do not occur prior to or in isolation from the broader community and history of exile which he inhabits.

Travel, then, is multivalent and non-idealised, and while Yasin claims affiliation with the 'mongrel humanity' that crosses Europe unwillingly, he simultaneously considers the opportunities that such an experience affords for re-seeing Europe as if through enlightened eyes and making connections that had heretofore remained veiled. Travel is described as moving between the hidden and the revealed, the *mahjoub* and the *zahir*, 'in the romantic tradition of reclining Taoists, wandering Buddhist monks searching for enlightenment . . . Like the Sufis condemned to forever tramp the roads of the world. Ibn Arabi's restless search for the *kashf*, the discovery' (11). Significantly, this journey is not one of economic necessity but rather of choice, a decision to leave behind earthly comforts and launch oneself into uncertainty. But the invocation of a religious purpose might seem like a romanticised rationalisation of travel, as Yasin is at a midway point in his life that leaves him restless and repeatedly suggests that his unmooring from Ellen is only a breaking point in a postcolonial life that he feels has always been fragmented and unsettled.

Nonetheless, the significance of thinking of this trip as a *hejira* lies less in its religious overtones than in the kind of insight that Yasin foregrounds. Quoting Ibn Arabi, 'the archetype of the eternal Sufi wanderer, who devoted much of his life to travelling the world in search of knowledge', Yasin notes that:

'The earth is not the true form of being, but something illusory.' The world we live in is a 'realm of signs' in which spirits, angels and djinns are made flesh. In dreams we pass beyond this physical realm into the real world, which otherwise cannot be seen. Ibn Arabi set off around the world hoping to awaken himself, to 'die' in a metaphorical sense so as to be able to see. (86)

Travel in this sense is equivalent to a hermeneutic, an interpretive perspective on the world which we might read as a 'realm of signs', deconstructing its illusions so as to capture and understand the nature of *djinns* that haunt us. Ibn Arabi's notion of awakening through this process echoes Walter Benjamin's argument in *The Arcades Project* [1982] (2002) for reading cultural spaces and practices as a process of awakening from the 'phantasmagoria' of capitalism that seduces us with its consumer items, decontextualised from the production process and presented as self-evident realities. In parallel, Yasin travels and reflects, wondering while wandering, in an attempt to awaken from the 'nightmare of history' that has marginalised non-European experiences and events.

This melancholy nomadism, which can also be seen in the context of the aforementioned interpretation of melancholy by Veličković, is portrayed by Yasin as more reflective of his condition than a settled life with a job and a family. Quoting Hafiz's line 'In my love's house . . . there is no peace in pleasure' he concludes, 'I feel that this is right, this is where we belong. Moving. Always moving' (278). But what does it mean to belong in movement? At the very least, Yasin's evasion of fixed identity and territory doesn't render this an inverse colonial travel narrative, where he might mimic Europeans visually and discursively mastering distant places, while also settling them physically. Also, he doesn't travel 'to see new places' but rather to rethink Europe, which he has 'known' for much of his life, from a different perspective (271). Mahjoub analyses movement from different perspectives rather unproblematically idealising it as a liberating experience for erudite migrants like Yasin. Movement is inescapable because of the histories of colonialism and impoverishment, but this realisation also makes it impossible for Yasin to belong in a national or territorial community, if such community is understood as sealed off within clearly delineated parameters. He does not belong in the imagined community of Europe, which maintains invisible borders against non-Europeans, any more than he belongs in the Sudan, a diasporic identity defensively preserved by his sister's family in the face of European racism. Belonging in movement, then, is not to be read merely as a permanently disenfranchised, existential condition – it is not so much that Yasin 'lacks' community – but rather as a choice, a possibility of traversing such communities and their borders to demonstrate their fissures and gaps. Early on, Yasin describes his predicament thus:

> I belong to that nomad tribe, the great unwashed, those people born in the joins between continental shelves, in the unclaimed interstices between time zones, strung across latitudes. A tribe of no fixed locus, the homeless, the stateless . . . My history is not given, but has to be taken, reclaimed, peace by solitary piece, snatched from among the pillars of centuries, the shelves of ivory scholarship. My flimsy words set against those lumbering tomes bound in leather in written in blood. My nation is a random list of places on the map that I have passed through, upon which I have no claim. Some might say that I have been assimilated, but they would be wrong. Others would say I am alienated and ought to be better integrated by now, but that too would be to miss the point. (4–5)

Neither assimilated nor alienated, Yasin is determined to unearth erased histories and experiences, claiming simultaneously the 'part of those who have no part' in dominant political discourses (Rancière 2004a: 11). During his travels, encountering people with whom he does not feel immediate kinship – for instance, his formerly drug-dealing brother Muk or the West Saharan refugee Haya – represent possibilities for provisional communities, which engender new insights even as they are steeped in asymmetries of misunderstanding and difference in social status. Mahjoub pushes readers towards such non-obvious communities and exchanges that claim their own place in the narrative, favouring agonistic relations filled with dissent and debate over harmonious communities based on resemblance and agreement. Haya, an uneducated young prostitute who unsettles Yasin with her violent reaction against racism in a French restaurant, undermines any idealisation of 'otherness' as automatic revolutionary radicalism. While Yasin wants to reclaim erased histories and insists on the importance of alternative education and erudition, Haya tells him they are too different and she 'can't eat his books' (223). More determined to reach a less precarious economic status, Haya 'wanted to eat proper French food', 'comfort and respectability, she was not a fashionable accoutrement' for alternative lifestyles (152).

Despite their similar cultural and geographic backgrounds, their temporary sojourn together isn't romanticised; Mahjoub continually underscores what separates them, highlighting the withdrawal of community and mapping the conditions of its (im)possibility. For example, Haya points out that men like Yasin 'don't marry our kind of women, they marry European women' (163). Yasin thus reaches out to Haya, but realises that there is a significant class and education barrier; nonetheless, he acknowledges this gap while simultaneously connecting the histories they have in common, and this is perhaps the only way that any transnational community can take (or claim) place in this novel of travel around Europe.

Mahjoub turns towards the past because migrants and exiles, upon entering host countries in Europe, 'lose their past . . . everything about them ceases to exist'. Furthermore, people in the host country assume that they barely need to know anything about the arrivals, and that their 'own history and culture have always been pure and unadulterated by outside forces' (Sévry 2001: 91). In this attempt to reclaim migrant histories to which European host nations are indifferent, but which inescapably involve them, Mahjoub also creates a subaltern, transcultural literary narrative that stretches across the European continent. In post-Cold War Europe, Mahjoub argues, 'we find ourselves divided, more fiercely than ever. The borders between the European states are dissolving, but there are new internal dividing lines: Between rich and poor, those who have a great deal and those who have nothing' (1997: n.p.). He observes that these subdivisions have affected literature as well, so that:

> Speaking across cultures is less popular than simply sticking to one's own crowd and telling them what they want to hear . . . Transcultural literature demands more, both of reader and writer. It does not have the support of those cheering waving crowds who would like you to be European or Third World, Black, or African or Arab. (ibid.)

Travelling with Djinns contributes to this demand for thinking beyond identitarian divisions and connecting the marginalised histories of underprivileged residents of contemporary Europe.

To conclude, in terms of the treatment of marginalised histories, Evaristo highlights the always-already multi-ethnic and multiracial history of Europe, mocking populist anxieties over the recent 'discovery' of non-Europeans at the heart of Europe. *Soul Tourists'* narrative perspective seems to favour integration in the sense that non-Europeans should claim Europe as a legitimate social and political home which they have long inhabited, as opposed to acting like uprooted migrants who have only just arrived. In turn, Sebbar stresses the importance of connecting different narrative lines of suppressed history to overcome colonial aphasia, both in terms of external and self-imposed silencing of colonial victims, and to rewrite national history at its core rather than remain relegated to the fringes. Despite the insistence on fostering a conversation between silenced personal memories and official historiography, *The Seine* envisages no possibility of articulating a unified, consensual historical perspective on traumatic colonial crimes. Mahjoub echoes the other two authors' preoccupation with linking the history of non-European erasure to the corresponding silences in mainstream historiography and epistemology. *Travelling with Djinns* locates the possibility of reclaiming erased history in re-translating the traces of non-European linguistic and cultural heritage as evidence of the centuries of continental migrations and exchange. This unearthed history, however, does not facilitate an articulation of a suppressed cultural identity, but is, rather, associated with belonging in movement, in melancholy nomadism, as a gesture of avoiding fixed identity markers.

Chapter 4

Postcolonial and Postcommunist Contact Zones in a United Europe

In the introduction I argue that, to understand the European Union's invisible borders and hierarchies of belonging, we should bring into conversation the differentially excluded experiences of postcolonial and postcommunist populations. This chapter explores the possible points of convergence where such conversations might happen in the context of existing and emerging literary texts that take on (post) Cold War Europe's attitude to its legacy of communism and experience of decolonisation. Following EU expansion into formerly communist countries, new economic migrants from the East have entered contact zones with established migrant populations from Europe's former colonies, facing similar prejudice and fear-mongering discourses about invasion to which postcolonial migrants have been subjected, often including a racialised component.[1] These contact zones have become the preoccupation of numerous contemporary literary and film narratives, but as British writer of Ghanaian background Mike Phillips observes of his novel *A Shadow of Myself* (2000), his decision to write about both Eastern Europe and decolonising Africa was met with surprise 'because as a black writer, I was expected to limit myself to thinking about the former colonies' (2010: 47). While contemporary literature and film, with increasing enthusiasm, irreverently crosses the borders between 'ethnically' and 'geographically' restricted topics,[2] postcolonial and postcommunist studies maintain separate objects of inquiry. Or, rather, as Hana Cervinkova notes, 'students of postsocialism look to postcolonialism for inspiration, but postcolonial scholarship does not seem to be too interested in what studies of postsocialism have to contribute' (2012: 159).[3]

Postcolonial studies have traditionally neglected the postcommunist part of the world, in part because many of these countries have not been considered colonies in the true sense of the word. However, many would argue that the EU has established a protocolonial relationship to its Eastern periphery by exploiting its more affordable labour and natural resources and by unilaterally setting the terms for economic development along neo-liberal lines without the possibility of negotiation.[4] It is therefore unsurprising that post-Cold War transitions to capitalism have been contemporaneous with an unprecedented flourishing of theoretical inquiries into the type of coercive, colonial-type mechanisms and assumptions that accompanied these, often seismic, social shifts. A detailed overview of such studies exceeds the scope of this book, but in brief, they have focused on comparisons to traditional colonial situations, indirect rule through economic and political domination, humanitarian interventions as neocolonial conquest, intersections between cultural and biological racism and historical discourses of prejudice that precede the Cold War.[5] Eastern Europe, as Larry Wolff (1994) asserts, was an immediate example of 'otherness' against which the Enlightened Western Europe constructed its identity in the eighteenth century, preceding the intensification of European colonialism around the world in the coming centuries.

According to Neil Lazarus, 'an adequate historicisation of colonialism has been hindered by the particular and historically specific "third wordlist" optic' that has underwritten work in postcolonial studies since its beginnings (2012: 120). If we reframe colonialism as the dynamic of inclusion into the profoundly uneven capitalist world system, Lazarus argues, we will be able to think about how this process unfolds in the 'second world' and overcome conceptually limiting geographic terms (west-east, north-south divide). From this perspective, the global spread of capitalism as a unifying factor in modern colonial endeavours is crucial to understanding political disenfranchisement and class stratifications of not only postcolonial but also postcommunist societies. The contemporary dynamic of this colonial legacy, now that 'Third' and 'Second' Worlds increasingly occupy the 'First' World, haunt Europe's conceptions of class, citizenship and belonging.

In Mike Phillips's and Dubravka Ugrešić's novels and essays, which are the central concern of this chapter, the dynamic of capitalism as colonialism itself becomes a unifying lens that refracts postcolonial and postcommunist migrants' shared experiences of discrimination in their adopted European homes, allowing us to trace similarities, correspondences and nodes of solidarity between them. While we can analyse such experiences by drawing on the interpretive tools of Orientalism and other discriminatory discourses on non-European 'others', we can also benefit from a more recent field of study which Ezequiel Adamovsky aptly terms Euro-Orientalism, entailing both Eastern Europe's historical image as a semi-European Orient and its current attempts to overcome this inferiority complex by disavowing the legacy of communism and joining the EU. According to Adamovsky, Europe's empire of capital relies on neo-liberal versions of Orientalism that 'has a distinctive class component' and constitutes 'a fundamental part of liberal-bourgeois ideology' (2005: 609). Analysing how Polish bourgeoisie project Orientalist stereotypes on less privileged classes, Michał Buchowski observes that 'internal societal orientalisation' presents impoverished workers and peasants as roadblocks to development, as the lumpenproletariat of postcommunism who are easy prey for nationalist ideologies (2006: 466–7). Their concerns about unemployment, according to Buchowski, are ascribed to laziness or habitual thievery under communism; while they are seen as mere objects of transitions, the entrepreneurial, progressive, urban middle classes become their true subjects, idealised agents of 'Westernisation'. In times of economic crisis, the poor become scapegoats for Eastern European middle classes, who blame them for the recession (Bohle and Greskovits 2009: 12).

Such insights about postcommunist transitions to capitalism, while arguing that racism underwrites the very establishment and articulation of neo-liberal class structures, also echo earlier postcolonial studies that explore intersections between classism and racism in colonial societies, with similar relationships between Europeanised comprador elites and less privileged classes assumed to be uncivilised. Nonetheless, as semi-European Europe, Eastern Europe has always been different from other colonial spaces in terms of racial, geographic and cultural proximity to Europe 'proper', which ensured that it can, at least in theory, strive to 'rejoin' Europe in the postcommunist period by claiming to be an integral part of its civilisation.[6] Simultaneously, postcommunist Europeans employ discriminatory discourses not only against internally 'uncivilised' others, but also against non-European migrants who increasingly settle this part of the continent. Finally, transitions to capitalism and (the possibility of) accession to the EU, driven by the need to overcome internalised Orientalist narratives which portrayed communist nations as underdeveloped, inefficient and even barbaric, are characterised by Eastern Europe's eager embrace of market economies accompanied by aggressive privatisation, disappearance of social welfare states and resulting waves of migration to Western Europe. Unlike old colonies, then, the new ones participate in active 'self-colonisation' in Alexander Kiossev's (1999) words, testifying to the consensual nature of Europe's empire.

To foster the much-needed dialogue between postcolonial and postcommunist studies and take into account such shared as well as divergent experiences of colonisation, I will employ the '(post-) Cold War' perspective as defined by Sharad Chari and Katherine Verdery: a unified interpretive framework aiming to explore worldwide effects of the Cold War ideology and undermine the traditional divide between 'Third' and 'Second' World studies (2009: 18). Enveloping Phillips's and Ugrešić's texts within this interpretive contact zone, I ask how the experience of communism and decolonisation can be thought together in a united Europe, posing alternative imaginings of community that unsettle both mainstream multiculturalism and neo-liberalism. In *A Shadow of Myself*, Phillips wanders through various European locales, including Prague, London, Berlin and Moscow, interweaving the histories of African struggles for independence and Eastern Bloc communism not only to shed light on these often neglected connections but also to interrogate the dominant narratives of Europe today. Essays in *Nobody's Home* (2008) and the novel *The Ministry of Pain* (2005), in turn, reflect Ugrešić's use of the experience of Yugoslav communism to mobilise 'outdated' discourses of class and identify neo-liberal mechanisms of exclusion and segregation that jointly marginalise postcommunist and postcolonial minorities in the context of the EU 'crisis.' As Veličković argues, such excursions into the 'prehistory' of post-Berlin Wall era are necessary in order to move away from 1989 as a frequently designated point of convergence between the two interpretive paradigms. Instead, she advocates a 'critical examination of communist alliances with anti-imperial struggles', which have been neglected by literary scholarship (2012b: 165).

But how does such prehistory affect alliances between contemporary postcolonial and postcommunist migrants in the EU? For instance, in Ai Kwei-Armah's play *Let There Be Love* (2008), which focuses on an encounter between a cantankerous, terminally ill West Indian man and a young Polish woman who has been hired as home help, conflicts abound. Having lived in Great Britain for decades, Alfred rehearses generic prejudices against Eastern Europeans as he hurls insults at Maria, who struggles with English and feels alienated from her adopted home. He subjects her to similar kinds of prejudice employed against West Indians and other postcolonial migrants in the post-war period. Nonetheless, as a friendship develops, he begins to empathise with Maria's homesickness, teaches her English and helps her escape an abusive relationship. Maria, in turn, brings about Alfred's reconciliation with his estranged daughters and, in an act of ultimate empathy, helps him commit suicide so that he doesn't have to die in hospital. Their gradual rapprochement, based on an interest in each other's backgrounds and common experiences of migration, grows into an alliance stronger than that offered by biological kinship: in the end, they have formed an alternative father-daughter relationship.

Despite the hopeful ending, this example illustrates the difficulty of idealising such new contact zones as optimistic harbingers of a more egalitarian Europe. Simultaneously, it is problematic to elide the highly idiosyncratic identities and situations portrayed within a generalising discourse about either postcolonials or postcommunists. In a similar way, the numerous differences and asymmetries among the protagonists of Phillips's and Ugrešić's texts, based on culture, race, gender or simply character, preclude the establishment of smooth alliances, or even empathy. These characters' exchanges result in collisions caused by misunderstanding and even eruptions of violence fuelled by racism and class resentment. They often occupy different positions of power, which results in non-reciprocal relationships. The violence of communing with others is the result of such disparities and imbalances, which I read via Maurice Blanchot's [1983] (1988) observations on the 'absent' community, where even seemingly socially equal encounters are traversed by irreducibly singular asymmetries of relating. For Blanchot, this does not mean community has failed; on the contrary, it demonstrates the impossibility of community understood as organic communion and reproduction of identitarian sameness, which, for him as well as Jean-Luc Nancy, carries potential for totalitarian closure.

However, the community that such reaching out to others engenders, albeit non-idealised, draws on their common experiences of colonial discrimination and highlights the continuing anticolonial potential of the communist idea. Phillips and Ugrešić also bring together their protagonists' variegated lifeworlds, including their ambitions, desires, vulnerability and sexuality alongside the more predictable features of migrant life, such as economic survival or cultural adaptation. They not only humanise them beyond the migrant stereotype, which often relies on victimhood and not belonging, but also challenge the expected portrayals of non-European migrants based on racial difference and Eastern European migrants based on economic impoverishment, which effectively keep their narratives separate according to difference in 'essential' identity.[7] I read these literary texts alongside Rancière's theories of political subjectification, especially his concept of disidentification from a given identity, which is one avenue of building (un)common alliances. Conversely, as we shall see particularly in Phillips and less overtly in Ugrešić, similarity and solidarity based on traditional kinship ties are constantly thrown into question.

By avoiding the debilitating tropes of not belonging, these texts, however, do not imagine the goal of belonging as inclusion in existing, countable political categories that would then have access to recognition in a multicultural state; nor do they desire the related inclusion into Europe's capitalist utopia. It is not about transcending one's marginalisation by occupying the centre. Rather, both authors attempt to redefine the terms on which one is able to belong by imagining communities gathering around non-filiative relationships while revisiting, critically, the historical legacies of socialism, anticolonialism and their equitable visions of society. While they are concerned with social equality, they revile the hegemonic ideals of multicultural harmony and co-existence in a neo-liberal Europe. In their texts, this hegemony operates through a violent policing of excessive difference into acceptable identities assumed to be flat and interchangeable; silences the histories of racial, class or other social antagonism, enforcing forgiveness; and replicates the capitalist logic of commodity exchange and reciprocity, where all 'ethnics' become equal when entering the market.

This puts in fresh perspective Phillips's and Ugrešić's insistence on highlighting the internal strife and violence even in imaginations of alternative communities, whose agents are immanently rooted in historically layered asymmetries of power. In Phillips, this violence is manifested through collective and individual crimes – especially those of colonial racism – across East and West Europe. He does not envision a way out of crime, but rather meticulously historicises it so as to de-pathologise it as a feature of 'uncivilised' societies. Ugrešić de-pathologises the violence and crime associated with variegated migrant communities of protest across Europe, while highlighting the invisible ravages wrought by neo-liberal economic immiseration and urban segregation. Rather than simply denouncing hostility or the absence of solidarity in the alternative communities they proffer, these authors' texts suggest the necessity of engaging with the histories of social disenfranchisement that both enable and impede the articulation of a common subaltern resistance to a neo-liberal Europe.

Crimes of prejudice: unavowable communities in *A Shadow of Myself*

Earlier I focused on 1961 as the year in which seemingly disconnected historical events converged to highlight interdependence between European colonialism, the Cold War and increasing immigration into Western Europe from European peripheries and colonies. In *A Shadow of Myself*, various narrative strands project outwards from another centrally important year, 1956, in which historical events inexorably change the protagonists' life trajectories. Phillips notes that the inspiration to write this novel came after listening to his brother, a 'passionate Marxist', describe his experience of studying in Russia. He started thinking about how Eastern Europe related to the Third World, since they were both used by the industrialised West in similar ways. The year 1956 illuminated links between these parts of the world because it marked 'the independence of Ghana, the invasion of the Suez Canal and the crushing of the Hungarian rebellion' (Sternberg 2001: 389–90).

The rich history of young people from the global African diaspora studying in the Soviet Union has not been the subject of many literary narratives. Mike Phillips foregrounds this interesting episode in Cold War politics, designed to aid in the struggle against Western colonialism and capitalism, so as to, as Eva Ulrike Pirker claims, 'open up a new space for the negotiation of "black" history, beyond the scope of . . . a "Black Atlantic" context' (2010: 138–9). In the novel, Kofi Coker, a Ghanaian who migrates to England, wins a scholarship to study in the Soviet Union thanks to his connections to prominent pan-African and anticolonial activists. He meets Khrushchev in 1956, after he is pressured into giving a 'fraternal speech' praising the accomplishments of the Soviet Union (230). The meeting with Khrushchev becomes his claim to fame, recalled frequently throughout the novel to emphasise the loss of Kofi's youthful potential and his ensuing lacklustre life in England, after this brief brush with world politics. The timing of Kofi's 'fraternal speech' is important because it symbolises his status as an unwitting pawn in the Cold War politics. As a former British colonial subject whose university education is made possible by 'fraternal' Soviet people, he must demonstrate support for the Soviet Union following its opposition to 'British and French invasion of Suez' and support for African countries' claims to independence (230).

The Suez crisis and Kofi's panegyric occlude another invasion of 1956: the Soviet suppression of the Hungarian rebellion, during which, as far as Kofi knows, 'Soviet troops had been invited by the Hungarian government to restore order' (230). While the Soviet government downplays one event in favour of another, Phillips brings the two into conversation not only to link the history of European communism to anticolonial struggles around the world, but also to stress the larger theme of contradictory, often doubled, meanings of each event depicted in the novel. Sober realisations about the violent underside of each seemingly innocuous event temper any idealism surrounding political as well as personal histories. Thus, Kofi's enchantment with comrade Khrushchev who warmly clasps his hand and hopes he 'had many good memories to take home' (241) is juxtaposed with former Gulag prisoner Alexy's observations that the same Khrushchev who 'condemned the excesses of former days' in 1956 'gave a real fire and brimstone speech about the Trotskyists and the saboteurs, enemies raising their hands against comrade Stalin' some years prior (233). Alexy's own fate as an idealistic black communist from the Caribbean, who married into Soviet citizenship and ended up denounced and imprisoned, foreshadows Kofi's subsequent expulsion from the Soviet Union. As a young man, Kofi is indifferent to politics and prefers to remain on the sidelines, so he is not charged with political disloyalty.[8] His expulsion, rather, reveals a racist underside of the Soviet regime: his relationship with his Russian teacher Katya, daughter of a prominent politician, is deemed unacceptable despite the official policy of anti-racism and welcoming of black students from newly independent African countries.

The novel is set after the dismantling of communism, but in the genre of thriller and crime narrative which Phillips favours,[9] it presents the 'prehistory' of Kofi's adult life in England as a mystery that gradually unravels. The narrative opens with the meeting of his two sons George and Joseph, who had not known of each other's existence. Joseph, Kofi's son from his marriage to Caroline in England, is a documentary film-maker invited to show his film in Prague. There he meets George, Kofi's son by Katya, a small-time crook and smuggler who lives with a Czech wife, Radka, and who has learned of Joseph's background from the newspapers. The two brothers eventually bring about a reunification of Kofi and Katya, neither of whom knows whether to trust the other as their sudden separation occurred under unresolved circumstances. As the mystery unravels, we learn that after Kofi was expelled from the Soviet Union, the authorities foiled Katya's plans to join him in Paris; instead, Katya was pressured into leaving the country and settled in East Berlin, so as not to dishonour her family with her pregnancy.

In this way, Kofi's sons learn more about their estranged (or in George's case absent) father's past, which turns him into a more complex figure than they had at first assumed. This narrative strand is complemented by Kofi's 'Diary of Desire', which reflects on his youth in the context of world political events: his meeting with pan-Africanists Kwame Nkrumah, Jomo Kenyatta and Ras Makonnen, his political maturation in the Soviet Union, and an intense love relationship with Katya that comes to an abrupt end with his expulsion in 1957. Underling the unlocking of these family and political secrets is the trauma of facing past crimes, not merely the legal and ethical crimes committed against Kofi and Katya, but rather the larger impossibility of innocence for all characters. George, Joseph and their families are complicit in the crimes sanctioned or necessitated by their communities, often as both victims and perpetrators.

The novel suggests that the characters must weather the consequences of some kind of criminal action whether they reside in east or west Europe, pre- or post-Cold War. However, while Phillips provides some background on Joseph's relatively uneventful life in London and the difficult relationship with his father, he gives markedly more space to the protagonists located across the former Iron Curtain – in Moscow, Prague and Berlin – whose lives abound in ethical dilemmas, navigating political intrigue and ensuring bare survival. For instance, Kofi's diary tries to come to grips with his naivety regarding Soviet politics, embodied in his unwavering trust in his dorm room-mate Valery, who was charged with spying on foreign students and in fact reported on his relationship with Katya. His other room-mate, a Zanzibari named Hussein, warned him against being too trusting since he was alert to the authoritarian tendencies of both Soviet communism and African anticolonial movements, prophetically stating, 'in my country and yours within a few years we'll be driving limousines and ordering executions the way the big men do here' (278).

The absence of trust in the most intimate relationships is a reoccurring theme in the novel, cutting in half marriages, love affairs and friendships. The scenario with Valery and Kofi is replicated in other relationships and other Eastern Bloc countries: thus, George is pressured by the Stasi officer Liebl into spying on 'fraternal' students from Africa at the university and later on a prominent East German professor, Silke Elsner, with whom he has a passionate love affair. Throughout the novel, George attempts to work through his guilt over unknowingly helping the Stasi to frame Elsner, whom he deeply loves. The Stasi use the photos of their affair to convince Elsner's husband, who defects to the West and expects her to join him, to renounce her, and she later commits suicide. No relationship in the novel is safe from similarly profound acts of betrayal and rupture: George also reports as well as cheats on Radka; Katya's father orders a violent beating and expulsion of the man she wants to marry; and Radka's university professor father is reported and imprisoned for supporting Charter 77, spending the rest of his life in obscurity and insignificance like Kofi.

In these episodes, characters of various postcolonial and postcommunist backgrounds reflect on their experiences of living in communist countries, roles they assumed in their respective societies, and political blueprints and power relations established during the Cold War that still haunt the postcommunist period. As each chapter relentlessly uncovers more histories of violence, it also stresses the characters' persistent need to process this shared trauma, either alone (through flashbacks and internal monologues) or in dialogue with others. Phillips emphasises the importance of claiming, as well as processing, the legacy of this period, which he presents in a far more nuanced way than it is portrayed in dominant narratives of

Eastern Europe – as straightforward state oppression, violence, inefficiency or as lost time to be erased by the promise of a better future in the European Union.

Rather than describing postcommunist and postcolonial protagonists as potential objects of Western compassion and rescue into the 'civilised' world, Phillips presents them as desiring, feeling and ethically conflicted actors in a complex world of allegiances. Although the state creates a system in which everyone is a potential enemy, some of these actors nonetheless make choices to be complicit with the system rather than go to prison or die. In this sense, they cannot be innocent: the position of speaking from a moral high ground is unavailable to them. And yet, they go on working, falling in love and having children, thus becoming victims of their own actions, since they are intimately involved with the very people they betray. Thus, although George feels that he can never live up to his father because Kofi 'would have had too much honour' for a career of a 'petty criminal and an equally petty informer', Kofi isn't fully innocent either despite his ignorance and victimisation, since he agrees to give the 'fraternal' speech in the face of the Soviet invasion of Hungary (329). However, this ubiquitous complicity with political crimes is rarely seen as individual aberration that should be unequivocally condemned; the novel highlights the limitations that social pressure places on individual agency. It abounds in expressions of understanding for the difficult compromises almost everyone has made, while acknowledging that they irretrievably ruin relationships.

For instance, Radka and George's marriage is doomed after she finds out that he informed on her and her best friend, with whom he also had a love affair. She recounts the story to Joseph using expressions of resignation, such as 'Everything was corrupt, even love' (126) and 'This was how we lived' (127). However, while she understands that 'It was hard for him to resist' the Stasi and 'There were no heroes', Radka cannot forgive him for conforming instead of self-sacrificing: 'I can't blame George for not being different, but I do' (127). In turn, Kofi feels compassion rather than anger towards Valery who 'had ruined his life' because he 'had probably had no choice, faced with the commands of an official like Katya's father' (339). Phillips suggests that the rewards of such conformism are also dubious: the lucrative engineering job that Valery receives in Siberia nearly freezes his feet off (390). While his lifelong connections help him become a corrupt billionaire in postcommunist Russia, Valery is

not portrayed as a stereotypically selfish apparatchik and later gang-
ster, standing above the rest of society which he callously manipu-
lates. Here again, the narrative privileges the sense of an individual's
embeddedness in social relations. When Valery arrives to drill oil in
Siberia, he disrupts community life like any other coloniser; however,
his 'main achievement' has nothing to do with engineering but rather
with 'his ability to keep the workers happy' by building housing,
ensuring scholarships for their children and organising film screen-
ings at the local Komsomol centre (353). Valery also gets Katya her
translation job in Berlin; and finally, he uses his influence to extricate
George from a dangerous conflict with Georgian gangsters who pur-
sue him for selling stolen Georgian paintings on the black market.

Perhaps my imbalanced focus on the Eastern half of Phillips's European novel thus far creates the impression that the author succumbs
to Euro-Orientalist stereotypes by projecting onto (post)communist
countries charges of endless crime and terror from the vantage point
of Western democracies. While *A Shadow of Myself* seemingly continues the literary trend of associating the post-Berlin Wall 'Wild East'
with crime, violence, chaos and/or excessive jouissance,[10] it is neither
sensationalist nor reductive, as I shall argue later. Rather, Phillips's
privileging of these now increasingly irrelevant histories is important
because it unites groups who are not seen as legitimately belonging
to Europe in a mode of 'minor transnationalism', to return to Lionnet and Shi's productive concept, which does not arise in opposition
to – and conceptual dependence on – dominant European historical narratives and centres of power but rather informs multilayered
and unpredictable lateral connections among the various margins.
George, Radka, Kofi and Katya are inextricably connected through
intimately shared histories – and ongoing experiences – of violence,
which Europeans who live on the other side of the former wall, the
novel implies, cannot quite understand or empathise with. In this
sense, Joseph is likely the loneliest character in the book, clueless not
because the East is 'inscrutable' in its terror, but because he is not an
insider to the tacit allegiances and common reference points that all
the other characters share.

For instance, Joseph feels frustrated because he cannot relate to
either Kofi or Lena, his lover from Bosnia, while Lena feels that Kofi
understands her because 'he had this experience. He knows how it
feels' (224). As a refugee, she feels closer to Kofi, who had an entire
life outside of Britain, than to Joseph, who is too much 'like the

English'. She complains, 'When I tell people here about myself they look at me like they're with a sick person. They're thinking, poor refugee, then they forget and they think, bloody foreigner' (223). Lena expresses the double bind of being either a victim or a nuisance, which fixes her migrant identity and prevents her previous life from being acknowledged in all its complexity. This sense of immediate connection that overshadows Kofi's long relationship with Joseph also crops up in Kofi's conversations with his newly discovered son George. Kofi empathises with George's pain over being a target of racist insults at school in East Berlin, where his race made him an outsider: 'He had the strange feeling that George was more like him than Joseph, and already he felt a kind of sympathy between them that was absent in his conversations with his younger son' (344). Similarly, Radka is first attracted to George because, like her, 'he was an outsider who played by the rules, and kept his feelings to himself' (87). And finally, 'because of George and Serge [George's son]', Radka and Katya 'share a common loathing for the ethnic bigotry which pervaded everyday life' (245) in Prague and Berlin.

Allegiances between these characters often have to do with their similar experiences of prejudice and exclusion rather than a common identity expressed in ethnic or racial terms. Phillips envisages the community that doesn't build around 'immanent unity', sublation of difference into a totality, and human essence articulated as generalised sameness, one that has no predetermined identity or even a common goal to affirm (Nancy 1991: 9). Instead, this community could perhaps be described by borrowing from Giorgio Agamben's reflections on 'whatever' community that communicates and exists not because they are tied by any 'condition of belonging . . . but by belonging itself' [1990] (1993: 84). Agamben's emphasis on belonging together, as it were, helps us move away from the language of victimisation or withdrawal from public space. In *A Shadow of Myself* the characters' common non-belonging to the larger community, understood as a unity of desirable individual identities and fundamentally fissured by bigotry and intolerance, does not represent a traumatising lack because of the alternative that their 'co-belonging' provides (Agamben 1993: 85). Moreover, such communities cannot be easily articulated in existing political language which trades in representable interests and identities. Agamben observes, 'they do not possess any identity to vindicate nor any bond of belonging for which to seek recognition'. This threatens to interrupt politics as usual since the state can 'recognise any identity', but not the singu-larities who belong without articulating an identity (85). Narrative imagination of such communities, rather than celebrating the subver-sive potential of resisting ideological cooptation, helps us rethink the very criteria and language of political belonging and representation in contemporary Europe.

By way of contrast, Phillips highlights the limits of a more main-stream, liberal multicultural version of community based on identi-fying with 'others' because it presumes a universal human essence with a different race or ethnicity as added features. Crucially, it also flattens unequal power dynamics, as well as social and political con-texts in which it unfolds. The novel explores this problem in Joseph's adaptation of his documentary for a multicultural TV series on out-siders in England, which features interviews with a group of Kofi's friends, ageing Africans who recount their experience of living in England after World War II. The producer criticises the first cut, an 'angry polemic in which the men described a hostile, oppressive soci-ety and the way they had survived it' (61), by saying that they are 'rambling through history' and 'talking about events at which they weren't present' (62). When Joseph defends the film's 'impersonal' note because it provides the men with distance from unpleasant events, the producer pressures him to produce a less gloomy ver-sion to 'give the audience characters with which they can sympathise and identify' (62). The resulting 'gallery of entertaining characters' is heart-warming and an audience success, but it disappoints Kofi and his friends because it erases their outrage at the insults and racism that the first version registers.

The impersonal details that evoke historical events and the asym-metries of power between the interviewees and their audiences are reduced to individualised testimonies of cultural difference, with which 'others' can safely sympathise, while transforming the abuses of (post)colonial racism into idealised narratives of accomplished multi-cultural coexistence. Commenting on Britain's continuing tendency to narrate the history of empire in terms of happiness, Ahmed notes that the 'melancholy migrant' who 'remembers other, more painful aspects of such histories threatens to expose too much'. Consequently, if rac-ism is 'preserved *only* in migrants' memory and consciousness, then racism would go away if only they would let it go away' (2010: 148). Here, however, melancholy migrants are not converted into forgiving citizens who identify with the multicultural nation; instead, Joseph is guilty of letting go of their memories when he edits them out of his documentary. Simultaneously, Phillips implies that the interviews might be insincere because the subaltern cannot be heard and the decades of living in Britain have taught the men to conceal 'their deepest feelings and beliefs from the whites' as 'an instrument of their survival' (60).

The narrative constantly betrays our expectations of identification based on a shared personal feature, whether it is expressed as nationality, race or a common, if different, humanity. Nonetheless, modes of identification are not lacking; on the contrary, they are multiple, shifting and contradictory, often serving not to entrench an identity but to disidentify from any predictable affiliation, which, for Rancière, represents 'removal from the naturalness of a place' and towards subjectification (2004a: 36). Modes of identification, friendship and attachment are so diverse in this community that they do not imply a stable ground or conditions for belonging, despite being categories recognised by mainstream political language (for example, black, Eastern European, German). Phillips mixes them freely to evoke modes of identification characterised by fissures, gaps and lack of closure. For instance, after Katya moves to East Berlin, she shuns other Russians rather than fraternising with them (248); identifying as a Brit, Joseph initially suspects George of being an Eastern European 'con man' and playing the race card to win sympathy (54). Frequent demands to self-identify in the novel result in fluid, uncertain allegiances: George identifies as German, although he is Russian-Ghanaian in terms of nationality and Czech in terms of residence (66). But this national identification isn't available to him because growing up in East Berlin he was referred to as a black Russian, which distanced him from mainstream society both as a racial 'other' and a political enemy.

This impossibility of firm identifications is highlighted in the conflicting meanings of the word shadow from the novel's title. A shadow can connote resemblance, and we can certainly find numerous parallel episodes in *A Shadow of Myself* that suggest similarity and continuity of experience among the Coker family members. George's experiences of racism at the university recall Kofi's own life trajectory; Joseph and George's similar-looking, white wives imply the brothers' surreal similarity as well as shared preoccupation with adapting to the dominant society (101); and Serge, carrying 'shadows' of Kofi's and George's blackness, is likely to suffer similar kinds of prejudice as his family members (73). But just as often, the word shadow highlights uncanny resemblances that entail a degree of strangeness, disturbing and even damaging to family relations. Serge's shadow of 'African ancestry' startles Joseph because, despite the 'dark undertone of his skin', Kofi's intense blackness is all but lost in his grandson: 'that this pretty, curly-haired white boy might be his grandson was strange and unsettling' (73). As a pale resemblance, the shadow here testifies to the loss that comes with social marginalisation, the cost of physically or symbolically passing for white in Europe. Serge is not quite white in relation to the dominant society, but his greater degree of whiteness severs the connection to his grandfather's Ghanaian heritage and experience of discrimination in post-war Europe. Finally, George comes to think of his brother Joseph as a negative shadow, a doppelgänger who becomes sexually involved with his wife (attracted to him as a superior version of George) and threatens to usurp his life (373).

These examples emphasise the complexity of (dis)identifications in contemporary Europe, which appear in traces across floating racial, ethnic, national, linguistic and cultural signifiers. Since such identifications are both subjectively provisional and vulnerable to external challenge, they reveal the lacuna at the heart of allegedly self-evident communal bonds: the impossibility of ever definitively proving one's belonging to a traditional – national or supranational – community assumed to be organic and grounded in a shared identity. Instead, the novel gathers communities that are united by their common experience of prejudice, colonialism and distance from the Western European ideal, as well as by the historical alliance between anticolonialism and communism, while underscoring the limitations of claiming solidarity based on racial identity politics divorced from its larger political circumstances.

Phillips has criticised 'black nationalism' as a 'mirror image of white racism' and a 'late flowering of European nationalism' (Sternberg 2001: 393). In the novel, even the ideals of pan-Africanism are betrayed in practice. Pan-Africanism intended to bring together anticolonial interests of black populations in Africa, the Caribbean and North America, not so much to affirm a common racial essence but to forge economic, political and cultural alliances. Kofi notes that, on the eve of the 1945 Pan-African Congress in Manchester, black American servicemen who frequented Makonnen's restaurants 'chose every opportunity when abroad to play the big man among poor people', looking down on Africans despite being 'slaves in their own country' (135). This lack of solidarity characterises relations between the two groups decades later: in postcommunist Germany, George quits his job renting cars at the airport because of American customers: 'mostly they treated you like shit on their shoe. The blacks are bad, too. They call you brother but then the way they act is the same as the whites' (103).

Phillips has argued that, instead of turning to race, nation or gender to understand contemporary migrations and movement of labour, it would be more accurate to track the movement of capital, 'go back to looking out where the money is' (Sternberg 2001: 392). We might place his insistence on the greater importance of economics than identity in conversation with Rancière's observation, regarding European racism towards immigrants, that:

> Today's immigrant is first a worker who has lost his [*sic*] second name . . . the form of a political subjectification of the count of the uncounted. All he now has left is a sociological identity, which then topples over into the anthropological nakedness of a different race and skin. (2004a: 118)

For Rancière, declaring class struggle an outdated concept has made invisible this 'gap between politics and sociology, between subjectification and identity' (119). While Rancière offers a critique of sociological identities as a road to subjectification because they are already 'counted' as existing political categories and do not address the broader dynamics of class, Phillips's novel, in fact, meticulously builds connections between 'politics and sociology', making it impossible to downplay some forms of subjectification in favour of others.

A Shadow of Myself does not treat race as an ineffective political category. Rather, it suggests that black nationalism is a problem only if it takes the commonality of race as a positive, immanent foundation for group identity, to the exclusion of all other forms of being-in-common. Such claims to commonality are not only politically restrictive since they exclude alliances not based on identitarian resemblance, but also foster an illusory sense of similarity since they privilege only one way of existing in the world, pure from adulterations by class, gender, life experience and so on. Instead, the novel highlights alliances around blackness as various experiences of prejudice, rather than as a foundational identity, which is non-restrictive and also makes it potentially open to alliances with other postcolonial and postcommunist subjects.

This shared legacy of racism unites the two halves of Europe, despite political decisions on both sides of the Cold War divide that have attempted to create greater inclusivity and respect for difference. As in *Travelling with Djinns*, Europe is united through its negative kernel, that which it disavows. Racism becomes the ultimate crime in the novel and a challenge for any European society. Joseph might feel more at home in increasingly non-white England than George does in the increasingly xenophobic Czech Republic, but these are differences in degree, rather than quality. Phillips thus brings into conversation different, but inextricably connected, experiences of otherness, which involve black as well as white characters. In the novel, there are no safe places in Europe; there are only places where one is less of a target than others. George enjoys moving from Berlin to Prague, while for Radka, this returns her to the painful memories of her childhood and greater prejudice to interracial couples: 'In Berlin people stared less. George's dress and manner marked him out as a native, like a camouflage for his colour. In Prague it was different. People feigned indifference, but they looked twice, seeing her with George' (255). While Radka idealises England as a place of greater multiracial equality where Serge would have a shot at a 'normal life' (125), relationships between black men and white women are also deemed uncommon. No one might directly comment on Joseph's marriage to Liz, but 'their presence in a room together could excite hostility or a prurient curiosity' (95).

In the London episodes, Phillips focuses on overt, systemic racism to African economic migrants in the post-war era as a continuation of colonial policies, and the more subtle contemporary operations of racism under the guise of multicultural recognition, as exemplified by the censoring of Joseph's documentary. In Eastern European locales, the state apparatus exhibits racist attitudes to African residents despite official policies of non-discrimination, as in the episodes where the Stasi exploit George based on his race. In the postcommunist period, Phillips implies, the ubiquitous crime associated with 'Wild East' privatisations partly results from this fundamental crime of racism. The narrative builds sympathy for George, who often comes across as blundering, irresponsible and greedy, by demonstrating ways in which a lifetime of being an outsider has involved him, first, in the Stasi crimes, and later, in crimes of economic survival.

Radka is unhappy with George for being unable to become like a 'Wessi' and swim the tide of economic opportunism post-unification (258); but as we have seen, he leaves his job renting cars because he feels humiliated by affluent customers who discriminate against him. When George attempts to sell the valuable Georgian paintings that his Russian cousin Valentin procures, he resorts to smuggling rather than selling them to a gallery because 'a black man who showed up trying to sell a painting which had no documentation would be looking for trouble' (24).

In his nuanced approach to thinking crime, Phillips cites Graham Greene as an inspiration, since he 'was not interested in crime as crime, but as a motive, a certain force in society' (Sternberg 2001: 392). *A Shadow of Myself* explores the conflicting social constructions of crime West and East to re-examine its 'role in society' and 'effect on individuals' (ibid.). The novel's conclusions are rather pessimistic: embracing rather than opposing crime allows one to climb to the top of the social ladder. Once acquired, such positions of power remain uncontested in the post-Cold War, democratic era. The novel documents various betrayals of hope for social justice: the eventual corruption of pan-Africanists Kenyatta and Nkrumah stands in sharp contrast with Hussein's uncompromising idealism, which lands him in prison in Uganda. Both Valery and Liebl become influential businessmen, their lack of scruples allowing them to navigate the aggressive process of privatisation during transitions to capitalism. While business thus becomes indistinguishable from crime in Eastern Europe, Phillips plays with the idea that, from the perspective of communist regimes, private ownership of the means of production, unrestrained profit and exploitation of labour inherently rely on the crime of violence and dispossession.

George voices this notion that crime is business as usual when he claims, 'We are not gangsters. We are just businessmen' (115). He rejects Radka's pleas that he become a 'proper Western businessman' by arguing that, 'In the West business was even more crooked . . . She was simply deceived by the skill with which they covered their tracks' (294). In terms of his outsider status as a black man and his lack of connections, George would be doomed to economic subsistence and social obscurity much like Kofi in England, if he believed in the myth of achieving affluence and increased economic opportunity through honest, hard work. But in neo-liberal Eastern Europe, class mobility is severely restricted: 'depressed and fatigued by the effort of finding work and shelter' (258), George decides to take Valery as his role model. Because Valery 'shaped himself to live in a horrible time and to get the best result', George is 'going to shape [himself] to live on top' of the world (386).

These kaleidoscopic perspectives that question dominant definitions of crime and emphasise social circumstances that produce it are largely presented to and for Joseph, and in a broader sense, for Western European audiences who might project crime onto Eastern Europe as a long-standing cultural feature. Joseph is not only exposed to executions, beatings and shady dealings through his involvement with George; he is also the interlocutor to whom George explains his admiration for Valery's business methods. These discussions and experiences contribute to Joseph's education, as it were, in terms of expanding his limited worldview, which excludes both his father's history as a colonial subject and his brother's experience of growing up in a communist country. Phillips thus shows the interconnectedness of various European histories across political divides, as well as the necessity of contextualising these histories within events unfolding in Africa and Asia.

Western definitions of crime come under scrutiny especially in an episode in which Joseph, kidnapped by Georgian gangsters who are pursuing his brother, is locked up with the illegal migrants they are trafficking. Salim, an Iraqi refugee who is considered an illegal, defends the Georgian traffickers to Joseph, saying, 'If the police came here now they would send us all back, Bosnian, Kurds, Africans, we have nowhere else to go' (309). Salim's current status as an illegal migrant, 'a rat in the cellar', is in sharp contrast with his earlier, carefree life: educated in Egypt and England, where he works for a time teaching English, he decides to travel around Europe and Asia (310). Because he ends up in Beirut at the time of increasing political instability and attempts to make his way back to Europe, he becomes a criminal from the perspective of European immigration law. In another episode, we learn that one of George's shady businesses in Prague has rather legitimate reasons: he converts old cars and vans into specialist transport vehicles to sell cheaply in Africa and Eastern Europe because they 'are very expensive to buy from Western Europe, and no one here makes them' (111). He exploits cheap labour to keep the costs down, but on the other hand he provides work to many unemployed, off-the-grid mechanics in Prague, 'Romanians, Bulgarians, Poles, Russians' (112).

Joseph concludes that George is 'up to his elbows in the castoffs of the Western world', a phrase which describes both the materials and labour he uses. The term castoff suggests an inferior, superfluous remainder which is expendable, aptly describing the scores of Eastern European migrants without work. George's scheme is thus enabled by the unequal distribution of economic power which makes Western European transportation vehicles too expensive for other countries to afford legally.

A Shadow of Myself foregrounds the often invisible social contexts which demonstrate how Western economic and political policies themselves engender crime. If we push this conclusion to its logical extreme, then George is correct when he observes that business as usual *is* crime. While bridging pre- and post-Cold War history, Phillips employs this provocative definition of crime to interrogate stereotypes of criminality associated with anticolonial and communist regimes and contemporary European projections of criminality onto undesirable populations from these backgrounds. The narrative discusses at length the various abuses perpetrated by the regimes in Eastern Europe and Africa; however, it also examines their shared legacy of anticolonialism, which was an attempt, however flawed, to forge a confident, independent identity that would be invulnerable to colonial discourses of discrimination. This subterranean historical current in the novel allows for reflections on missed opportunities, which resulted in a gradual dismantling of the ideals of social justice and equality.

This forgotten history of Europe, in conversation with anticolonial movements around the world, stands in sharp contrast with the contemporary entrenchment of neo-liberal capitalist Europe, which has not fully confronted the continuing impact of its colonial empires. Most of this alternative history is recorded in Kofi's diary, which enhances the sense of its obscurity, since Kofi writes in solitude and without an audience in mind. Two strands of memory dominate Kofi's writing, sharing the general theme of anti-racist politics: his meeting with the pan-Africanists in Manchester and experiences in his multicultural Moscow dorm. Kofi is ambivalent about the pan-Africanists, as much as his father, who sees them as fanatics, 'dreamers unhinged and deceived by the education they had pursued among the whites'. And yet, it is precisely their seemingly rash idealism, their decision to do what common sense deems impossible, that enchants Kofi: 'there was something extraordinary about this gathering of black men who were so conscious of their own importance, and of their mission'. They convince the Manchester mayor to approve the conference although the 'whole purpose of the participants was to kick white men on their asses out of the continent' (156–7).

Such brazen demands, refusal of subservience and confidence in the struggle for freedom are in sharp contrast with Kofi's dead-end career as a black ship stoker in England. Their enthusiasm worlds novel, unheard-of possibilities, promising to redress centuries of class exploitation and racist violence. The microcosm of such a world already exists in Makonnen's restaurant in Manchester, aptly titled *The Cosmopolitan*, graced with a mural depicting the 'Chinese, Indians, and Africans, and white men and women, all of them marching or running, straining towards some object, the muscles and sinews of their necks and limbs standing out' (133). Embodying the common fight against capitalism and imperialism, Makonnen's restaurant gathers not only Africans, but also African Americans, Jews, Eastern Europeans, trade union members and communists. This new perspective on colonial hierarchies allows Kofi to understand similar geopolitical positionings of the Soviet Union and Ghana: he highlights the need for the two countries to unite in anticolonial struggle, mocking British stereotypes of Russians as 'barbarians' because the 'British and their friends were liars who described the world in terms which would keep us quiet' (131).

This unity of purpose through anticolonial internationalism characterises Kofi's dorm at Moscow university, where, despite subsequent betrayals and disillusion, 'most of the boys had open minds and a dream inside them about going back as engineers or scientists to build the bridges and dams and turbines which would power their independence and abolish the poverty' from which they came (131). The possibility of a community where the different races fraternise and fight for equality extends beyond the dorm, in unofficial encounters, despite official prohibitions against Russians fraternising with foreigners and random acts of racist violence. In the middle of a Moscow street, 'a toothless man had stopped [Kofi] and shook his hand'; Katya explains, 'He wants to welcome you' (144).[11] In another episode, Kofi meets abjectly poor Russian peasants in the countryside; they invite him in for a meal, showing interest in his life trajectory and asking if he is from the same country as Paul Robeson, the famous African American anti-imperialist activist with resilient sympathies for the Soviet system (186).

Phillips almost obsessively returns to these unpredictable scenes of connecting, which transpire in spaces characterised by poverty, seediness and even violence. The protagonists tend to be outcasts with respect to the dominant social order, whether in terms of race, occupation or political affiliation. In the novel's Russian episodes, these scenes evoke a sense of solidarity among the 'people' composed of the socially abject, which flies in the face of the more heroic representations of community or internationalism in Soviet socialist realist narratives, for instance. The shadow of this possibility of connecting, articulating a community of the 'uncounted' which restores the 'part of those who have no part, a part or party of the poor' (Rancière 2004a: 11), infuses the present with hope in episodes that take place in contemporary Europe, where we follow George, Valentin and Joseph to similarly marginalised urban spaces. Echoing Kofi's greeting by a Russian man as he strolls around Moscow, Joseph greets Roma families in Prague streets because he feels kinship with them (121). While Kofi and Katya feel most at ease at Moscow's Central Market, immersing themselves in a mix of languages and cultures of 'swarthy, leather-skinned brown people, or dark-eyed women', in contemporary Hamburg, George and Valentin frequent 'the haunt of Turks and Arabs, Africans, dockworkers and whores . . . and the newer outcasts – Russians, Uzbekis, Chechens, Croats, Serbs, and Kosovars' (180, 34). The concept of the shadow, then, transcends interpersonal relations in the novel to connect decentred perspectives of outcast communities, who are invoked in official discourses of diversity (whether Soviet or EU) but whose actual lifeworlds remain beyond their purview. If Europe's community is to be rethought and reimagined to include its erased Cold War histories, such (un)common places provide a starting point. From East to West, these peripheral communities multiply to the point that firm geographic designations become impossible, since different cities featured in the novel are continually likened to one another.

The existence of these multifarious postcommunist and postcolonial migrant communities is haunted by the history of what once united them, the anticolonial internationalism exemplified in the novel by the pan-Africanist conference and Soviet university scholarships for students from Western European colonies. As Jopi Nyman observes, Phillips not only 're-imagines the radical past of Afrocentricity and progressivism not popular today', but also urges 'the readers to remember the utopian promise of the narrative of socialism, and especially its promises of belonging and equality' (83–4). Phillips enjoins the audience to think back to this history soberly and without idealisation, but also with a view to preserving the kernel of its neglected yet persistent potential, which may find a different manifestation in the future. Kofi frequently notes that his past life seems unreal and cannot be taken seriously, suggesting a broad marginalisation of leftist discourses and practices, including the impossibility of addressing class inequalities in neo-liberal Europe. His meandering but ultimately successful reunion with Katya and the meeting of the two brothers open up the horizon of hope that such history will be rescued from oblivion and brought to bear upon the present. What enables the protagonists to make sense of the past is the creation of this microcosmic community which must negotiate it together rather than in isolation, even if their relationships are asymmetrical and agonistic.

As we have seen, the novel highlights asymmetry and conflict to complicate potential idealisations of any community predicated on common resemblance or interests, whether familial, racial or multicultural. Engaging with Nancy, Blanchot similarly rejects assumptions that community can achieve organic communion or absolute mutuality; he insists that community is always-already absent, which, however, does not mean that it has failed. Blanchot thinks of this absent community as a relation between irreducibly different singularities who, in an exposure to one another, encounter the unpredictable, including a 'violent disymmetry', both 'the fissure and the communication' (1988: 22). Inspired by a Levinasian understanding of ethical relationships as excessive and lacking in reciprocity, Blanchot observes that, even in situations of social equality, the self looks at an irreducible other, rather than same encountering same, so that one is never on fully equal terms with another (3). He emphasises this to move away from thinking community as marked by harmony and interchangeability, which create the possibility of sacrifice of any mortal singularity to the immortal idea of the collective. *A Shadow of Myself* centres on such imbalanced encounters, even when the characters are on more or less socially equal terms, so as to highlight the irreducibility of singular difference. However, it pushes the thinking of 'violent disymmetry' beyond abstract irreducibility of difference by suggesting that power differential and agonistics are inherent to relationships between seeming equals.

The Soviet Union is an interesting case from this perspective, as it gestures, at least, to a radically inclusive community of sociologically different others who are declared equal economically and politically. But its concept of equality as generalised sameness embodies precisely the totalitarian potential that both Nancy and Blanchot criticise as 'immanence of man to man' that sublates the sacrifice of others to the common good (Blanchot 1988: 2). The former Gulag prisoner Alexy's shockingly optimistic message to Kofi embodies this aporia:

> In twenty-five years nothing has happened to me, because of my colour, even in the camps. But even if it had, it wouldn't matter. When you go back to Africa, tell them that this system offers more freedom to more people. If they imitate the West, what they'll have is a ruling class working for the Americans. The hope is here . . . Without Stalin and Beria, this would have been a paradise. (282)

By accepting rather than condemning his own sacrifice to the state, Alexy chooses to highlight the sense of hope reflected in my first description of the Soviet Union. He praises the potential of equality that was lost in the turn to community as totalitarian communion, implying that the fight against colonialism is an unfinished, imperfect project that remains relevant despite the failings of communist regimes. Registering a sense of hopefulness that pervades both Alexy's and Kofi's perspectives, which cannot be tempered even by the subsequent disappointments, Phillips here captures the ambivalent attitudes of black leftists towards the Soviet Union, especially in the first half of the twentieth century. In her analysis of black activists' and intellectuals' experiences and impressions of the USSR, Pirker implies that although they saw it as another empire, with authoritarian tendencies, they also believed it represented a hopeful alternative to Western empires because it was based on the ideals of racial equality and social justice. For instance, W. E. B. DuBois wrote, 'Russia alone has made race prejudice a crime; of all great imperialisms, Russia alone owns no colonies of dark serfs or white' (Pirker 2010: 125). Echoing Alexy, Langston Hughes chose to focus on changes in everyday lives of ordinary people rather than comment on Stalin's leadership and Soviet politics. He suggested that his relatively kind evaluation of the new country, more positive than his white fellow traveller Arthur Koestler's, may be due to its unique anti-racist politics:

I think most idealists expected too much of Russia in too short a time . . . Some things irritated these people much more than they did me. Just as the dirt in Central Asia upset Koestler, so it upset me. Dirt without Jim Crow was bad – but dirt *with Jim Crow, for me,* would have been infinitely worse. (Pirker 126)

I do not argue, however, that the novel suggests an exoneration of the Soviet Union or the community as that which both protects us and inevitably demands our sacrifice. Rather, it presents us with a challenge to find a way out of this aporia, preserving the kernel of the fight for social justice while imagining communities that are not grounded in a mandatory, common 'essence'. The ethical injunction to 'make race prejudice a crime' and 'offer more freedom to more people' haunts the novel, especially when we contrast George's observations about contemporary African migrants in Europe with Nkrumah's hope for Africans to live with dignity. Namely, George resents undocumented African migrants in Hamburg for scuttling about the city like 'rats', 'their breaths furred and stinking, their bodies racked with the pain and exhaustion of how far they had come, their skins and hair grey with the dread of long nights locked in the hold of a ship' (5). The presence in Europe of so many Africans anxious to escape their countries betrays Nkrumah's promise that, 'When we're running things . . . boys like [Kofi] will be making a life for themselves and building our country instead of crossing the sea locked up like rats in an iron cage' (137). The images of Africans as rats on the ship invoke the slave trade as much as illegal border crossings and undignified jobs. In the prosperous European Union, they represent 'human flotsam' patronised by Europeans like 'exotic sights', which makes George feel angry and humiliated since it destroys his childhood fantasy of Africans as 'tall and heroic presences' looking into 'far and beautiful distances' (4–5). Aside from George's clear embarrassment over his African roots, his reactions also betray a resentment of powerlessness: of playing to Europe's patronising gaze. Agency lies perhaps in claiming the hope for dignity and using historical precedent for inspiration.

The novel's final gesture towards such hope lies in portraying Serge, Katya and Kofi's grandson, as multicultural European and African offspring that may confidently claim belonging in Europe. The novel here permanently moves away from black nationalism and postcolonial black diaspora as viable pathways to belonging since both privilege ideas of displacement, nomadism and attitudes to 'cultures as separate and alien to each other' (Phillips 2009: 144). After a youthful preoccupation with not fitting in, George concludes that the idea of firm roots is false: 'You can belong where you choose to belong' (345). Given the novel's nuanced treatment of the problem of discrimination, this is not a facile affirmation of the victory of individual agency over social prejudice. Rather, Phillips envisions community as a matter of choice – as continuous practices of living together, in a host of exchanges that complicate definitive identifications by race, ethnicity or culture, rather than a destiny of fitting in an a priori defined, static community. He insists on belonging rather than exile, in Rancière's sense of 'outcasts' belonging 'twice over' in acts of 'political impropriety': 'belonging to the world of properties and parts and belonging to the improper community, to that community that egalitarian logic sets up as the part of those who have no part' (2004a: 137).

While traditional conceptions of community, as critiqued by both Nancy and Blanchot, are based on inherent sacrifice of any one singularity to an organic communion with others, non-filiative communities in Phillips are also lacerated by antagonism and violence. The novel does not offer a way out of violence, manifested in so many institutional and symbolic crimes: it suggests crime is, after all, a 'force in society' as Phillips notes. Even in the absence of institutionalised crimes or crimes underlying the very foundation of political community, violence permeates everyday interactions because of diverse power differentials. Nonetheless, as Phillips said, 'the thing about Europe is that poets still have to invent it' (Sternberg 2001: 388) and his own invention in *A Shadow of Myself* revises the concept of community, registering increasing migrations not only in Great Britain but Europe in general. When visiting Germany, Phillips observed that it was easy to live there but difficult to 'belong'; the only possibility of belonging 'together' was in company with other outsiders living a 'strange "in-between" life' (Sternberg 391). This has become paradigmatic of Europe, where the growing mixed-race population harbours possibilities for affinity between groups, for instance 'Turks in Berlin' and 'Afro-Caribbeans in London', based on 'the way of life, the way of seeing things' (Sternberg 388). The novel's final question, then, can be articulated as a challenge to think belonging as a version of lateral subaltern transnationalism, while simultaneously addressing material alienation from economic and political circuits of power.

Storming the EU fortress: communities of disagreement in *Nobody's Home* and *The Ministry of Pain*

Critical responses to 'post-Yugoslav'[12] writer Dubravka Ugrešić have envisioned her work as a single voice reflecting national preoccupations over loss and factional identity after the wars in former Yugoslavia. However, recently, scholars have begun to situate Ugrešić's work in a much broader context that speaks to concerns shared by many countries faced with articulating a place in the new European Union. Ugrešić's postcommunist literary production increasingly moves away from a sense of lonely horror and melancholic attachment to her disappearing country and instead places the Yugoslav tragedy in a global postcommunist and newly relevant EU context.[13] Even the early texts, such as *Have a Nice Day* (1995) and *The Culture of Lies* (1998), which map the route of her 1990s exile, already offer a perspicacious analysis of the emerging New World Order in which the 'Balkan'[14] wars are but one instance of the fashionably derogatory ethnicisation of alterity in the market of cultural difference, where cultural chauvinism dangerously overlaps with multiculturalism. Nonetheless, this increasing focus on analysing transnational politics – especially identities fostered by neoliberal capitalism and the aftermath of postcommunist transitions – informs more forcefully and confidently Ugrešić's essays collected in *Nobody's Home* and the novel *The Ministry of Pain*.

In these texts, Ugrešić increasingly moves away from, though by no means abandons, her focus on meticulously articulating the trauma of losing the phenomenological and intellectual space once known as Yugoslavia. *The Ministry of Pain*, in the words of Stephenie Young, both depicts and itself performs the function of literature 'as an arbiter between trauma and recovery' (2010: 90).[15] This novel follows the exilic trajectory of a Slavic literature professor who, like Ugrešić, leaves her Zagreb teaching position for a temporary one in Amsterdam, and decides to dedicate her class, populated by Yugoslav refugees of various nationalities, to reconstructing languages, memories and practices of everyday life in the shared country that is fast disappearing. This project proves traumatic for many students, which exposes its conceptual limits; however, beyond this transnational project of a broken people, the narrative imagines solidarity with numerous 'others' of various ethnic and racial backgrounds, who similarly haunt European metropolises. This gesture of transcending the trauma of one's immediate national tragedy in favour of developing a broader contemporary perspective on otherness in the EU also informs the essays in *Nobody's Home*, which comprise Ugrešić's reflections on the failures of EU multiculturalism and rampant class inequalities.

Articulating transnational connections and possible solidarities is particularly important to Ugrešić in the context of EU's insistence on both liberal multiculturalism and the preservation of individual national identities. For Ugrešić, the allegedly progressive EU multiculturalism does more to segregate than connect, more to downplay other sources of disenfranchisement than to empower politically. The EU portrayed in her texts suffers from a democratic deficit, both because actual voting citizens feel distant from EU circuits of power and because the most vulnerable populations, typically postcolonial and postcommunist citizens and migrants, remain excluded from many of its economic and political privileges. If Phillips unearths the history of racism towards and economic marginalisation of Europe's 'others' in order to question dominant stereotypes of violence associated with these groups, Ugrešić imagines Europe's future as one punctured by violent protests by a 'tribe of millions, déclassé and inured', expressing their rage in 'the multitude of demonstrations that have pointed to ever-increasing social stratification' (2014: 124). Ultimately, while Phillips scrutinises Europe through the history of violence, Ugrešić predicts violence as Europe's future.

Ugrešić dissects the discourses of Europe's deficient democracy which aim to silence the protesting migrant demos: if these protests turn violent, their demands cannot be admitted into the legitimate political sphere because their expression is seen as altogether 'other' to the Eurocentric narrative of individual rights and democratic participation. In the last decade, these groups have become increasingly vocal and aware of their shared predicaments with disenfranchised citizens across the EU: significantly, French 2005 *banlieue* riots were often invoked during Greek 2008 protests and the anti-austerity movement that began in 2010,[16] while Spanish *indignados* waved Greek, Tunisian and Egyptian flags during 2011 protests. Not only are such forceful insurrections taking Europe by storm, but many are also featuring, for the first time in recent history, united fronts of citizens and migrants.[17]

Ugrešić's texts on the new Europe explore this problem of political representation for those who cannot be heard because they are a priori dismissed as anarchic or immature. As kaleidoscopic reflections on both spoken and written expressions of anger, helplessness and displacement, *The Ministry* and *Nobody's Home* call for the ethics of recognising the clamour of violent protest as political discourse rather than an illegitimate path towards empowerment. These texts cognitively map a transnational community of protest against a neo-liberal Europe, which abandons a facile multiculturalism in favour of connecting disparate migrants whose voices are received in EU government circuits as so much jarring noise. Like Phillips, Ugrešić questions dominant definitions of crime, suggesting that neo-liberal disenfranchisements of Europe's most vulnerable populations, including the ravages of shock-therapy transitions to capitalism in Eastern Europe, have engendered both survival mechanisms and protests that are denounced as criminal.

Growing economic woes across Europe have brought into relief the problem of EU democratic participation, especially in the shape of mass protests against neo-liberal reforms, EU treaties, austerity measures and racist policies in migrant neighbourhoods. EU as well as local national authorities' responses to popular protests in the last decade evince an anxiety that the demos might participate in the first place by resorting to occupying the streets to voice its dissatisfaction and demands. In such situations, official political statements and news coverage often feature spectacular images of burning cars and Molotov cocktails, using the pretext of violence to discredit and mute the protests while defending the right to peaceful, 'civilised' assertion of dissent.

For instance, the peaceful marches against the Iraq war in 2003 painted the image of Europe that is committed to democratic participation, non-violent resistance and diplomacy. In depictions of such protests, civilisation often codes as whiteness, European rules of genteel and mature political debate or middle-class status.[18] It is in this context that the violent 'riots' which happen in neighbourhoods populated by non-European residents appear as isolated events that concern merely the municipalities or countries in which they occur: such protests are not 'of Europe', as violence itself has become disassociated from the European tradition. El-Tayeb argues, for instance, that when the 2005 *banlieue* riots broke out, they weren't welcomed as expressions of democratic spirit but rather observed anxiously as if to ask if this catastrophe can happen in any European country. The diversity of the protesters and complexity of motives were generally reduced to markers of aggressive young masculinity and Muslim faith clashing with European values (2008: 661).

The problem of violence is treated with similar discomfort in philosophical reflections on contemporary forms of protest which situate themselves on the left of the political spectrum. Hardt and Negri (2004) privilege the concept of 'multitude', a composite, diverse assemblage which non-violently storms the neo-liberal Empire by claiming the streets and deserting quotidian duties. The multitude acts in-common, taking advantage of connectivity and networking that underlies regular labour activity and investing it in the cause of creativity, fairness and equality. The multitude is not an immature 'people in training' but rather self-organised and 'maddeningly elusive, since it cannot be entirely corralled into the hierarchical organs of the political body' (192). Significantly, migrants are seen as a crucial group comprising the multitude: though they 'often travel empty-handed in conditions of extreme poverty', they 'are full of knowledges, languages, skills, and creative capacities' (133). Designating the contemporary metropolis, a hybrid, excessive product not of 'general will but common aleatoriness', as a proper battleground for multitude, Negri in particular looks to the migrant as a figure of hope, 'what is to come', 'giving meaning to solidarity' (2002: n.p.). However, since the primary mode of the multitude is 'love of humanity', violence, incoherence and anarchy are denounced as inappropriate modes of being-in-common, degrading the multitude to crowd mentality: 'The crowd or the mob or the rabble can have social effects – often horribly destructive effects – but cannot act of their own accord' (Hardt and Negri 2004: 50, 100).

In *Commonwealth* (2009), Hardt and Negri further develop the concept of love as ontologically constitutive in that it produces the common: 'Love is the power of the poor to exit a life of misery and solitude, and engage the project to make the multitude' (189). 'Good' love is distinguished from various types of 'bad' love, such as love of the same (one's own race or nation). While they acknowledge that love can be ambivalent and turn into its opposite, they still consider the social tendency towards love and building the common as immanently present. This suggests that, if there is violence and anarchy, they originate from the always-already present love that has been corrupted. However, assuming that multicultural love is a primary mode of being of this ideal political assemblage inevitably results in denouncing the actions of multitudes that, for instance, burn down European metropolises.

The loaded terms rabble and mob used in *Multitude* suggest that enlisting in the multitude may be a matter of political maturity, which draws a problematically clear line between the ability to self-organise and susceptibility to external manipulation. *Common-wealth* revises the earlier negative position on the 'the crowd, the mob, and the masses', implying that there is a 'possibility of recuperating these social formations when their indignation and revolt are directed and organised' (243). Thus, while Hardt and Negri defend the much maligned spontaneity and naivety of French *banlieue* riots, they insist that the multitude must be 'trained in love', 'organise antagonisms against the hierarchies and divisions of the metropolis, funnel the hatred and rage against its violence' (260). This revision, nonetheless, is still haunted by the fear of disorganised antagonism and preserves the tendency towards a prescriptive 'training in love'. Unwittingly, it echoes classist and racist preferences for liberal, civilised and well-organised protests discussed above. Complicating this vein of thinking, Étienne Balibar observes that antiglobalisation militants somewhat idealistically believe that migrants may constitute a mass base of organised resistance to Empire, as if 'the ultimate point in insecurity and oppression of uprooted migrants can automatically be translated into an avant-garde movement' (2003a: 43).

Hardt and Negri's multitude as a blueprint for an alternative transnational community is based on love and cooperation seen both as immanent and as implicit conditions of belonging. As we have seen, Agamben criticises communities conceptualised around such conditions of belonging while preferring the 'whatever' community of singularities that 'co-belong without any representable condition of belonging', such as the 1989 Tiananmen Square protesters (1993: 85). In my discussion of this dynamic in Ugrešić, I will move away from Hardt and Negri and towards the idea of belonging together not only without a representable identity, but also without conditions. The latter idea is closer to Blanchot's concept of non-utilitarian, unpredictable 'camaraderie without preliminaries', a relationship of love which doesn't even need love to sustain it and exists even when love is impossible or unfelt (1988: 32, 34).

Coming from a leftist perspective that appears less uncomfortable with antagonism, the absence of love and revolutionary violence,

Žižek argues that contemporary discourses denouncing various types of 'subjective violence' enacted by 'social agents, evil individuals, disciplined repressive apparatuses, fanatical crowds' distract our attention from the invisible and anonymous, but powerful and systemic violence of global capitalism (2008: 10–14). Žižek writes prior to the violent terrorist attacks across European metropolises in recent years, but his – as well as this chapter's – focus is not so much on murderous attacks deliberately targeting civilians but rather on mass street protests that may entail violence to objects or humans. Thus, the fascination with *banlieue* protests, for instance, merely fetishises the effects of the larger dynamic of social and economic violence that, as a result, remain safely in the shadows. However, like Hardt and Negri, Žižek denounces the kind of mass violent protest associated with French *banlieues* or the 2005 Danish cartoon controversy as ultimately ineffective because it is inarticulate. Sociologists and philosophers who ascribe any meaning to it are patronising wishful-thinkers, since this is a 'zero-level protest' that 'demands nothing', a 'meaningless outburst' that lacks a utopian project, and 'an implicit admission of impotence' akin to terrorist suicide attacks (2008: 75–6, 81). Žižek employs the same phrasing to describe the 2011 London rioters, arguing that they fit the '"Hegelian" notion of the rabble'. Their violence isn't revolutionary or self-assertive but instead preoccupied with looting, a 'manifestation of consumerist desire violently enacted' (2014: 121, 125).[19]

That Žižek contrasts these 'meaningless,' almost instinctive 'outbursts' of violence to nostalgia-tinged May 1968 protests, which were allegedly articulate and carried utopian promise, seems symptomatic of a similar civilisational coding at work in the idealisation of anti-Iraq war protests. Reading Ugrešić, then, can help us examine this notion of inarticulateness in the context of EU protests: specifically, what it means that violence strips them of any ability to signify. Also, we must ask how and why economic desperation and disenfranchisement incite social trauma rather than love, just as (post)colonial discrimination and social hierarchies ossify into inescapably asymmetrical, agonistic relationships in Mike Phillips's Europe. This line of thinking presents an alternative to expecting the 'rabble' to grow up, in a teleological manner, into the trained multitude of 'civilised' cooperation. However, it does not endorse violence as a strategy or as the only possible mode of a disenfranchised minority's political expression.

Indeed, Ugrešić suggests that Europe's main democratic challenge is to allow for its disposable groups to articulate their antagonism even if it leads to a radical restructuring of the EU.

Based in Amsterdam, Ugrešić meticulously analyses the mechanisms of power in the burgeoning EU, primarily assumptions and ideals at work in the prevailing discourses advocating unification and its self-portrayals as a multicultural, democratic beacon. Never one to reject the utopia of communism only to wholeheartedly profess belief in the utopia of the EU, Ugrešić complicates what she sees as an all-too-easy reconciliation with economic exploitation and forgiveness for historical wrongs within Europe. In *A Shadow of Myself*, this sense of reluctant, but quiescent reconciliation to historical wrongs arises from the continuity of corruption, racism and class discrimination across the various geographic and temporal divides. The victims and perpetrators continue to occupy the same symbolic space and positions of differential power; from this perspective, antagonism and conflict become ethical acts of rebellion against the prevailing discourses advocating coexistence and forgiveness.

Recounting a visit to a New York nail salon where Vietnamese employees courteously service American customers, Ugrešić reflects on a similarly surprising lack of antagonism in the wake of the Vietnam war: wondering if the salon is a 'place of symbolic global reconciliation', Ugrešić ironically suggests the Vietnamese might be calling on 'all of us to show some compassion for their partner in the historical chain of trauma between the coloniser and colonised, the exploiter and exploited, the power-monger and his victim' (2008: 135). The climate of reconciliation dominates, also, postcommunist Eastern Europe which Ugrešić portrays as 'occupied' by EU and global capitalism. Indeed, the EU comes across as empire-light, a consensual empire which is difficult to unmask *as* empire because its 'occupation is sensual, exciting, and pleasurable; if it hadn't been, someone would have objected already' (99). This apathetic resignation and growing consensus around the EU as an unquestionable good is precisely the problem Ugrešić attempts to highlight.

In *The Ministry*, Amsterdam emblematises the subtlety of this pleasurable neocolonial exploitation: in the city which the novel's narrator Tanja Lucić describes as steeped in the aesthetic of kitsch, 'live Barbies – young women from Moldavia, Bulgaria,

Ukraine, Belarus' and 'Eastern European Kens who had come to this Disneyland to entertain the grown-up male children here' are indifferently consumed as 'alien flesh' (79). Throughout much of the book, Lucić reflects on 'infantile urban exhibitionism' that prompts the Dutch to display a variety of toy-like objects from their windows, as in a gesture of fingerprinting, or signalling, their belonging in the city (29). The entertainment industry of prostitution, much like Amsterdam's residents' kitschy personal items, are, in their 'cuteness', beyond good and evil – flattened into the commodity fetish, they occlude their political meaning, the trajectory of sexual trafficking from the crumbling postcommunist states. As David Williams notes in his reading of the novel, 'in a Europe united by commerce, the West will provide the cash, and the eastern body will be a tradable commodity' (2013: 104). Estranging the city through a nightmarish Benjaminian lens – offering disturbing images of a surreal, grown-up playground – Lucić retrieves this silenced political context, which she mourns as a 'generalised human loss: Like a Balkan keener I wailed my agony over one and all, only my agony was mute' (233).

The Ministry is preoccupied with this traumatic muteness, the loss of language with which to describe not only the agony of Yugoslav wars, but also the general untranslatability of the experience of communism in Western European exile. This lack of common reference points evokes Kofi's sense of isolation and inability to share his diary that preserves the 'unreal' history of pan-Africanism and communist internationalism which is incomprehensible to Western audiences. Similarly, it is impossible for Lucić to communicate the 'deaf, dumb, and blind pain' of Yugoslav war crimes (143). The only way to express the pain in its 'speechlessness', and uselessness, is to scream it. This failure of language marks the very inability to speak of the experience of communist Yugoslavia, which has disappeared as a referent, shattering the symbolic order that sustained it. Yugoslav refugees in Amsterdam speak an extinct language, 'half swallowing their words . . . and uttering semi-sounds', like 'linguistic invalids' (4). While Lucić's student Igor praises Holland as a 'a country without pain', a 'big blotter' that 'sucks up everything – memories, pain, *all that crap*' (207), this unbearable lightness of forgetting is stubbornly counteracted by the narrative that revives the Yugoslav dinosaur by collecting memories, as haphazard and half-baked as the language to which they belong.

In *Nobody's Home*, Ugrešić similarly assumes the position of a postcommunist migrant subaltern, whose pain over the breakup of Yugoslavia is silenced in the dominant historical reductivism accompanying the transitions to neo-liberal capitalism. She points out how Yugoslav intellectuals, to be accepted by the international community and justify the country's breakdown, had to 'cultivate *false memory syndrome*' and transform themselves into 'victims of communism' (165). But something is indeed lost in this process: Ugrešić wonders how she can disabuse a Dutch bartender who, brainwashed by the 'media and widely-held beliefs', calls Yugoslavia 'Tito's dictatorship' (204–5). She doesn't know how she can explain that in the post-Yugoslav 'democritatorship' she has to fight for the rights she 'had enjoyed freely in the communist dictatorship? The right to gender equality. The right to reproductive choice . . . The right not to declare my nationality. The right not to hate my neighbour' (206).

Prevailing European stereotypes of communism, therefore, are also to blame for this silencing. Ugrešić portrays the EU as invested in preserving the myth of political and economic superiority over both its Eastern fringes and former colonies through insistence on multicultural unity and consensus building, preemptively managing the crisis of identity that is increasingly 'occupied' by multitudes of migrants. In light of official emphases on the need for consensus and getting along – and anxieties about its absence, as in popular oppositions to the EU Constitutional Treaty, the Lisbon Treaty and austerity measures – Ugrešić's critique appears heretical, unnecessarily prickly and uncooperative. However, I propose reading this disagreement via Rancière's positive valorisation of the concept, as the moment when politics happens. For Rancière, the focus on consensus, while appearing as a pillar of democracy, subscribes to the logic of policing and the foreclosure of egalitarian change:

> Police is first an order of bodies that defines the allocation of ways of doing, ways of being, and ways of saying . . . it is an order of the visible and the sayable that sees that a particular activity is visible and another is not, that this speech is understood as discourse and another as noise. (2004a: 29)

Politics, conversely, occurs with disagreement, 'an extremely determined activity antagonistic to policing: whatever breaks with the tangible configuration whereby parties and parts or lack of them are defined', so that 'it makes visible what had no business to be seen and makes heard a discourse where once was only place for noise' (30). Ugrešić's texts thus argumentatively and aesthetically mark the possibility of politics in the EU, against the management of crisis taking shape as the 'consensus police'. She articulates into the political sphere those who are often managed through a discourse of cultural differences into visible, acknowledged ethnic minorities based on an a priori determined identity. Because this mode of representation displaces their disenfranchisement in the context of EU economic and political privileges, Ugrešić advocates a radical disidentification from given identities. As we have seen, in *A Shadow of Myself*, disidentifying from the 'naturalness of place' (Rancière 2004a: 36) and imagining new modes of subjectification is necessitated by the sheer proliferation and elusiveness of identity markers, which are, nonetheless, inevitable. For Ugrešić, such markers are also inescapable, invariably looming as external impositions, but her narrative emphasis is often their meticulous deconstruction and subjective rejection.

Žižek too echoes Rancière's concept of dissensus when he acknowledges that the *banlieue* protest in France, though inarticulate, was such a fundamental attempt to achieve visibility to the system in which these French residents have no part. The violence was thus not only necessary to draw attention to their overlooked plight, but also to reject the exclusionary frame of recognition and pose the zero-degree question of potential dialogue: 'Do you hear me?' (2008: 79). Ugrešić furthers a critique of EU cultural identity politics as its primary mechanism of policing and maintaining this exclusionary frame of recognition which renders undesirable requests invisible: Europe 'treats culture as her principle ideological glue, to rearticulate and reglue herself' (2008: 154). The focus on culture as ideology turns European integration into a positive strategy of protection as well as containment of supposed cultural differences. However, because this stated respect for difference parades as a 'mask for chauvinism', it effects only a false reconciliation and democratic participation of all (253). European unification thus appears as rather lacklustre and uninspired, and Europe seems fatigued at the end of old utopias as it announces a thoroughly commodified, dull, mass-market utopia of multiculturalism, where 'the feeling of joy seems to be lacking' (253).

The politics of recognising diverse cultural identities is no less problematic than the insistence on a unified European identity. Ugrešić likens the European market of cultural differences to the Eurovision song contest, notorious for its transparent politicisation, spectacular kitsch and affirmation of cultural stereotypes (139). As with the prostitution industry in *The Ministry*, cultural difference is here flattened into a mere spectacle:

> The cultural bureaucracy of the EU is perpetuating . . . *me Tarzan, you Jane* . . . formula for acknowledging various cultural identities . . . As long as someone who is Moroccan lays something *Moroccan* on the counter, whatever that means, and we lay something *European* out, whatever that means, all is right with the world. (145)

To achieve visibility in the host nation, one can also employ culture as a utilitarian currency to profit from one's merits, one's safely packaged difference: 'culture can serve as *an identity help-kit,* as a shadowy point of self-respect and mutual regard, or as a blank surface onto which meaning can be inscribed and read' (153).

While the sticky concept of cultural difference illuminates Europe's inability to live with difference as an ethnically or racially unmarked category, *Nobody's Home* and *The Ministry* trace the contours of a postnational, global capitalist dynamic that the EU, with its insistence on national and cultural identities traditionally conceived, both occludes rhetorically and fails to account for politically. Metropolitan migrants who have no clear national identity thus have to wait for a European 'melting pot, which would erase state borders, and national and ethnic divisions,' and hand 'people a European passport . . . making them European citizens' (2008: 156). More significantly, 'A language which would include the overlapping interests of numerous groups, trans-local solidarities, cross-border mobilisations and post-national identities does not exist yet' (149).

Ugrešić's aesthetics moves towards developing and performing such a language in order to articulate, in-common, the globally relevant demands of subaltern cosmopolitans who 'have no part' and who belong together without a filiative resemblance. To coin this innovative, poetic discourse of disagreement, Ugrešić grapples with identifying new structures of power and class formations which seem elusive and therefore absent, or at least benign when compared with old centralised forms of governance. She wonders who the exploiters are today: 'Today they are invisible, so perhaps this is why people seem to think there aren't any. Do they exist? Are there classes? To which class does he belong? Who are his enemies? And what is with his allies?' (292). This quandary remains disorienting and vague, without being forced into a clear resolution. More recently, reflecting on 2011 London protests, Ugrešić comments on the youth and lack of educational opportunities for many of the protesters, 'whose futures have been stolen' but who don't know 'who their real enemy is any more', resorting to 'vandalism' as 'the only means of articulating their fury' (2014: 123–4). Ugrešić's narratives create connections among the disenfranchised groups by highlighting their common alienation and poverty rather than cultural difference, while demonstrating how frustration manifests as indiscriminate vandalism in a political situation where centres of power seem invisible or at least dispersed.

In *The Ministry*, Tanja Lucić identifies with the silenced, muted immigrants on Amsterdam trains to such a radical extent that she confuses her own image with that of another passenger lost to the external world while listening to his 'silent music'. It is 'as if I'd been watching myself in the glass, as if I'd seen myself but couldn't hear myself' (31). Her identity already unmoored and her former language disabled, she enters a new collective configuration in this transitory space par excellence, where Amsterdam residents temporarily come together in the here and now, forced to confront one another. This scene dampens ideals of multicultural coexistence in European metropolises, but doesn't register antagonism either; rather, it captures a mood of indifference and isolation, perhaps even more damning than open confrontation. The passage combines the images of a 'dark-skinned young man poring over a textbook of Dutch for foreigners . . . [who] turns toward the window, mumbles a few words to himself', 'a young Chinese couple chewing gum in synchronised motion, their faces grey and mouselike' and 'a tired Moroccan Madonna with a boy in her lap' (31). It is significant that, unmoored and silent like Lucić, they all keep to themselves, not having a language in common; however, it is the external narrative perspective that desires affiliations among people of such seemingly incongruent backgrounds and concerns (taking care of family, or learning Dutch). The differentiating cultural and ethnic markers are scattered across their descriptions; nonetheless, they are united by attributes that signal their alienated participation in global capitalism (tired, grey, mouselike) and by the glaring absence of a common language to express their pain, to scream it, as it were. It is as if the narrative highlights their common non-belonging, but implies that despite this shared predicament, the only community they can form is transitory and indifferent.

Ugrešić's narratives about Amsterdam persistently wander away from its adult playgrounds catering to tourists to depressing spaces of immigrant consumerism, such as flea markets and rundown super-markets, recalling Phillips's penchant for highlighting the proliferat-ing urban spaces of grey economy as both the repressed underside of Europe and as prefigurations of its future community. Lucić is drawn to such spaces by 'vague magnetism', 'the strong scents of spices from beyond the seas' and 'seedy vendors of cheap clothing' (193). In *Nobody's Home*, Ugrešić is similarly drawn to shop for cheap consumer items at a Dutch bazaar, noting the immigrant shoppers' common superfluous status vis-à-vis the state: 'They are all of them "trash," stripped of any awareness of their position. Clever politi-cians and the even cleverer clergy have slipped them a toy to play with: the right to religious, national, ethnic identity' (227). While this statement problematically suggests general ideological turpitude, the scathing depiction of abject disenfranchisement can also be read as a performative echo of right-wing sentiments that migrant minorities are merely excessive 'waste', a 'drain' on affluent European societies. In a situation in which superfluous immigrants consume superflu-ous trash items, the sociality of being in-common exhausts itself in a corporate context which creates the only public space. Suggesting that corporations organise even communal life in Holland, Ugrešić notes that the Dutch supermarket Albert Heijn is often the only store in Amsterdam's urban ghettoes, 'its single public space' which peo-ple frequent having no other choice (2008: 119). Ugrešić's depic-tion significantly dampens Negri's hope that contemporary migrants can inhabit the city with dignity and claim its inhospitable streets in unpredictably creative as well as peaceful ways, creating a vanguard solidarity movement.

Nonetheless, Ugrešić's emphasis on this common activity driven by poverty also becomes a discursive space for Rancière's dynamic subjectification, rather than a static marker of one's 'group' iden-tity, precisely because she creates innovative connections among a burgeoning underclass at the heart of European utopia, locating political potential in the 'count of the uncounted' (2004a: 118).

As an exile, then immigrant herself, Ugrešić is drawn to this portion of Dutch society more than to any other, performatively aligning her sympathies with the underpaid and underprivileged. She emphasises similarities in economic impoverishment between postcommunist migrants and other migrant groups, including those from the former colonies, along with similar types of racism suffered at the hands of the host society. Thus, Ugrešić notes, 'Pole' has become a ubiquitous designation for any Eastern European in Holland and associated with 'criminal behaviour' and 'human trash', which renders them disposable like the migrants described in the flea market scene above (2014: 27). Fanning local resentment against the latest migrant groups, the right-wing Partij voor de Vrijheid launches a website 'cordially inviting Dutch citizens' to discuss the following questions: '*Do you have problems with recent arrivals from Central and Eastern Europe? Have you lost your job because of a Pole, Bulgarian, Romanian, or some other Eastern European?*' (ibid.).

Developing a transnational perspective, Ugrešić also places the rampant class stratification of postcommunist transitions in a contemporary European context, where neo-liberal reforms continue to increase income and employment gaps between European and non-European residents. Thus, *The Ministry of Pain* offers a scathing critique of the privileged 'transition mutants' of postcommunist societies, 'progressive and aggressively young, the well-paid commissars of *European integration and enlargement*, the harbingers of the new world order' (235). These *engagé* yuppies specialise in alleviating the blows of privatisation and democratisation, while 'living off the misfortunes of the people they help' (234). Educated in what the narrative derides as 'Eurospeak', they obliterate complex histories and antagonisms of their countries by disseminating everywhere the fashionable terminology of globalisation that 'manages' conflict: '*management, negotiation technology, income, profit, investment, expenses, hidden communication* and the like' (236). They even adjust their personalities to fit the requirements of an upwardly mobile corporate labourer: '*hardworking, communicative, loyal, discreet . . . and skilful in coping with stressful situations*' (236).

In other words, they benefit from renewed social differentiation that has spawned an enormous postcommunist underclass, 'a nameless mass of slaves down below' (237). These are the economically superfluous multitudes that rummage through trash for food, sell their kidneys and turn to prostitution in their societies' transitions to capitalism. Ugrešić italicises the words of corporate Eurospeak to signal that this is the hegemonic language which needs to be contested because its seemingly universal validity leaves the impoverished nameless and silent. This is the policing structure of European democracy: configurations of accepted expressions recognisable as language rather than noise.

To make significant egalitarian demands in this context, the underclass who have no part must, as Rancière says, make 'heard a discourse where once was only place for noise' (2004a: 30). In *The Ministry of Pain*, Ugrešić posits a collective first-person political subject typically assumed to be making noise, as she antagonistically rehashes European anxieties about uncouth, violent non-European minorities who produce animal sounds rather than human language:

> We are barbarians. We have no writing; we leave our signatures on the wind: we utter sounds, we signal with our calls, our shouts, our screams, our spit. That is how we mark our territory. Our fingers drum on everything they touch . . . We bawl at weddings and wail at funerals, our women's convulsive voices battering the concrete facades like tempests. We break glasses and go bang: firecrackers are our favourite toy. Sound is our alphabet, the noise we produce being the only proof that we exist, our bang the only trace we leave behind. We are like dogs: we bark. (228)

The narrator's self-inclusion into the 'we' of this enunciation recalls Yasin's identification with the 'we' of 'the nameless body of mongrel humanity' that has transgressed Europe's borders in Mahjoub's *Traveling with Djinns* (173). This formation of subjects unified through their exclusion from a discourse rather than through an a priori party, group identity or ethnicity assumes the tone of threat through self-annunciation, making visible the contingency of existing political configurations. For Rancière, these articulations of dissension are at once 'arguments and world openers, the opening up of common (which does not mean consensual) worlds where the subject who argues is counted as an arguer' (2004a: 58). At the end of the novel, the protagonist has disidentified again from this group to occupy a new subject space and point to the parallel exclusion of post-Yugoslav subjectivities that overflow visible ethnic categories recognised by the EU:

> Then I open my mouth and let out the words . . . I flicker my tongue like a fairy tale dragon, and it forks into Croatian, Serbian, Bosnian, Slovenian, Macedonian . . . I shatter the glass with my voice like Oskar Matzerath. I secrete the words from my mouth like ink from a cuttlefish. (255)

The rhetorical construction of a collective first-person Yugoslav identity through the country's linguistic diversity brings forth less a multicultural people, understood as a collection of ethnic groups and predicated on the existence of ethnically marked, separate individuals, and more a multitude of singularities in-common where self is not separate from other, where a tongue can simultaneously speak a number of (now officially separated) languages. As Nancy reminds us, while relations between individual subjects involve an experience of juxtaposition, including recognition of mutual similarities or differences, singularities relate through 'exposing-sharing' which effects 'a mutual interpellation of singularities prior to any address in language (though it gives to this latter its first condition of possibility)'. This does not imply juxtaposition or separation, but exposition to communication, to the outside, which Nancy sums up as '*you shares me*' (1991: 29). Since exposure is inseparable from communication or the 'sharing of voices' (Nancy 77), Ugrešić rebuilds the diverse Yugoslav community as an event of singularities indiscriminately sharing one another's languages, without the need to (mis)recognise one's 'self' in the 'other', moving away from the concept of an individual subject detached by specific ethnic, cultural or linguistic properties.

Additionally, the intimations of a desperate need to be noticed and accounted for in public discourse, in both passages quoted above, intensify into inhuman auditory and tactile violence, where 'civilised' language is deterritorialised by the animalistic and the monstrous. This noise can be dismissed as inarticulate or destructive just as Oskar's screaming is seen as childish and unnatural in the Nazi Germany of Grass's *The Tin Drum*, or as Malik Solanka's unconscious tirades are treated as lunatic ravings in the complacently imperialist New York of Rushdie's *Fury*. In contrast, Ugrešić not only implies that noise must be heard as discourse, but that interlocutors must show respect and empathy for the singularity of enunciation which is alien to traditional forms of political discourse. In the first passage, therefore, Ugrešić introduces a number of communicative gestures that would typically be labelled too emotional, meaningless or disturbing – shouts, bangs, spit. She deliberately mobilises Eurocentric anxieties that associate such expressions with otherness qualified as fundamentalist Muslim, patriarchal or violent, recalling El-Tayeb's observations on hegemonic interpretations of *banlieue* protests in France.

The larger connection that Ugrešić's narrative makes is that the violence of the physical and rhetorical breakdown of Yugoslavia into ethnic groups parallels the violence of EU multicultural discourses that categorise migrants into separate minority groups. Against this ethnic labelling, or stigmatisation as '"the beneficiaries of political asylum," "refugees" ... "the fallout of Balkanisation," or "savages"', Ugrešić also insists on using the collective first-person pronoun to highlight post-Yugoslavs' shared loss and predicament, as well as shared responsibility for processing memories of the lost country: 'The country we came from was our common trauma' (2005: 52). Yugoslav refugees gain agency and a new language that counteracts their silencing both at home and in Holland when they substitute the neutral first-person pronoun for official ethnic labels. Once Yugoslavia disappears, its inhabitants become Yugos, or '"our people." The possessive pronoun also came in handy when referring to the language they spoke together ... to avoid its former, now politically incorrect name of Serbo-Croatian, they called it simply "our language"' (13). The persistent use of 'we' and 'our' throughout the narrative obviates discourses of national identity that are simultaneously solidifying in post-Yugoslav space. It also echoes the 'we' that connects subaltern migrant groups in the EU into an assertive, possibly dangerous, collective that seeks to gain visibility in public discourse: 'We are barbarians ... Our young men are wild and sullen, full of anger ... [they] hurl stones at car windows; they steal whatever they can lay their hands on' (227).

To return to Žižek's reflections on the meaninglessness of violence in various EU protests, the problem, he argues, is not so much violence per se – its seeming irrationality can also be seen as a Badiouian 'event', a rupture that occurs without having been anticipated to exact social justice – but that it isn't truly emancipatory because it has no programme for the 'day after' of political restructuring. A similar argument takes place in Hardt and Negri's *Commonwealth*.

In its long-term impotence, therefore, shouts, bangs and stones hurled at car windows do not signify enough. However, Walter Benjamin's [1921] (1986) reading of political protest, especially his differentiation between localised and general strike, helps to complicate such arguments. For Benjamin, a localised strike, as merely 'an external modification of labour conditions', remains in the domain of lawmaking, thus allowing for a perpetuation of state violence (what Žižek might call invisible, systemic violence) (291). Conversely, a general strike is 'anarchistic' and interrupts the very system of lawmaking (292). While the state focuses on the effects of a general strike to denounce it as violent – or, while Žižek and Hardt and Negri focus on the 'day after' of protests to accuse them of lacking vision – for Benjamin, a general strike seen as a 'pure means' is non-violent in the sense that, just by virtue of happening, it interrupts the systemic violence of the state (292). The question, therefore, is not what is the purpose of all the lost lives, burnt cars and destruction of living space in EU protests, but rather, how does the noise of protest signify as a 'pure means', as an event? How does it change relationships in a social space by traumatising as well as addressing others who may not hear the protesters' demands otherwise?

In an essay entitled 'Sobs', Ugrešić reflects on such forms of address when witnessing other people's pain in everyday situations in which the one who witnesses and the object of the gaze are separated by an uncomfortably visible state of heightened emotional disturbance. Faced with a violent lovers' fight or a sobbing madwoman in Amsterdam, the narrator feels a strange, obsessive sympathy which leads to reflections on the subaltern positions of people whose misfortunes are muted by the contemporary media culture. For the narrator, teletechnological mediation abstracts the organic embodiment of pain: misfortune reaches us 'through our television screens, filtered . . . for mass consumption' and 'leaves us indifferent' (2008: 56). Like Oskar Matzerath, the sobbing madwoman is 'an accountant for world pain. Maybe every night she registers in an invisible ledger all the pain that has happened in the world, and in the morning she publishes aloud all that she had written down' (57).

Hence, when she encounters pain directly, persecuted by sobs and shouts, the narrator finds it ethically impossible to ignore the drama: she must respond, at least by pausing to reflect on it. Yet, the possibility of an unambiguously charitable political act, rather than media-induced indifference, is suspended in the tension between the narrator's privilege to explore such a reflective gesture and the spontaneous, ineluctable materiality of the woman's sobs or the lovers' rage. The tension over knowing how, precisely, to act in an ethically demanding situation is heightened through the narrator's double position as both a subaltern who desires to be heard as she flickers her dragon tongue and a privileged metropolitan who writes widely disseminated texts, abstracts misfortune and witnesses mediated pain. She both empathises and engages with those seen as merely making noise and highlights her distance from them in terms of uneven social privilege and the asymmetry of political situatedness.

The ambivalence of this double exposure characterises a similar encounter between Lucić, a university professor, and three young boys who attempt to rob her with a pocketknife. The boys' description is uncannily similar to that of the collective 'we' of migrant men as well as post-Yugoslav refugees mentioned earlier in the novel, connecting them to the unheard noises of protest: 'All three had the dark, sullen look of grown men' and then one of the boys aimed 'his black pupils at my face, he let out a long, piercing cry full of hate . . . as unexpected and powerful as an electric shock. It came from some unknown depths, some unknown darkness' (2005: 241). While Lucić becomes the immediate – and gendered – target of this accusing cry, she uses attributes throughout this passage that de-individualise hate and separate it from the specific situation, signalling a larger social context beyond this violent event, in which blame is not easily ascribed. Lucić thus reacts to the incident as 'both moving and dreadful', acknowledging both fear for her life and empathy with the attackers (241). Ugrešić's texts suggest that the tensions present in such encounters obligate one to walk the thin line between refusing one's privilege of representing subaltern expressions in tired colonial epithets that reproduce existing hierarchies (for instance, calling *banlieue* migrant protesters 'scum' or blaming Greek 'profligacy' on their 'Balkan' mentality) and denouncing destruction and murder as actions that cause more pain to others.

The main question emerging from this discussion, then, is how to create a viable community of protest and resistance around differentially subaltern positions within the EU. This crucial question hovers above Hardt and Negri's concept of multitude and the spontaneous ascription to its assemblages of primary, or at the very least, prescriptive bonding through multicultural love rather than tension, enmity or withdrawal of solidarity. *Nobody's Home* and

The Ministry of Pain forward a transnational perspective that connects the seemingly isolated position of postcommunist subalterns to those of other marginalised, often postcolonial, EU minorities. Although in this way the texts' narrators disidentify from their 'natural' groups, and move towards a cosmopolitan multitude gathered around shared economic strife, Ugrešić does not dissolve existing asymmetries of power and disparate interests in a transcendental, utopian vision of peaceful coexistence. We might read this gesture as a refusal to obscure antagonism at the heart of modern Europe; also, the existence of asymmetry and divisiveness can be both a fundamental social experience and a tool for political mobilisation, bringing various incompatible positions into conversation. Downplaying antagonism would lead to conceptualising political community as organically united and consensual rather than divisive, a warning that underlies Jodi Dean's (2012) critique of any community of protest that inadvertently adopts neo-liberal notions of flexibility, coexistence and inclusiveness, including Hardt and Negri's multitude or the US Occupy movement.[20]

An alternative Europe, thus, may start with a politics of disagreement and antagonism, through a critique of all those European intellectuals who will gradually stop writing about 'themes of exile, passports, and visas', discouraged by the 'enthusiasm for unification and the code of political correctness' (Ugrešić 2008: 158). Ugrešić particularly faults Eastern European intellectuals for having become 'passionate supporters of post-postmodernism . . . the ideology of cynicism, games . . . the carnivalising of ideology and politics'. Thinking ideology as entertainment parallels her reflections on depoliticising immigration in Amsterdam through the aesthetics of kitsch, which results in an infantile, ahistorical utopia. Here too, if 'we proclaim that everything is a game, we cease to be responsible. We become children' (173).

From that perspective, the austerity protests that shook many European countries over the last decade might help renew political commitment and diversify European protesting publics. Instead of reproducing dominant power discourses that 'cynically' dismiss the significance of protests, portraying them as immature or destructive, we could take the cue from Greek bank employees, whose joint statement denounced violence, yet gave strong support to the *raison d'être* of the austerity protests. Namely, after three bank employees died in a fire started by the protesting crowds in May 2010, the bank employees went on strike. Rather than distancing themselves from the protesters or echoing the government line, their union accused disastrous government policies of pushing people to the brink of committing such desperate acts of violence.[21] In other words, rather than simply recuperating what Žižek calls 'subjective violence', they portrayed it as reactive, and argued that emphasising it in public discourse throws a veil on the much more systematic, yet invisibly deadly dynamics of neo-liberal violence perpetrated by the Greek government.

Chapter 5

Epilogue: Memories of Yugoslavia and Europe to Come

As we have seen, Dubravka Ugrešić re-members the dismembered Yugoslavia through a rhetorical construction of a collective first-person Yugoslav identity articulated in a language described only as 'ours'. Despite the country's rich diversity of languages and dialects, she suggests that the conceptual tools of liberal multiculturalism which has become the dominant way of explaining the multi-ethnicity of socialist Yugoslavia in the wake of its demise misses not only the country's idiosyncratic economic and political system, but also the extent to which Yugoslavia cannot be reduced to a collection of distinct and internally consistent, albeit interconnected, cultural or linguistic groups. Ugrešić's frustration at being unable to explain this to her European interlocutors is symptomatic of the larger problems of the (mis)translations of political terminology: because the state itself was officially a federation of 'nations and nationalities', the separate nation states that resulted from it seem to have merely deducted the federation part. To contest this reductive understanding, Ugrešić rebuilds the diverse Yugoslav community as an event of singularities indiscriminately sharing one another's languages, without the need to (mis)recognise one's 'self' in the 'other'. Forking her tongue, she suggests a host of identifications that coexist fluidly and in-common, without clearly defining relationships or groups. This understanding of community calls into question the adequateness of popular rhetoric about promoting cultural understanding or negotiating religious differences in the Balkans, which presumes the (co)existence of always-already distinguishable groups defined by various identity markers as the central feature of the region.

While Ugrešić by no means idealises the former Yugoslavia as a state, her discourse is nonetheless more nostalgic than that employed by the NSK State in Time project, discussed at the beginning of this book. Drawing parallels between Yugoslavia and the European Union, the NSK alert us to the totalitarian potential that exists in the very conceptualisation of the state and the tools it employs to ensure its survival. Nonetheless, the type of sociality in-common which Ugrešić remembers, and which implies a degree of social justice and egalitarianism, is not entirely monopolised by hegemonic representations of the state in so far as it has survived its demise. The last decade, especially, has seen the phenomenon of intensifying recreations of a Yugoslav 'community without community' which emanates from the absence of the state, often through a disidentification from state signifiers. In part this stems from nostalgia for the lost principles of a shared Yugoslav social and cultural space in the face of fervent, solipsistic nationalisms in the region and the social fragmentations of neo-liberal capitalism. It articulates itself through cultural and intellectual events, including exhibitions, concerts, theatre productions and conferences.[1] The invocation of Yugoslavia also underpins unofficial, civic, virtual and physical associations,[2] which often assume a critical attitude to the former state but also advocate the reinstatement of social benefits lost in its wake, such as subsidised education, healthcare and workers' protection, as well as the commitment to solidarity, community and internationalism.

Striking in all these initiatives is the absence of state-related terminology and the attempt to define veritably spectral connections in the post-Yugoslav space that cannot be easily harnessed into an institutionalised project. For instance, the multi-ethnic cast of the theatre production *Rođeni u YU (Born in YU, 2010)* criticise official discourses that place a taboo on positive imaginings of Yugoslav life. This production soberly explores questions of repressed memories of life in Yugoslavia, including both pleasant and traumatic personal histories, both stale socialist sloganeering and a sense of hope and purpose.[3] The actors explain they eagerly participated in this project because they embrace Yugoslavia not as a country but as a 'cosmopolitan concept' that was regularly undermined by 'tribalism' and as a 'cultural milieu' shaped by common historical experiences which survived the state's dissolution ('Rođenima u Yu zabranjeno sjećanje' 2010: n.p.). For the association 'Naša Jugoslavija', in turn, Yugoslavia denotes an 'attitude', a 'way of life', and a 'mode of being together' which represents a 'potential for interdependence' that was only partially realised in the former state. Yugoslavia translates into 'heterogeneity', 'openness to difference' and 'creative dynamism', which comprise a historical legacy and thus, responsibility of the people who fall under its purview.[4]

This paradoxical legacy of the absence of (state) community, of an ephemeral being-in-common, has also inspired several regionally influential texts by Vuk Perišić. Laboriously dismantling typical explanations of Yugoslavia's demise, Perišić suggests that the argument that Yugoslavia couldn't survive because it was 'an artificial state' overlooks the inherent artificiality of all states. In a philosophically innovative gesture, Perišić counters the claim that Yugoslavia fell prey to nationalist tribalism because it 'failed to foster a Yugoslav nation'; he recuperates this alleged failure as the single greatest success of the country: 'To be a Yugoslav was never . . . a national but a civic and international, or more precisely anational choice' (2011a: n.p.). For Perišić, Yugoslav signifies not a supranational (but still national) identity, like the one embodied by the term American or like an imagined future identity in the EU, but rather the absence and withdrawal of any identity understood as a given: Yugoslavia becomes an anational choice. The demise of Yugoslavia as a state, with the accompanying 'kitsch' insignia like the anthem, flag and the cult of Tito, is beneficial to this Yugoslav idea, which cannot be coopted by any institutionalised discourse (2011b: n.p.). Once 'one's own' state disappears, one begins to see every state as 'alien': Perišić argues that the state is always-already an 'alienated apparatus of power and deception', which resonates with NSK's attitude to the state. This critical perspective to the state is crucial to a democratic culture (ibid.).

In the conclusion to this book, I explore the multivalent phenomena of re-membering former Yugoslavia so as to highlight the potential that interrogating and rethinking this project carries for conceptualising a radically different European Union. I will dwell in more detail on one example of such remembrance, the Subversive Festival in Zagreb, which revisits the break-up of Yugoslavia by placing it in the context of European and global socialist initiatives and histories. My intention is not to idealise Yugoslavia as an idea or way of being – this would problematically echo the idealisation of Europe discsussed in the introduction. However, common threads in this remembrance – subaltern, uninstitutionalised community as an alternative to hegemonic state mythology; being-in-common despite the absence of a common identity; and a critical attitude to the state – merit further analysis and discussion. By way of analogy, we might imagine the effects of such a politics of disidentification within the EU, where even the label European would no longer designate self-differentiation from 'others' and where the identity politics tradition-ally associated with individual European states would be critically assessed. Lastly, invoking Yugoslavia also represents a refusal to abandon the now-underground politics of social(ist) equality, the welfare state and solidarity, which underwrote the European unifica-tion project itself for much of the twentieth century.

At present, the dominant association between Yugoslavia and the European Union is a negative one. In light of the economic crisis and explicit conflicts among European states, a host of academic and pop-ular texts have compared the EU to Yugoslavia as an admonishment of failure should it not successfully resolve its problems. Yugoslavia here looms as a negative doppelgänger, foretelling the 'Balkanisa-tion' of the Union that is beleaguered by the same centrifugal forces as the erstwhile federation: intensifying nationalism and separatism, economic disparity between north and south, mutual resentment and stereotyping and mounting debt.[5] Additionally, Yugoslavia is seen as providing a lesson to the EU in terms of the difficulty of balancing autonomy and unity, especially with a view to ensuring representa-tion of diverse interests and democracy.[6]

However, while the EU is diagnosed as a democratically deficient union, pundits are quick to point out that a multiparty EU is none-theless fundamentally different from socialist Yugoslavia, which was a one-party state.[7] A discernible anxiety about Europe being infected by the same nationalist bug as Yugoslavia also permeates the discus-sions of separatist politics in the EU. John Feffer warns that Europe's 'dystopian future could be glimpsed' from its 'eastern borderlands' (the collapse of not only Yugoslavia but also of the Soviet Union and Czechoslovakia); 'the world is upside down' because 'Instead of Eastern and Central Europe catching up to the rest of the EU, pockets of the "west" have begun to fall behind the "east"' (2015: n.p.). Despite the dystopian scenarios contained in the scare-word 'Balkanisation', Robert Hayden argues that the EU cannot fall prey to a civil war understood as a battle over territory or the practice of ethnic cleansing, since Europe completed its ethnic cleansing by 1945. According to Hayden, immigrants, the most disenfranchised minority who have the most reason to rebel, are so spatially dispersed that they could not lay claim to any clearly defined territory (2011: n.p.). His argument, however, does not take into account the separatist politics of European minorities, such as Catalans or Scots.

In spite of their frequently sensationalist titles and implicit warnings against becoming like the Balkan 'other', many of these negative comparisons nonetheless appear well founded – the substantial parallels are difficult to ignore. Perhaps inadvertently, such comparisons demonstrate the inherent instability of states riven by indebtedness, social inequality, disappearing safety nets, right-wing politics and bureaucratic inefficiency. Tim Judah notes that even EU democracy is no safeguard against chauvinist nationalism, since, after all, nationalists were voted in during multi-party elections in Serbia, Croatia and Bosnia (2012: n.p.). However, this projected repetition of history with a difference occludes the extent to which the Yugoslav federation that began to fragment by the end of the 1980s and the European Union that came into its own in the early 1990s are antagonistic, even mutually exclusive, social projects. This was encapsulated both in the commonly stated desire of seceding republics to leave Yugoslavia and join Europe, as well in the victory of a certain set of values internally seen as European – nationhood (understood along ethnic rather than federalist lines), private enterprise, market competition, democracy, individual rights – over the values of socialist Yugoslavia, which partly allowed the aforementioned practices, but also controlled their implementation. Temporally, one succeeds the other; for the EU to thrive, Yugoslavia had to disappear. I suggest that this shift (in the context of other regime changes in Eastern Europe) also marks a definitive transition from a socially egalitarian Europe to a neo-liberal Europe.

Revisiting the memory of the Yugoslavia that disappeared, then, becomes a subversive act which disturbs normative narratives of political community and economy contained in the EU vision of European affairs, as well as in self-legitimising discourses of the successor states. As Tanja Petrović convincingly argues, postcommunist countries, including Yugoslavia, had to rid themselves of the legacy of socialism in order to have a future in the EU due to the dominant perception of socialism as primarily a totalitarian system that is likened to fascism, rather than seen as antagonistic to capitalism or liberalism (2012: 10, 83). Paradoxically, European discourses which encourage the erasure of the legacy of socialism also dangerously

diminish its role in antifascist struggle; in turn, this engenders revi-
sionist histories that absolve local fascist movements, although anti-
fascism is one of the founding ideas of modern Europe (11). What,
then, is the significance of memorialising the defunct Yugoslavia,
whose ideology projected a vision of an egalitarian, antifascist, inter-
nationalist Europe? What kind of cultural and political potential, if
any, does this carry both for the region and for Europe?[8]

Often, the modes of remembering Yugoslavia through a commodification of its popular culture, consumer items and official symbols
are interpreted as sentimental, private and apolitical. Such apparently individual, nostalgic ways or remembering are patronised as
politically harmless or berated as politically ineffective, depending
on one's critical attitude to the post-Yugoslav status quo. A classic
example of the commodification of state symbols is the ubiquity of
souvenirs and paraphernalia that market the Yugoslav flag, pioneer
attire and images of Tito, as well as bars and restaurants that exploit
communist insignia in their decors. In *Titostalgija* (2010), a comprehensive study of the extraordinary popularity of the cult of Tito manifested in a range of (quirky) cultural practices, Mitja Velikonja notes
that their mostly private, unofficial nature results in explicit denials
of Yugonostalgia and interpretations of this phenomenon as 'apolitical, stripped of ideological baggage' (24). Just as often, the over-
whelming, persistent popularity of Yugoslav-era music in the region
is described as innocuous; for instance, young people who listen to
such music simply want to have a good time and in no way 'relate
to Yugoslavia' (144). Alternatively, this effortless embrace of music
is accused of 'trivialising and commodifying the Yugoslav legacy',
which is reduced to uncritical, affective recycling of mass culture,
blocking a responsible inquiry into both the positive legacies of the
country and tendencies that led to its demise (Petrović 2012: 133).

A similar accusation could be brought against the travelling exhibition *Long Live Life!*, which started in 2013 in order to document
'the good life' in former Yugoslavia through everyday objects and
practices, including music, sports, newspapers, advertisements and a
wide variety of consumer goods. This popular exhibition addresses
Yugoslav ideology by, for instance, including a section on the socialist youth brigades and recreating a typical classroom, complete with
a map of Yugoslavia and a portrait of Tito, but its stated goal is
cautiously apolitical.[9] While the text accompanying exhibition pieces
is playful and ironic, the overall tone of the exhibition is overtly

nostalgic in that the guestbook in the 'classroom' asks the visitors, 'Why was life good back then?'[10] This tendency to idealise could be seen as exploiting the contemporary climate of economic uncertainty and disenfranchisement so as to proffer a safe, unblemished image of the past, where communist ideology is merely an appendage (or even a marketing strategy) to everyday objects. Yugoslavia not only becomes graspable through such objects – it becomes the 'object' of history itself, watered down into a politically correct concept instead of remaining a dynamic, transgressive force that can disturb the present. *Leksikon YU Mitologije* [The Lexicon of YU Mythology], a website project subsequently published as a book (ed. Andrić et al.), whose purpose echoes the aforementioned exhibition, attracted similar critiques of idealising Yugoslavia. *Leksikon* reflects collective authorship, soliciting unofficial, personal memories of the 'mythology' of everyday life in former Yugoslavia, privileging them over entries on politics or history. Muharem Bazdulj warns that it dismisses the existence of Yugoslavia as a 'political fact, regressing into private gossip' (Petrović 2012: 132), while Sandro Siljan faults it for peddling a 'pathetic and non-conflict imagination' which idealises the past (2012: n.p.).

Contrasted with this nostalgic, romanticising narrative of the lost country is a pragmatic, rational narrative of contemporary post-Yugoslav rapprochement, which is seen as inevitable given the similar languages, cultural background and shared histories. For instance, Judah speaks hopefully of the 'Yugosphere' which has supplanted not only the former Yugoslavia but more importantly the solipsistic nationalisms in the region, re-establishing broken ties in the interest of economic, political and cultural cooperation. In Judah's discussion, the Yugosphere, unlike Yugonostalgia, looks to the future, redefining the region outside of the parameters set by the erstwhile shared socialist homeland (2009: n.p.). Petrović notes that for Judah, the Yugosphere flourishes only because of the 'dictates of the market', while he entirely discounts the common Yugoslav history that gives rise to shared 'emotions or affinities' (2012: 118). In this way, Yugosphere is in consonance with European integration; it is emptied out of affective content which appears as insignificant and immaterial in the face of the more pragmatic concerns of neoliberal market competition. Larisa Kurtović, however, provides a corrective to Judah's description of the Yugosphere as a novel phenomenon occasioned by the 'logic of profit' by historicising South

Slav connections that both preceded the actually existing Yugoslav state (the idea of unification that dates back to the nineteenth century), as well as coexisted with its dissolution in the form of anti-war movements (2010: 10).

I have very briefly outlined the dominant – nostalgic/paralysing and modern/entrepreneurial – explanations of the resurgence of Yugoslav memories and connections to argue that they neutralise the political signification of affects by dismissing them as private, ineffable, sentimental or impractical. Commodification and ideali-sation that flatten out historical complexities may not be the most constructive ways to address the legacy of the former country, but even in those instances, the 'consumers'' responses are haunted by the excess of political dissatisfaction which cannot be given voice in the hegemonic discourse that validates neo-liberal-capitalism-cum-nationalism by pathologising this memory as 'communist nostalgia' (Todorova 2015: 95). Virtually all modes of memori-alising Yugoslavia which I have researched, regardless of their genre or mode of dissemination, have as a common denominator a cluster of ideological values whose disappearance is mourned: workers' rights, solidarity, welfare policies, social egalitarianism, economic security, 'brotherhood and unity',[11] anticolonialism and Non-Alignment in international politics. Whether remembrance is explicitly political or not, this common denominator can be a productive, dynamic conceptual category in interrogating the hegemonic values in the region and inspiring political alternatives in the European Union. The goal is not to prove that Yugoslavia indisputably carried out these principles into practice but rather to promote a critical conversation on the former country and its ideology, including its accomplishments, drawbacks and surviv-ing utopian potential. Velikonja thus redeems the maligned word nostalgia by suggesting that remembering Yugoslavia is not only about reinterpreting or reinventing the past, but also creating new meanings and contexts, available to the young generations who were born after Yugoslavia but share a vision of a more equitable world with the older generations (2010: 167).

From this perspective, visitors' reactions to even the allegedly apolitical exhibition *Long Live Life!* are valuable in identifying the desires associated with both the past and the present, which can yield innovative paths to political subjectivisation. Both the exhibi-tion pieces and guestbook entries identify Yugoslavia not with an immanent (multi)national identity, but rather with 'the good life' articulated through pleasure, friendship, collective action, hobbies and a broad sense of empowerment.[12] What could be described as specifically Yugoslav biopolitics nonetheless represents a challenge to the contemporary necropolitical regime of neo-liberal capitalism founded on the dispensability of human labour and needs. *Leksikon YU Mitologije* carries similar potential in capturing the pleasurable practices of everyday life that both arise from as well as exceed state ideology, primarily focusing on common culture, relationships and habits – the shared symbolic order which interpellated the Yugoslavs. The nostalgia implicit here, I argue, is not so much for the lost objects recorded in these idiosyncratic archives, but rather for their mythical aura: for the lost activities and affects with which they are associated. This interpretation could extend to the popularity of Tito memorabilia as well. Despite its allegedly apolitical edge, Titostalgia, Velikonja argues, may be 'subconsciously political' not only because Tito is a political figure par excellence but also because endorsing Tito is a 'gesture of protest' against 'nationalism, submissive *integration with Europe*, neo-liberalism, conservatism, traditionalism, clericalism' (2010: 145). Titostalgia also signifies the mobilisation of common goals of the left persuasion, and 'against the injustices of globalisation, capitalism, militarism . . . US unilateralism, NATO and the EU' (146–7).

The communities of remembrance that former Yugoslavia engenders cannot be explained as expressions of identities conceptualised through the philosophical categories of liberal multiculturalism. Aside from the ubiquitous 'brotherhood and unity' slogan, there is scant recourse in the aforementioned discussions to notions of (multi) ethnic identity, the nation or even cultural mixing. Rather, Yugoslavia today denotes heterogeneity, protest and broad social justice, less a reified statist destiny than inheritance, hope, choice and chance. It contains the kernel of an alternative sociality-in-common discussed throughout this book. Moreover, a refusal to idealise the former state underlies many of these archival gestures. It is evinced in a critical perspective that relies on humour and ironic distancing, the questioning spirit of 'positive cynicism' (169) and the estrangement of socialist ideology as a fantasy structure, where even Tito figures as more a myth and legend and less as an actual politician. The interrogation of historiography through irony not only hinders dogmatic thinking about the past – what Svetlana Boym (2002) theorises as

conservative, 'restorative nostalgia' – but also mocks the deadly serious, aestheticised nationalist histories of post-Yugoslav states.

Thus, even in the institutional absence – and in criticism – of
the former state, its spectral legacy survives in the existence of a
post-Yugoslav community which, like the NSK State in Time, engenders non-material sites of memory such as websites, literature and
the arts, although it has also occupied material sites where Yugoslav history has been erased, as the 2011 'History Lesson' attests.[13]
The virtual associations and forums where the Yugoslav legacy is
discussed not only acknowledge that the region is haunted by the
ghost of the state that is persistently declared dead, but also provide
an alternate reality of cross-national modes of relating within the
official spaces of the separate states. More importantly, they represent perhaps the most comprehensive network of connections to the
large post-Yugoslav diaspora, people who left the country following
its demise and who may still consider themselves Yugoslav. This is
not to idealise the power of the virtual world, especially as access to
the internet depends on one's social status,[14] but it might be productive to further explore this space not only as an archive of Yugoslav
memories, but also as a potential site of post-war 'truth and reconciliation', accessible to more participants than any local initiatives
currently taking place. For instance, Tomislav Longinović proposes
that digital spaces could be 'valuable modes for storing testimonies
of the victims and their loved ones, ensuring that the forgetting is
not enforced as part of new state entities after the final dissolution
is over' (2001: 122).

My argument that seemingly apolitical sites of remembering
Yugoslavia have political implications, even if unacknowledged
or unsayable in the dominant regime of representation, is further
strengthened by an explicit shift towards politicising Yugoslav
memories in recent years. One example is protest against the material erasure of socialist history, exemplified by the 'History Lesson'
intervention and the murals and graffiti by the Kurs collective,
which memorialise Yugoslavia's battle against fascism and its ideals of justice and egalitarianism.[15] Also, the post-Yugoslav music
scene has seen a rise in self-organised choirs which perform old
songs about anti-fascism and worker solidarity, popular in Yugoslav
times, revisiting these issues in the context of neo-liberal precarity and nationalism. The choirs collaborate and perform across the
former Yugoslavia with a political message that overtly invokes the

legacy of socialism and expresses solidarity with marginalised social groups.[16] Similarly, some rock musicians, many of whom opposed the war and nationalist parties, have engaged in leftist political activism using music to spread their message. Mladi Antifašisti (Young Antifascists) music collective published a compilation of antifascist rock and roll, with the goal of reminding the younger generations of the legacy of Yugoslav anti-fascism since fascist thinking 'as the guardian of capitalism' has become internalised in post-Yugoslav societies (Jagatić 2013: n.p.). Finally, it is crucial to mention intensifying political protests by workers and students in virtually every post-Yugoslav state that invoke the rights to labour protection and free education, articulated in the ideological register inherited from socialist Yugoslavia.[17]

These examples of re-membering overtly refuse to give up the legacy of egalitarianism and solidarity not merely as Yugoslav but rather as European legacies, so as to intervene in hegemonic narratives about a neo-liberal EU as the only viable future for Balkan nations. We can therefore develop more hopeful parallels between Yugoslav and European legacies which can help us think about alternatives to the continuing ascendance of deregulated markets and financial capital, (neo)colonial policies and investment in Eurocentric narratives of identity. For instance, commenting on the surprisingly massive, cross-ethnic labour protests in Bosnia and Herzegovina in 2014, Marina Antić suggests that the country's status as the 'extremely subjugated periphery of global capital', masked as a process of Europeanisation, produces the starkest awareness of the inequalities underpinning the European discourse of democracy and belonging (Dragojević 2014: n.p.). Similarly, Igor Štiks implies that Bosnia and Herzegovina is not only the most obvious symptom of EU's imperialism which favours its 'deindustrialisation', 'debt slavery' and a 'weak state', but also that its self-organised plenums, 'actually impacting elected officials, putting participatory democracy in practice', show 'what Europe should be' (2014: n.p.).

In theory as well as practice, a vibrant example of thinking former Yugoslavia alongside with thinking Europe is the Subversive Festival in Zagreb, which has been taking place annually each May since 2008. While this popular festival is situated in the Balkans as the current periphery of European and global capital, it reinscribes this space via the historical legacy of Yugoslav socialism and the politics of Non-Alignment which can inspire conversations about alternatives on the continental level, turning the Balkans into a provisional 'centre' of left-oriented political philosophy, art and activism. The fortnight event includes a one-week film festival which features a wide variety of feature films and documentaries, both (post)Yugoslav and international, representing alternative, dissident and aesthetically experimental cinema, thematically consonant with the festival's annual topic. The other week is dedicated to a conference comprised of a diverse array of participants and discussion formats, including lectures, panel discussions, forums, interviews, collaborative workshops and seminars for university students.

The Subversive Festival has grown into one of the most prominent progressive events, gathering acclaimed intellectuals and activists such as Gayatri Spivak, Michael Hardt, Slavoj Žižek, Saskia Sassen, Antonio Negri, Bernard Stiegler and Vandana Shiva, among others. It has also 'served as a platform and network for progressive movements from all around the Balkans and Eastern Europe as well as a bridge between these movements and wider European and global actors' (*Subversive Festival* 2008–17: n.p.). All programmes are free and open to the general public with the exception of evening lectures and panels.[18] This likely affects the composition of the audience attending the evening events, possibly excluding the economically marginalised groups whose rights the conference ostensibly champions. Since I am interested in the general format and potential of the Subversive Festival in the context of my broader discussion of the EU, I have not researched the audience compositon beyond anecdotal observations at the 2015 Subversive Festival, where I noticed that many students as well as some rural and blue-collar workers attended evening lectures. In terms of walks of life, interests and politics, this is nonetheless a remarkably diverse festival, including a broad spectrum of different and sometimes opposing positions on the left, and addressing topics as various as local and global protests, environmental protection, feminist politics, LGBT rights, (neo)colonialism, the European Union crisis and the politics of Non-Alignment.

While each conference features a variety of themes and participants, it subsumes them under a broader umbrella topic, typically addressing pressing events of global concern. The selected current issue is brought into conversation with a significant historical event which the conference revisits and rethinks from the contemporary perspective. Thus, in 2010, given the intensifying crisis of capitalism, the conference theme was 'The Collapse of Neoliberalism and the Idea of Socialism Today'. Exploring the implications of contemporary socialism-inspired movements involved an interrogation of the failures of historical socialism across Eastern Europe, including, for instance, Yugoslav totalitarian tendencies exemplified by the Goli Otok camp for political prisoners, operational from 1949 to 1956. Inspired by the Arab Spring, the 2011 conference addressed the theme of decolonisation, analysing the contemporary emancipatory struggles alonsgside historic anticolonial movements. This conference also marked the fiftieth anniversary of the inaugural conference of the Non-Aligned Movement in Belgrade, which envisioned an anticolonial politics based on the solidarity of formerly oppressed peoples, seeking an alternative to the Cold War blocs and nuclear race. This gesture not only revisited the historical legacy of anticolonial alignments worldwide, but also reminded post-Yugoslavs of the crucial role that their country played in both founding this movement and promoting its goals. To mention a few more examples, the 2012 conference placed into conversation the US Occupy movement and anti-austerity protests across the EU and the Balkans, imagining possibilities for a new politics of the commons, both locally and globally. Finally, the 2014 conference addressed the (im)possibilities of empowerment and freedom (including the situation of undocumented migrants), in the information era marked by the technologies of surveillance and control.

Attending the eighth annual installment in 2015 provided me with an opportunity to observe closely both the conceptual and practical structure of the festival. While the festival was thematically dedicated to 'micropolitics and revolt' in the context of looming environmental and humanitarian disasters, and the necessity of forging alliances between struggles for climate and labour justice in Europe and globally, both the daily forums and evening events encompassed a number of recurrent and overlapping concerns. A prominent theme in the panels focusing on the post-Yugoslav space, in light of the seventieth anniversary of the victory over fascism, was the historical revisionism that aims to dismantle the Yugoslav antifascist ideology, considered through the lens of a renewed popularity of right-wing politics, struggle over LGBT rights and (im)possibility of supranational labour solidarity. For instance, the panel entitled 'Antifascism after All: Between Revisionism and Street Right' [*sic*] tackled the problems of historical erasure, centring not only on the anniversary of the annihilation of European Nazism but also on the, largely uncommemorated, sixtieth anniversary of the Bandung Conference, which marked an important step towards the Non-Aligned Movement. The panelists thus argued for revisiting the legacy of antifasicst as well as anticolonial politics as the only hope for the region. Simultaneously, they placed post-Yugoslav events in the broader context of flourishing right-wing politics across the European Union, drawing a parallel between contemporary austerity measures and the 1930s economic crisis during which the interests of big capital and right-wing parties coincided in warding off the threat of leftist revolt.

The conference also hosted a variety of forums for thinking and forging practical alliances among left movements in the Balkans, which involved representatives of student, worker, trade union and environmental associations. Here again the Yugoslav legacy was seen as helpful in terms of overcoming separate nationalisms (portrayed as top-down discourses, employed to dispossess the majority) because it provided a language in-common, not through ethnic or cultural similarities but rather through a familiar ideological register inherited from the history of anti-capitalism. Simultaneously, however, the panelists subjected the Yugoslav political hierarchy and bureaucracy to scrutiny, proposing alternative models of organising, including non-hierarchical networks united through a common policy focusing on socio-economic issues, incomplete democratisation and historical revisionism. Finally, the Balkans were placed in a larger context of fighting for non-commodifiable commons in Europe, which necessitates both environmental preservation and labour justice. Here the interrogations of dominant EU economic models arrived from the broader periphery: representatives of various Balkan states as well as of Greece, Ireland and Spain, which bear the brunt of austerity measures and increasing inequalities. Panelists discussing post-Yugoslav microbattles for the commons argued for a re-invigoration of the Yugoslav socialist tradition of self-management and the notion of a public good. In the larger EU context, this fight for greater participatory management of resources and environmental protection was reflected in a series of panels on the proposed EU-US Transatlantic Trade and Investment Partnership (TTIP), demonstrating how further deregulation and corporate free trade would be impenetrable to democratic checks and balances. These panels were complemented by a workshop on the drafting of a European Citizens Initiative petition against TTIP.

I proffer the Subversive Festival as a model venue for rethinking the EU from the post-Yugoslav perspective not merely because of its overtly political content and its refreshingly thorough, meaningful interrogation of Yugoslav socialism, but also because the regional divisions mean that the Festival straddles the EU border, connecting inside and out, member states with non-member states. It mobilises the question of the border physically as well as philosophically, bringing into sharp focus the very liminality on which hegemonic EU narratives hinge. At the same time, the legacy of Yugoslav connections helps to highlight the artificiality of this border in alternative imaginations of community, projecting out to other European peripheries, as well outward to other continents, via the history of international Non-Alignment. Furthermore, this interdisciplinary festival straddles the line between art and activism, aesthetics and politics, which has been the guiding premise of this book, whereas in the context of my earlier discussion of Yugonostalgia, this gesture undermines the alleged binary between private (aesthetic) and collective (political) modes of remembering. In terms of narrowly regional concerns, it provides a safe intellectual as well as affective space for a responsible and comprehensive evaluation of the socialist past, which would transcend both its pragmatic dismissals by nationalist elites and nostalgic adulations by the dissatisfied citizenry. As Larisa Kurtović observes, preoccupied with surviving personal and collective war traumas, post-Yugoslav societies have not been able to meaningfully evaluate Yugoslav socialism and think about what 'can and should follow' this system (2010: 10).

In terms of the EU, the Yugoslav themes and modes of community that the Festival both mobilises and models could provide a way out of the double bind of neo-liberalism and identity politics, which, as I have argued throughout, provides the basis for both nationalist and multicultural imaginings of community. In this case, community is conceptualised through relationality, multicentrism and networking, as being-in-common in a struggle for the commons, which indirectly echoes the Yugoslav model of community, built around a politics of dissensus – antifascism, anti-capitalism and Non-Alignment.[19]

We can perhaps see Yugoslavia as an attempt to think community through a Derridean 'politics of friendship', even love, despite not having a common identity, all the more desired now that its successor states continue to rely on a politics of hatred and competitiveness (Perica and Velikonja 2012: 251). To paraphrase author Viktor Ivančić (2011), we should not think Yugoslavia is dead just because it has ceased to exist.

Notes

Introduction

1. See, for instance, Tzvetan Todorov on European identity:

   Europeans seem to have less national pride than Americans, thanks among other things to the strong presence of the past in their memory. They know that their nations were responsible in the past for catastrophic political decisions, the establishment of dictatorships, and the exploitation of subjugated peoples. That may explain why the self-critical reflex is more widespread among European countries than in American society. (13)

   Although he later criticises the EU for participating in NATO interventions around the world, he does not see this as a matter of national pride or imperial supremacy.
2. See Delanty, Uricchio, Pim den Boer et al., Hassan and Dadi and Sassatelli (2009).
3. Such collections examine literary and/or film narratives about migrancy in relation to Europe's (post)coloniality, but typically compile individual essays that focus on specific national contexts, rather than Europe as a whole. Examples include *Migrant Cartographies: New Cultural and Literary Spaces in Post-Colonial Europe* (ed. Ponzanesi and Merola 2005), *Racism Postcolonialism Europe* (ed. Huggan and Law 2010), *Migration and Literature in Contemporary Europe* (ed. Gebauer and Schwartz Lausten 2010), *European Cinema in Motion* (ed. Berghahn and Sternberg 2010), *Deconstructing Europe: Postcolonial Perspectives* (ed. Ponzanesi and Blaagaard 2013) and *Postcolonial Transitions in Europe* (ed. Ponzanesi and Colpani 2015). The exception to this rule are several cultural studies monographs, *Screening Strangers: Migration and Diaspora in Contemporary European Cinema* (Loshitzky 2010), *Tracking Europe: Mobility, Diaspora, and the Politics of Location* (Verstraete 2010) and *In Permanent*

Crisis: Ethnicity in Contemporary European Media and Cinema (Celik 2015). Finally, *Afroeurope@ns: Cultures and Identities* (ed. López 2008) argues for a comparative analysis of diasporic African literature in Europe in order to transcend national postcolonial frameworks.

4. These metaphors abound in critical analyses of the EU. Consider, for instance, Probst's claim that 'the idea "people of Europe" is still a phantom, and the EU is not a collective political body rooted in a political revolution or in a founding act, set up by the people of Europe' (2003: 52).

5. The narrative of integration and progress, where war and colonialism are relegated to the past, also underpins the House of European History, which opened in Brussels in 2017 under the auspices of the European Parliament.

6. See Passerini for an overview of these challenges.

7. See De Master and Le Roy, as well as Bunzl. Erik Jones (2007) argues that most contemporary European parties, regardless of political affiliation, are tough on immigration and immigrant crime and try to outperform one another in showing their determination to control it.

8. See Franz.

9. This move to a general Muslim identity is also an internal mode of diasporic self-identification and creation of community, comparable to the mobilisation of black identity as oppositional politics among disparate postcolonial communities in Britain. Tibi (2010) reflects on this ethnicisation of Muslim identity, arguing that its emergence is partly a reaction to Europe's own invocation of the spectre of Islamism.

10. Twentieth-century anti-Semitism constructs Jews as racial others, whereas earlier discourses of anti-Judaism treat Jews as primarily religious and cultural others. Also, while Bunzl commends the EU Monitoring Centre on Racism and Xenophobia for criticising Europe's perceived Christian essence and declaring a joint battle against anti-Semitism and Islamophobia, he argues that they assume a problematic continuity in anti-Semitic sentiment, which has undergone major shifts. Contemporary European anti-Semitism emerges primarily among disenfranchised Muslims who equate it with anti-Zionism. In this version, Jews are attacked not because they do not belong in Europe but precisely because they are seen as part of the 'European hegemony' that marginalises Muslims in Europe and Palestine alike (2005: 504).

11. See Asad.

12. Nonetheless, the politically variegated, evolving Europe of course is not a homogeneous or static political entity. For instance, in 2009, the Council of Europe criticised as racist and discriminatory the Swiss

referendum that imposed the ban on the construction of minarets. In 2010, the Council passed a resolution against the general ban on burqa (favoured by Belgium and France) on the basis of feminist and human rights.

13. Hansen explains:

> Of interest too in this context is that the EU territories and Spanish possessions, Melilla and, in particular, Ceuta, increasingly have come to serve as hubs in the Union's escalating fight against the so-called mounting problem of illegal immigration from Africa and elsewhere . . . the Spanish government, with support from the EU, has invested some 120 million dollars in the building of a radar system in the Strait of Gibraltar, which . . . is designed to serve as 'a sort of electronic wall across the strait' and so provide vital assistance in Spain's and the EU's fight against 'illegals' and 'clandestine asylum seekers'. (2002: 487)

14. On the former topic, see Mitchell Cohen. Morocco officially applied to join the then-European Community in 1987, but was rejected; the country has since (unsuccessfully) renewed its bid on the basis of potential Turkish entry into the EU.

15. Behr argues that EU's system of governance is not unique but rather 'embedded in the 19th century legacies of imperial rule from which it has inherited political ideas and practices'. The EU wants to become 'a new Empire, concentrating political power and wealth . . . extending its borders to the East and defining and enacting universal standards of statehood' (2007: 242).

16. El-Tayeb argues:

> The massive deindustrialisation of European urban centres since the 1980s especially affected migrant and minority communities . . . As a consequence, a working migrant population has been replaced with a multiethnic underclass that represents an example of what Étienne Balibar and others have called 'disposable populations,' considered superfluous from the moment they are born, with no realistic prospect of being integrated into the system. (2008: 664)

17. Postcolonial and other non-European residents and migrants are at a much higher risk of unemployment than European nationals. See Kogan and Franz for comparative studies of Western European states that have significant immigrant populations. When it comes to postcommunist states, Central European countries have generally fared

better than Balkan states and former Soviet republics, but everywhere there is a steep increase in income inequality and the working poor. See Bohle and Greskovits, as well as Orenstein.

18. Gill says that 'the restoration of capitalism has brought about a catastrophic decline in the standard of living and the quality of life for the vast majority' of Eastern Bloc populations, 'with women, children and the elderly particularly hard hit'. Declining birth rates and a dramatic drop in life expectancy have been compounded by 'a steep increase in murder, suicides, crime rates, and domestic violence, and a rapid increase in income inequality' (2003: 58).

19. See Marciniak.

20. See Boatcă (2012).

21. Colour-blindness, or a ban on ethnic and cultural data collection and consequent legislative action (as in France), can lead to an effacement of unofficial and official racist acts towards specific groups perceived as different. See Alec G. Hargreaves.

22. Cardús argues that 'we are experiencing a crisis in multicultural and multiethnic models that have proved politically unviable, or at least insufficient' (2010: 69). Instead of achieving fluid and layered pluralism in Europe, multiculturalism has been used to erect 'barriers to the integration of newcomers' and 'turn cultural origin into a closed community in which residents obtain the protection of the welfare state, but only on condition of maintaining their characteristic community in isolation' (65).

23. See Ruud Koopmans et al. for a comparative analysis of major European host societies' immigration policies, citizenship laws and cultural expectations for new residents.

24. I agree with Rancière's criticism of Nancy's conception of 'being-with' as primary or originary, as the always-already of social existence. In conceiving of community that takes place as the dissolving of existing political consensus, Rancière cautions that this is not the 'community of some kind of being-between, or an *interesse* that would impose its originarity on it, the originarity of a being-in-common based on the *esse* (being) of the *inter* (between) or the inter proper to the esse' (2004a: 137). To avoid replacing one originarity (of the subject) with another (of the between), I posit it as a re-inscription of the political symbolic order rather than as a basic condition of existence.

25. See Derrida [1997] (2000).

26. See Derrida's critiques of Blanchot's and Nancy's unreflexive sexism in theorising community in *The Politics of Friendship* [1994] (2005a) and *Rogues: Two Essays on Reason* [2003] (2005b).

Chapter 1

1. For a comprehensive overview, see Birringer's (2003) analysis of major directions in Europe's performance art in relation to articulating European identity and various hierarchies it harbours.
2. Černý defended his sculpture saying,

   > I am seriously very pro-European. It would be a great pity if Europe would not be able to take this as a bit of satire and irony. If we are strong as Europe it should be OK for one nation to make fun of other nations. (Charter 2009: n.p.)

3. As it is clear from the discussion of the Cultural Capital of Europe (as well as events such as the Eurovision Song Contest and the EU Prize for Literature), the EU of course works on nurturing a transnational, Europe-wide cultural sphere. However, *Entropa* suggests that national boundaries and mythologies are by no means dissolved or even undermined in such supranational imaginings; it chooses to foreground the former over the latter as if to hold up a mirror to the EU.
4. For more information and analysis of Futurist and Vorticist manifestoes, see Caws (2000).
5. A number of European Parliament members supported Černý's project, arguing that Europe must embrace politically incorrect art which can potentially hurt European feelings by employing cynicism and parody. EP members' statements are available online at <http://www.europarl. europa.eu/sides/getDoc.do?type=IMPRESS&reference=20090206STO 48713&format=XML&language=EN > (last accessed 23 August 17).
6. This video game can be accessed at <http://www.frontiers-game.com> (last accessed 23 August 17).
7. Schleuser also participated in a collaborative artistic publication, *Taking the Matter into Common Hands: Contemporary Art and Collaborative Practices* (ed. Billing et al. 2007), which reflects on the possibilities and advantages of collaborative artistic interventions rather than individual artistic work.
8. Fornäs discusses related invocations of European history by examining activist and artistic appropriations of the EU flag which hint at the Union's anti-democratic, former communist and/or fascist elements (2012: 143–4).
9. See <www.borderacademy.org> (last accessed 23 May 2013).
10. Another German performance art and activist collective, The Centre for Political Beauty, has invoked similar historical precedents in addressing the current migrant crisis. CPB have launched the 'Kindertransport' initiative for Syrian refugee children and moved the white crosses commemorating the victims of the Berlin Wall to the external EU borders,

in solidarity with future victims. The group, which employs art as a 'fifth state power', argues 'that the legacy of the Holocaust is rendered void by political apathy, the rejection of refugees and cowardice. It believes that Germany should not only learn from its History but also take action.' See <http://www.politicalbeauty.com> (last accessed 23 August 2017).

11. More information about micronations can be found at <http://www.micronations.net/> (last accessed 27 May 2015).

12. That the state as such is rooted in repressive power is implied in the Berlin Congress's 'Atomic Declaration of Dependence', where the delegates anarchically call for the state's and their own dissolution:

> The state is the manifestation of Kitsch. We hereby disassociate ourselves from your coffee-scented dog-breathed manifestations and unilaterally declare the dissolution of ourselves and the elimination of time through the timelessness of Kitsch. We find your bourgeois adoration of time and form repulsive and degenerate.

See <http://times.nskstate.com/the-other-congress-declaration/#more-464> (last accessed 23 August 2017).

13. The acceptance speech is broadcast in IRWIN's 'NSK Garda' presentation, available at <http://dictionaryofwar.org/concepts/NSK_GARDA> (last accessed 23 August 2017).

14. For Nancy, literature in this sense is a practice of writing and 'sharing of voices' that highlights our being-in-common beyond any figure of identity (1991: 77). Literature both articulates the plurality of singular voices and interrupts any mythical narrative that tends to 'ground' community and foreclose multiple possibilities of communities to come.

Chapter 2

1. Recent films dealing with urban segregation and racism have employed the registers of apocalypse, dystopia and action-adventure to suggest that these heavily policed death worlds are sites of civil war and camp-like imprisonment. See, for example, Pierre Morel's *District B13* (2004), set in a Parisian *banlieue*, Áron Gauder's *The District!* (2004), set in a poor neighbourhood in Budapest and, beyond Europe, Neill Blomkamp's *District 9* (2009) and *Elysium* (2013).

2. See Leban.

3. The 2014 film *Liquid Traces: The Left-To-Die Boat Case*, directed by Charles Heller and Lorenzo Pezzani, assembles the trajectory of the boat recorded by surveillance technologies to make the victims visible and

turn the sea into a 'witness for interrogation'. The film can be viewed at <https://vimeo.com/89790770> (last accessed 23 August 2017).

4. Lalami decided to write *Hope* after she read an article 'in the back pages of the French newspaper *Le Monde* about a group of migrants who lost their lives crossing the Strait of Gibraltar' (Montuori 2011: 20). As a politically engaged writer, Lalami regularly publishes cultural commentary and opinion pieces on migration in *The Nation*, *The New York Times*, *The Washington Post* and elsewhere. While her literary work is best known in the United States – in 2015 she was nominated for the Pulitzer Prize for Fiction – she has received increasing critical attention from international scholars working on migration narratives, Mediterranean studies, Anglophone Arab studies and gender criticism. In an essay about Binebine, Hakim Abderrezak calls the genre of writing about clandestine Mediterranean migration 'illiterature', a politically engaged tool which breaks the taboos of silence in both Europe, which often dehumanises illegal migration, and Morocco, 'which cultivates its image as a touristic haven' (2009: 462). An early example of 'illiterature', *Welcome to Paradise* was shortlisted for the Independent Fiction Prize in 2004, while another Binebine novel, *Horses of God*, was turned into a film and became Morocco's entry for Best Foreign Language Film at the 2013 Academy Awards.

5. See Gržinić (2008) for parallels between Europe's fascist past and contemporary neo-liberal creation of death worlds.

6. See Flesler and Suárez-Navaz.

7. Abderrezak notes that the rise of clandestine migration results from Spain's 'fortification' of the Mediterranean through its 1991 decision 'to end Moroccans' privileged status to enter Spain without a visa and the implementation in 1998 of the Sistema Integrado de Vigilencia Exterior (SIVE, Integrated System of External Vigilance)', a hi-tech surveillance system along Spanish coasts (2009: 461). On the other hand, to accommodate the surge in migration, Spain has signed agreements with Senegal, Gambia, Mali and Mauritania to offer limited-term work visas to workers from these countries (Montuori 2011: 2).

8. As Jonathan Smolin explains:

> The name of the phenomenon in Moroccan Arabic – hrig, which means 'burning' – implies not simply setting one's identification papers on fire before getting on the patera in a desperate attempt to avoid repatriation if arrested by the authorities. It also expresses a metaphorical burning of the past, a total rejection of the emigrant's life in Morocco. (2011: 75)

9. The unemployment rate for young Moroccans with a university degree is at 30 per cent. Recent research indicates that about 40 per cent of Moroccan migrants are university educated (Montuori 2011: 125–6).

10. In 2009, Crialese visited Lampedusa, which had by then become a major EU frontier, patrolled by the coastguards and littered with migrant boat wrecks. While there, 'a boat reached Lampedusa with over 70 people on board. Only five of them had survived. Among these only one female: Timnit T.' He cast Timnit in *Terraferma* so as to tell a story without using words like '"clandestine" or "emigrant" or "foreigner"' which, he observed, meant nothing to people like her (*Terraferma Presskit* 2011: 5).

11. See Scherer and Polleschi.

12. In 2013, an Italian fisherman saved forty-seven migrants but was prevented by coastguards from saving all the people who needed help ('Italy Immigration Law' 2013: n.p.). In 2007, two Tunisian fishing boat captains were arrested for rescuing forty-four migrants and bringing them to Lampedusa despite being blocked by Italian coastguards from entering the port. They were acquitted in 2011 (Frenzen 2011: n.p.).

13. See Friese (2012). Also, livelihood on Mediterranean islands in general is in crisis because of growing human populations which have upset the ecological biodiversity, aided by the perilous 'consequence[s] of global warming, sea level change, changes in precipitation, increased frequency and intensity of storms, soil erosion, and diminished soil fertility' (Past 2013: 58).

14. See Van't Klooster and Friese (2008).

15. Friese reports, 'tourists do not encounter the migrants. They are blocked at the sea, brought to a mole, separated and instantly brought to the Centre' (2008: 11). However, 'Lampedusa in Festival', an event that combines films, exhibitions and performance art to examine the politics of migration, has managed to bring these disparate groups on the island together as participants in a critical dialogue on the festival's themes (see Ianniciello).

16. It is, however, problematic that Crialese focuses most of his attention on a stereotypically vulnerable migrant – the selfless, pregnant woman – to invoke empathy in the movie. The film itself highlights the differential treatment of pregnant mothers as recipients of charity and single young men as disposable bodies that seem interchangeable.

17. The media abound in images of such encounters on Spanish, Greek and Italian beaches, but perhaps one of the most poignant images contrasts African migrants perched on Melilla's razorwire-fence border with oblivious golfers on the other side (see Kassam).

18. Like *Terraferma*, *Eternity and a Day* received numerous critical accolades and was screened widely on the festival circuit. It won the Palme d'Or and the Prize of the Ecumenical Jury at the 1998 Cannes film festival.

19. Employing a discourse of nationalist Hellenism in opposition to the diversity of the Ottoman Empire, the independent Greek state completed population exchanges and expulsions of non-Greek citizens such as Turks, Albanians and Macedonian Slavs in the first half of the twentieth century. This carries over into contemporary policies of withholding citizenship from non-Greek residents and imposing the Greek language, culture and Eastern Orthodox religion on ethnic minorities (for more information, see Koundoura). Hellenism has also been appropriated by the rest of Europe as both the continent's glorious past and future fulfilment of its Eurocentric trajectory; predictably, this idealisation has clashed with Europe's 'disappointment' with actual Greece.

20. See Frontex migratory routes map at <http://frontex.europa.eu/trends-and-routes/migratory-routes-map> (last accessed 23 August 2017).

21. Before the recent economic meltdown that fuelled EU's racist discourses on Greek 'corruption' and 'profligacy', Great Britain and the United States backed right-wing forces during the Greek Civil War and the Colonels' dictatorship under the pretext of battling communism.

22. The 12.5km anti-migrant fence along the Evros river, at the Greek-Turkish border, was built in 2012.

23. See Featherstone and Ifantis.

24. See Constantine Giannaris's films *A Place in the Sun* (1995), *From the Edge of the City* (1998) and *Hostage* (2005), Panos Karkanevatos's *Borderline* (1993), Stavros Ioannou's *Roadblocks* (2000) and Theodoros Nikolaidis' *Kalabush* (2002).

25. Horton claims that Angelopoulos 'exaggerates history' for the purposes of the film since Solomos was 'an avid collector of Greek words' and 'quite fluent in Greek' (1997a: 214–15). Nonetheless, each poet that Angelopoulos invokes in this and other films is *xenitis* in a way: George Seferis grew up in Turkey, Dyonisios Solomos lived in Italian-occupied Zakynthos and Alexander Cavafy in Alexandria. This portrays the Greek national body as fundamentally marked by dislocation and diaspora.

26. For instance, the December 2008 protests were named the 'New December' ('ta Nea Dekemvriana'), evoking the December 1944 battle between British-led troops and Greek left-wing guerrillas. Also, 'by the mere fact of mass participation, the December events evoke the famous student uprising against military rule in November 1973' (Kalyvas 2010: 352).

27. For instance, a Maltese couple have used their boat to search and rescue migrants in the Mediterranean (McKenzie); an Austrian hotel offers jobs and training to refugees (Johnstone); a German couple have launched a website where prospective hosts can be paired up with refugee room-mates (Sarhaddi Nelson).

Chapter 3

1. A number of more positive foundation narratives have also provided a basis for a common European identity, as is the case with any traditional nation. For studies that explore articulations of European identity and its foundation myths see Delanty, Padgen, Fligstein and Bottici and Challand.
2. Rigney offers a different historical trajectory, claiming that in the post-1989 period, Europe also had to incorporate the memory of Stalinist terror which presented a competing site of 'atrocity and victimhood' in addition to the Holocaust (2012: 613).
3. Arat-Koç argues that Europe has ignored mainstream racism and anti-Semitism and consequently 'never seriously confronted its colonial and racist history', by projecting racism onto the 'worst excesses' of Nazism (2010: 190).
4. Italy's apology to Libya came with a reparation deal through which access to oil and gas were to be exchanged for basic infrastructure building; Germany apologised for colonial-era massacres in Namibia without offering compensation; Great Britain apologised for the torture of Kenyan Mau Mau rebels and offered limited compensation to victims; and France acknowledged the brutal and unjust rule in Algeria.
5. See also the virtual project 'Museum with No Frontiers' (<http://www. museumwnf.org>, last accessed 23 August 2017), which alternates online exhibitions on the shared histories of Europe and the non-European world. Finally, see Basso Peressut et al. (2013) for a comprehensive analysis of European museums' engagement with history in light of both emigration and immigration.
6. See Brozgal and Kathryn N. Jones.
7. Brozgal hopes that this declassification 'augurs a new era of critical activity', especially since in the absence of archives, historical accounts which began emerging in the 1980s relied on 'FLN archives, eyewitness testimony, and coroner's records' to 'ground analyses often in contradiction with one another' (2014: 37). Sebbar's novel is a fictional representation of this process of piecing together an archive based solely on eyewitness accounts.

8. See House and MacMaster. Also, notable films on the event are documentaries *Le Silence du Fleuve* (1991) and *Une Journee Portee Disparue* (1992) and feature films *Mon Colonel* (2006), *La Trahison* (2005) and *17 Octobre 1961* (2005).

9. When Michael Levine's *Ratonnades d'Octobre* (1985) was published, 'some bookshops refused to display Levine's title' which resulted in a 'low-scale impact'. Didier Daeninckx reports that, when his novel *Meurtres pour Memoire* (1984) came out, 'everyone was incredulous, I had to provide proof and show my sources' (House and MacMaster 2006: 289).

10. The book has since garnered extensive popular and critical attention; today, Sebbar is considered a major Francophone writer and was awarded the Officer of the Order of Arts and Letters in 2016.

11. See Kathryn N. Jones and Mortimer.

12. See Vambe.

13. House and MacMaster note that this was fairly common practice: Algerians who offered eyewitness accounts of 17 October 'had not volunteered their wartime memories to their own children before then' and when they gave interviews, 'it was often in front of their children who then heard about their parents' stories for the first time' (2006: 271).

14. Also, the novel combines as valid various kinds of knowledge: Louis conducts his research at Parisian libraries, whereas Amel turns to oral accounts, absent from historical records.

15. Evaristo has won numerous fellowships and honours at home and abroad, and her work has garnered significant critical and popular attention. She is the recipient of various literary awards, and her books have been nominated 'A Notable Book of the Year' thirteen times in British newspapers. See the author's website (www.bevaristo.com) for more information.

16. For instance, see Habib (2008) for a discussion of African presence in Renaissance England. For an overview of other prominent publications and events, see Muñoz-Valdivieso (2009).

17. For a comprehensive study of Shakespearean references in *Soul Tourists*, see Muñoz-Valdivieso (2012).

18. Tournay-Theodotou also places the novel in the context of EU expansion and negotiations of diversity, noting that Evaristo's singular contribution in the context of black British writing has been to include the 'history of continental Europe' (2011: 108).

19. See Hooper. Nonetheless, the novel playfully evokes colonial travellers in referencing E. M. Forster's *A Passage to India* (1924) and Lawrence of Arabia.

20. Burkitt's (2007) reading of *The Emperor's Babe* as a postcolonial post-epic offers productive insights into *Soul Tourists*' re-imagining of the epic genre.

21. While *Travelling with Djinns* is not as acclaimed as the previous two novels discussed in this chapter, Mahjoub's work in general has been translated into a number of languages and awarded several prizes, including *The Guardian* African Short Story Prize, the St Malo Prix de l'Astrolabe and the Mario Vargas Llosa Premio NH de Relatos.

22. Mahjoub is also difficult to categorise as a minority writer within the context of a specific nation. He writes in English, but has lived in the Sudan, Great Britain, Denmark and Spain.

23. According to Steiner, in Mahjoub, 'The space between languages then could become the site of alternative subjectivities, for transformation and self-translation, because it resists the limitations imposed by possessive communities of belonging', but forays into cultural translation also 'assert the limitations of relation, especially under conditions of disorientation, physical violence and the impact of regimes of power' (2008: 50).

Chapter 4

1. For instance, the figure of a 'Polish plumber', representing the threat of cheap labour from Eastern Europe that would 'steal' Western European jobs, was exploited during 2005 EU Constitution referendum debates in France. Also, see Korte et al. (2010) for an overview of Orientalist attitudes towards Eastern Europe and their current permutations in the context of European integration.

2. Aside from texts discussed in this chapter, see novels such as Abdulrazak Gurnah's *By the Sea* (2001) and Tomáš Zmeškal's *Biography of a Black and White Lamb* (2009); plays such as David Edgar's *Pentecost* (1994), Ai Kwei-Armah *Let There Be Love* (2008), Richard Bean's *England People Very Nice* (2009); films such as Damjan Kozole's *Spare Parts* (2003), Ken Loach's *It's a Free World . . .* (2007) and Želimir Žilnik's documentaries *Fortress Europe* (2000) and *Logbook Serbistan* (2015).

3. For examples of postcolonial scholarship that has engaged postcommunist studies, see Chioni Moore (2001) and Spivak (2006). Recent journal issues aimed at fostering a broader dialogue between postcolonial and postcommunist studies suggest that this exchange might intensify. See 'On Communism, Colonialism, and East-Central Europe', *Journal of Postcolonial Writing* (2012) and 'Consensual Empires', *Journal of Narrative Theory* (2014).

4. See Dokuzović and Freudmann; Marjanović.

5. While much scholarship addresses the discursive constructions of Eastern Europe as a whole, the wars in former Yugoslavia and the concomitant 'Balkanist' discourse have inspired studies that deconstruct derogatory representations of the Balkans. See Hammond, Wolff, Melegh, Böröcz, Boatcă, Marciniak, Zarycki, Todorova (1997), Goldsworthy, Bjelić and Savić, Blagojević, Kovačević (2008) and Korte et al.

6. Nonetheless, discriminatory language towards Eastern Europeans is often racialised: their whiteness is 'dirty', unkempt and poorly dressed, replicating, as Veličković notes, 'class disgust which operates on poor white working-class bodies', as in the case of 'chavism' in Great Britain (2010: 197).

7. Phillips complains that black British writers, 'only notable for the colour of our skins', have been expected to produce the 'drama of race', 'where the drama that is demanded of East Europeans is the drama of difference – a drama rooted in the distinction between rich and poor' (2009: 146). His play *You Think You Know Me but You Don't* (2005) betrays such expectations as its protagonist Victor, a Romanian immigrant, addresses his audience in an exceptionally lyrical and erudite monologue, which is not stereotypically expected from someone working a series of low-paid jobs in Great Britain.

8. Pirker argues that, despite receiving university stipends from the Soviet Union, African intellectuals often accepted these offers for practical rather than ideological reasons (2010: 133).

9. Phillips is best known for a series of four crime novels featuring black journalist Sam Dean, which have earned more popular attention than *A Shadow of Myself* (see López Rodríguez). Also, he has explored the history of multicultural Britain in several non-fiction collections, *Windrush: The Irresistible Rise of Multi-Racial Britain* (1998) and *London Crossings: A Biography of Black Britain* (2001). Nonetheless, *A Shadow* has attracted critical attention because of its depth of political awareness and incisive analysis of social and political changes in Europe following the Cold War.

10. Notable representatives of this genre are Jonathan Franzen, *The Corrections* (2001), John Beckman, *The Winter Zoo* (2002), Arthur Phillips, *Prague* (2003), Charlotte Hobson, *Black Earth City: When Russia Ran Wild (And So Did We)* (2003), Wendell Steavenson, *Stories I Stole* (2004), Tom Bissell, *God Lives in St. Petersburg: And Other Stories* (2005), Gary Shteyngart, *Absurdistan* (2006) and A. D. Miller's *Snowdrops* (2011).

11. Reflecting on intensifying racism against non-whites in postcommunist Russia, Evaristo reminds that Langston Hughes similarly 'experienced

[Soviet] Moscow as a place of welcome'. In *I Wonder as I Wander* (1956), Hughes says:

> On a crowded bus, nine times out of ten, some Russian would say, 'Negrochanski Tovarish – Negro comrade – take my seat!' On the streets queuing up for newspapers, for cigarettes, or soft drinks, often folks in the line would say, 'Let the Negro comrade go forward.' (Evaristo 2008: 6)

12. I use this term because it is Ugrešić's preferred, if intentionally humorous, label in the EU literary market of enforced ethnic self-definitions. She suggests this term as an (im)possible identity marker (see Kovačević 2007).

13. This shift has mirrored Ugrešić's increasing relevance as a globally significant author: once the first woman to win the prestigious NIN Literary Award in former Yugoslavia in 1988, Ugrešić became the Laureate of the Neustadt International Prize for Literature in 2016.

14. Since the 1990s wars in former Yugoslavia, which came to represent the Balkans as a whole, much has been written about the derogatory 'Balkanist' discourse, which relies on stereotypes of intolerance, underdevelopment and savagery. See note 5 in this chapter.

15. See also Korljan.

16. See Kornetis and Pourgouris.

17. See Kalyvas.

18. See, for instance, Jürgen Habermas and Jacques Derrida's (2003) joint declaration on the Iraq war. They argue that a united Europe should balance out US hegemony and optimistically look to the future of Europe in which its best legacies will flourish: commitment to democracy, separation of church and state, social equality and distrust of force and technology. This declaration also discusses Europe's self-destruction in the two world wars and the crimes of European colonialism, but suggests that Europe has overcome its violent past: it congratulates Europe on peaceful mass protests against the Iraq war, which resounded around the world.

19. Žižek contrasts these 'impotent' riots, implicitly working class, with the (similarly violent) 2010 British student demonstrations, implicitly middle class, and praises students for sending a 'clear' message that they 'reject the proposed reforms to higher education' (2014: 121).

20. Dean furthers a sharp but sympathetic critique of protests which emphasise networking and horizontality over centralisation and hierarchy for resembling the adaptability of 'communicative capitalism' (2012: 66). Nonetheless, she considers the Occupy movement valuable in that it articulated the antagonism of the 99 per cent against the wealthy 1 per cent, exhibited commitment to the 'new, demanding, and

unceasing practice of occupation' and provided a vanguard for mobilising collective opposition to inequality (217).

21. See 'Greek bank staff strike over deaths' (2010).

Chapter 5

1. For a comprehensive overview, see Perica and Velikonja, Kurtović and Petrović.

2. See Mazzucchelli and Longinović.

3. This play addresses nationalist, patriarchal and linguistic violence in times of peace as well as war. Selma Spahić's play *Hipermnezija* (2011) similarly disenchants Yugoslav multiculturalism by featuring childhood memories of Serbs, Albanians, Bosniacs and others about both the war violence and the ethnic, gender and sexual discrimination that preceded it.

4. See <www.nasa-jugoslavija.org> (last accessed 19 August 2017).

5. See Ames, Stojanov, Ehl, Tempelman and Mencinger.

6. See Accetto.

7. See Lane.

8. In my discussion, I explicitly privilege the interpretations of Yugoslavia as a singular entity, which contained the elements of both capitalist and communist regimes, but which cannot be conceptually reduced to either one. If it had been just like any other capitalist country, its memory would not need to be so aggressively expurgated in the wake of its disappearance and onset of real existing capitalism. Had it been just like any other socialist country, it would be difficult to explain away strong ties to the capitalist bloc, broad exposure to capitalist consumer goods and culture, liberal policies on travel to capitalist countries or tolerance of private enterprise. Tellingly, the 2011 Brussels exhibition 'Thinking Yugoslavia 20 Years Later' explores and addresses these three common interpretations of the Yugoslav project: socialist, capitalist and singular.

9. The exhibition organisers hope that the older visitors will be reminded of a 'happy time' in their lives; the younger visitors will learn about their (grand)parents' lives; and tourists will become acquainted with the 'most intriguing' period in our recent history. See <http://www.ziveozivot.com/index.php/zivi-zivot/posetioci> (last accessed 24 August 2017).

10. See 'Vremeplov kroz svakodnevicu druge Jugoslavije' (2013).

11. This type of cross-Yugoslav, socialist solidarity was supposed to transcend narrowly ethnic, religious and linguistic identification. Perica remarks that brotherhood and unity was 'Yugoslav civil religion' (2004: 100).

12. Readers' comments on 'Vremeplov kroz svakodnevicu druge Jugo-slavije' (2013) illustrate this, as well as supplement the sampling of the guestbook entries included in this article. To the question 'Why was life good back then?', the responses included 'Because the music was good'; 'Because people were happier and more sincere'; and 'Because we were Tito's pioneers'.

13. In 2011, a group of activists, art historians and artists staged a 'History Lesson' on the occasion of the removal of the 1964 plaque from Dom Omladine Beograda (Belgrade House of Youth), which attributed the opening of this cultural centre to Socialist Yugoslavia's authorities and Tito's support. It was replaced with a plaque which attributes its recent reconstruction to Belgrade city authorities and the US government. Commenting on the erasure of socialist history, the group remarked that Yugoslavia was a state full of contradictions and betrayed expecta-tions that devolved into bloodshed, but that 'among the people . . . there was that spirit of togetherness and brotherhood, in which they sincerely believed . . . [Yugoslavia] was our chance' (Petrović 2012: 110).

14. Zinaic is sceptical about the effectiveness of cyber projects that memo-rialise Yugoslavia since only about half of Serbia's households, for instance, have Internet access (2015: 214).

15. The Kurs collective say that their artistic work, which draws on archi-val images and tropes, sheds a critical perspective on contemporary 'historical revisionism, precarity, and flexible employment policies'. See <http://www.udruzenjekurs.org> (last accessed 24 August 2017).

16. See Petrović, Perica and Velikonja.

17. See Horvat and Štiks.

18. The price of a ticket for a 2015 evening lecture was the local equivalent of three euros and thirty cents (with discounted rates for students), which approximates the price of a movie theatre ticket in Zagreb.

19. Karamanić (2015) develops this argument in his lecture.

Bibliography

Abderrezak, Hakim (2009), 'Burning the sea: clandestine migration across the Strait of Gibraltar in Francophone Moroccan "illiterature"', *Contemporary French and Francophone Studies*, 13:4: 461–9.

Accetto, Matej (2007), 'On law and politics in the federal balance: lessons from Yugoslavia', *Review of Central and East European Law*, 32: 191–231.

Adamovsky, Ezequiel (2005), 'Euro-Orientalism and the making of the concept of Eastern Europe in France, 1810–1880', *The Journal of Modern History*, 77: 591–628.

Agamben, Giorgio [1990] (1993), *The Coming Community*, Minneapolis: University of Minnesota Press.

Agamben, Giorgio [2003] (2005), *State of Exception*, Chicago: University of Chicago Press.

Ahluwalia, Pal (2004), 'Empire or imperialism: implications for a "new" politics of resistance', *Social Identities: Journal for the Study of Race, Nation and Culture*, 10:5: 629–45.

Ahmed, Sara (2000), *Strange Encounters: Embodied Others in Post-Coloniality*, New York: Routledge.

Ahmed, Sara (2004), *The Cultural Politics of Emotion*, New York: Routledge.

Ahmed, Sara (2010), *The Promise of Happiness*, Durham, NC: Duke University Press.

Alami, Ahmed (2012), '"Illegal" crossing, historical memory and postcolonial agency in Laila Lalami's *Hope and Other Dangerous Pursuits*', *The Journal of North African Studies*, 17:1: 143–56.

Ames, Paul (2012), 'The Balkanisation of Europe?', *Global Post*, 16 October, <https://www.pri.org/stories/2012-10-16/balkanization-europe> (last accessed 1 May 2016).

Amine, Laila (2012), 'Double exposure: the family album and alternate memories in Leila Sebbar's *The Seine was Red*', *Culture, Theory and Critique*, 53:2: 181–98.

Anderson, Perry (2009), *The New Old World*, New York: Verso.

Andrić, Iris, Vladimir Arsenijević and Đorđe Matić (eds) (2004), *Leksikon YU Mitologije*, Belgrade: Rende.

Arat-Koç, Sedef (2010), 'Contesting or affirming "Europe"? European enlargement, aspirations for "Europeanness" and new identities in the margins of Europe', *Journal of Contemporary European Studies*, 18:2: 181–91.

Arns, Inke (1996), 'Mobile states | shifting borders | moving entities: The Slovenian artists' collective Neue Slowenische Kunst', *Agora8: ABrt Documents* <http://agora8.org/InkeArns_MobileStates/> (last accessed 12 March 2017).

Asad, Talal (2000), 'Muslims and European identity: can Europe represent Islam?', in Anthony Pagden (ed.), *The Idea of Europe: From Antiquity to the European Union*, Cambridge: Cambridge University Press, pp. 209–28.

Balibar, Étienne (2003a), 'Europe: an "unimagined" frontier of democracy', *diacritics* 33:3/4: 36–44.

Balibar, Étienne (2003b), *We the People of Europe?: Reflections on Transnational* Citizenship, Princeton: Princeton University Press.

Balibar, Étienne (2010), 'Europe: final crisis? some theses', *Theory and Event*, 13:2, <https://muse.jhu.edu/article/384016> (last accessed 5 March 2015).

Balibar, Étienne (2016), 'Europe at the limits', *Interventions: International Journal of Postcolonial Studies*, 18:2: 165–71.

Banerjee, Subhabrata Bobby (2008), 'Necrocapitalism', *Organisation Studies*, 29:12: 1541–63.

Banton, Robyn (2014), 'Dire, voir, savoir: remembering the paris massacre in Leila Sebbar's *La Seine était Rouge*', *Contemporary French and Francophone Studies*, 18:4: 360–8.

Basso Peressut, Luca, et al. (eds) (2013), *European Museums in the 21st Century*, Milano: Politecnico di Milano.

Bataille, Georges [1967] (1991), *The Accursed Share: An Essay on General Economy*, vol. 1, New York: Zone Books.

Behr, Hartmut (2007), 'The European Union in the legacies of imperial rule? EU accession politics viewed from a historical comparative perspective', *European Journal of International Relations*, 13:2: 239–62.

Benhabib, Seyla (2002), *The Claims of Culture: Equality and Diversity in the Global Era*, Princeton: Princeton University Press.

Benjamin, Walter [1921] (1986), 'Critique of violence', in Walter Benjamin, *Reflections: Essays, Aphorisms, Autobiographical Writings*, ed. Peter Demetz, New York: Schocken, pp. 277–300.

Benjamin, Walter [1982] (2002), *The Arcades Project*, Cambridge, MA: Belknap Press.

Berghahn, Daniela, and Claudia Sternberg (eds) (2010), *European Cinema in Motion: Migrant and Diasporic Film in Contemporary Europe*, New York: Palgrave Macmillan.

Bhambra, Gurminder (2016), 'Whither Europe? postcolonial versus neo-colonial cosmopolitanism', *Interventions: International Journal of Postcolonial Studies*, 18:2: 187–202.

Bilefsky, Dan (2009), 'With sharp satire, enfant terrible challenges Czech identity', *The New York Times*, 5 September: A8.

Billing, Johanna, Maria Lind and Lars Nilsson (eds) (2007), *Taking the Matter into Common Hands: Contemporary Art and Collaborative Practices*, London: Black Dog Publishing.

Binebine, Mahi (1999) (English trans. 2003), *Welcome to Paradise*, London and New York: Granta.

Birringer, Johannes (1996), 'The utopia of postutopia', *Theatre Topics*, 6:2: 143–66.

Birringer, Johannes (2003), 'A new Europe', *Performing Arts Journal*, 75: 26–41.

Bjelić, Dušan, and Obrad Savić (eds) (2002), *Balkan as Metaphor: Between Globalisation and Fragmentation*, Cambridge, MA: MIT Press.

Blagojević, Marina (2009), *Knowledge Production at the Semiperiphery: A Gender Perspective*, Belgrade: Institut za kriminološka i sociološka istraživanja.

Blanchot, Maurice [1983] (1988), *The Unavowable Community*, Barrytown, NY: Station Hill Press.

Boatcă, Manuela (2012), 'The Quasi-Europes: world regions in light of the imperial difference', in T. E. Reifer (ed.), *Global Crises and the Challenges of the 21st Century*, Boulder: Paradigm Publishers, pp. 132–53.

Boatcă, Manuela (2013), 'Multiple Europes and the politics of difference within', *The Worlds & Knowledges Otherwise Project*, 3:3, <https:// globalstudies.trinity.duke.edu/wp-content/themes/cgsh/materials/WKO/ v3d3_Boatca2.pdf> (last accessed 5 August 2017).

Bohle, Dorothee, and Béla Greskovits (2009), 'East-Central Europe's quandary', *Journal of Democracy*, 20:4: 50–63.

Böröcz, József (2006), 'Goodness is elsewhere: the rule of European difference', *Comparative Studies in Society and History*, 48:1: 110–38.

Bottici, Chiara, and Benoit Challand (2013), *Imagining Europe: Myth, Memory and Identity*, Cambridge: Cambridge University Press.

Boym, Svetlana (2002), *The Future of Nostalgia*, New York: Basic.

Brancato, Sabrina (2009), 'From routes to roots: the emergence of Afro-Italian literature', in Marta Sofía López (ed.), *Afroeurope@ns: Cultures and Identities*, Newcastle upon Tyne: Cambridge Scholars Publishing, pp. 52–64.

Bratsis, Peter (2010), 'Legitimation crisis and the Greek explosion', *International Journal of Urban and Regional Research*, 34:1: 190–6.

Brozgal, Lia (2014), 'In the absence of the archive (Paris, October 17, 1961)', *South Central Review*, 31:1: 34–54.

Buchowski, Michał (2006), 'The spectre of Orientalism in Europe: from exotic other to stigmatised brother', *Anthropological Quarterly*, 79:3: 463–82.

Bunzl, Matti (2005), 'Between anti-Semitism and Islamophobia: some thoughts on the new Europe', *American Ethnologist*, 32:4: 499–508.

Burkitt, Katharine (2007), 'Imperial reflections: the post-colonial verse novel as post-epic', in Lorna Hardwick and Carol Gillespie (eds), *Classics in Post-Colonial Worlds*, Oxford: Oxford University Press, 157–69.

Butler, Judith (2004), *Precarious Life: The Powers of Mourning and Violence*, New York: Verso.

Cafruny, Alan W., and Magnus Ryner (eds) (2003), *A Ruined Fortress? Neoliberal Hegemony and Transformation in Europe*, Lanham, MD: Rowman & Littlefield.

Carbacos Traseira, María (2012), 'A straight elliptical wobble: Afro-European transculturalism, and Jamal Mahjoub's *Travelling with Djinns*', in Russell West-Pavlov et al. (eds), *Border-Crossings: Narrative and Demarcation in Postcolonial Literatures and Media*, Heidelberg: Universitatsverlag Winter, pp. 187–200.

Cardús, Salvador (2010), 'New ways of thinking about identity in Europe', in Roland Hsu (ed.), *Ethnic Europe: Mobility, Identity, and Conflict in a Globalised World*, Stanford: Stanford University Press, pp. 63–83.

Caws, Mary Anne (2000), *Manifesto: A Century of Isms*, Lincoln: University of Nebraska Press.

Celik, Ipek (2015), *In Permanent Crisis: Ethnicity in Contemporary Media and Cinema*, Ann Arbor: University of Michigan Press.

Černý, David (2010), *Personal Website*, <http://www.davidcerny.cz/start.html> (last accessed 20 February 2013).

Cervinkova, Hana (2012), 'Postcolonialism, postsocialism, and the anthropology of East-Central Europe', *Journal of Postcolonial Writing*, 48:2: 155–63.

Chari, Sharad, and Katherine Verdery (2009), 'Thinking between the posts: postcolonialism, postsocialism, and ethnography after the Cold War', *Comparative Studies in Society and History*, 51:1: 6–34.

Charter, David (2009), 'David Černý Says Hoax EU Sculpture Inspired by Monty Python', *Times Online*, 14 January, < http://www.timesonline.co.uk/tol/ news/world/europe/ article5518579.ece> (last accessed 12 February 2013).

Chebel d'Appollonia, Ariane (2002), 'European nationalism and European Union', in Anthony Padgen (ed.), *The Idea of Europe: From Antiquity to the European Union*, Cambridge: Cambridge University Press, pp. 171–91.

Cheliotis, Leonidas (2013), 'Behind the veil of philoxenia: the politics of immigration detention in Greece', *European Journal of Criminology*, 10:6: 725–45.

Chioni Moore, David (2001), 'Is the post- in postcolonial the post- in post-Soviet? Toward a global postcolonial critique', *PMLA*, 116:1: 111–28.

Chow, Rey (2002), *The Protestant Ethnic and the Spirit of Capitalism*, New York: Columbia University Press.

Cohen, Brianne (2012), *Contested Collectivities: Europe Reimagined by Contemporary Artists*, dissertation, University of Pittsburgh.

Cohen, Mitchell (2014), 'L'Étranger: "The French Intifada," by Andrew Hussey', *The New York Times*, 27 June, < https://www.nytimes.com/2014/06/29/books/review/the-french-intifada-by-andrew-hussey.html?mcubz=3> (last accessed 30 May 2017).

Cooper, Robert (2001), 'The next empire', *Prospect* (October): 22–6.

Croes, Rob (2008), 'Imaginary Americas in Europe's public space', in William Uricchio (ed.), *We Europeans? Media, Representations, Identities*, Chicago: Intellect Books, pp. 23–43.

Dean, Jodi (2012), *The Communist Horizon*, New York: Verso.

Debord, Guy [1967] (1995), *The Society of the Spectacle*, New York: Zone Books.

Delanty, Gerard (1995), *Inventing Europe: Idea, Identity, Reality*, New York: St. Martin's.

Deleuze, Gilles, and Felix Guattari (1996), *What is Philosophy?*, New York: Columbia University Press.

De Master, Sara, and Michael K. Le Roy (2000), 'Xenophobia and the European Union', *Comparative Politics*, 32:4: 419–36.

Derrida, Jacques [1978] (1990), 'Violence and metaphysics: on the thought of Emmanuel Levinas', in Jacques Derrida, *Writing and Difference*, New York: Routledge, pp. 79–153.

Derrida, Jacques [1997] (2000), *Of Hospitality*, Stanford: Stanford University Press.

Derrida, Jacques [1994] (2005a), *The Politics of Friendship*, New York: Verso.

Derrida, Jacques [2003] (2005b), *Rogues: Two Essays on Reason*, Stanford: Stanford University Press.

Derrida, Jacques, [1993] (2006), *Spectres of Marx: The State of the Debt, the Work of Mourning and the New International*, New York: Routledge classics.

Dokuzović, Lina, and Eduard Freudmann (2011), 'Fortified knowledge: from supranational governance to translocal resistance', *The EU between Free Market and Fascism: A Reader*, Ultrainput, 3 May: 16–40, <www.ultrainput.com> (last accessed 4 June 2012).

Dotson-Renta, Lara (2012), *Immigration, Popular Culture, and the Re-Routing of European Muslim Identity*, New York: Palgrave Macmillan.

Doyle, Laura (2014), 'Inter-imperiality: dialectics in a postcolonial world history', *Interventions: International Journal of Postcolonial* Studies, 16:2: 159–96.

Dragojević, Rade (2014), 'Marina Antić: emancipacijski potencijal Principova čina traje do danas', *Novosti*, 6 July, <http://arhiva.portalnovosti.com/2014/07/marina-antic-emancipacijski-potencijal-principova-cina-traje-do-danas> (last accessed 30 June 2016).

Drakulić, Slavenka (2009), 'Grand coup de toilette', *The Guardian*, 18 January, <http://www.guardian.co.uk/commentisfree/2009/jan/18/eu-politics-bulgaria-italy> (last accessed 13 February 2012).

Ehl, Martin (2013), 'The EU will end up like Yugoslavia and other Slovenian reflections', *Transitions*, 2 July, <http://www.tol.org/client/article/23845-the-eu-will-end-up-like-yugoslavia-and-other-slovenian-reflections.html?print> (last accessed 1 May 2016).

El-Tayeb, Fatima (2008), '"The birth of a European public"': migration, postnationality, and race in the uniting of Europe', *American Quarterly*, 60:3: 649–70.

El-Tayeb, Fatima (2011), 'The forces of creolisation: colourblindness and visible minorities in the new Europe', in Françoise Lionnet and Shu-Mei Shih (eds), *The Creolisation of Theory*, Durham, NC: Duke University Press, pp. 226–52.

Erlanger, Steven (2010), 'Racial tinge stains world cup exit in France', *The New York Times*, 23 June, < http://www.nytimes.com/2010/06/24/world/europe/24france.html?mcubz=3> (last accessed 13 February 2017).

Eternity and a Day (1998), film, directed by Theo Angelopoulos. USA: New Yorker Video, 1999.

Étienne Balibar and Antonio Negri on the Constitution of Europe: Notes from a Seminar in Rome (2004), trans. Arianna Bove, <http://www.generation-online.org/p/fpbalibar3.htm> (last accessed 21 August 2017).

'European conscience and totalitarianism' (2009), *European Parliament*, 2 April, <http://www.europarl.europa.eu/sides/getDoc.do?pubRef=-//EP//TEXT+TA+P6-TA-2009-0213+0+DOC+XML+V0//EN> (last accessed 14 May 2017).

Evaristo, Bernardine (2005), *Soul Tourists*, New York: Penguin.

Evaristo, Bernardine (2008), 'CSI Europe', *Wasafiri*, 23:4: 2–7.

Fanon, Frantz [1952] (1967), *Black Skin, White Masks*, New York: Grove Press.

Featherstone, Kevin, and Kostas Ifantis (1996), *Greece in a Changing Europe: Between European Integration and Balkan Disintegration?*, Manchester: Manchester University Press.

Feffer, John (2015), 'The European Union may be on the verge of collapse', *TomDispatch*, 28 January, <http://www.tomdispatch.com/blog/175948> (last accessed 20 March 2017).

Felski, Rita (2012), 'Introduction', *A New Europe?*, special issue of *New Literary History*, 43:4: v–xv.

Flesler, Daniela (2008), *The Return of the Moor: Spanish Responses to Contemporary Moroccan Immigration*, West Lafayette, IN: Purdue University Press.

Fligstein, Neil (2009), *Euroclash: The EU, European Identity, and the Future of Europe*, Oxford: Oxford University Press.

Fornäs, Johan (2008), 'Meanings of money: the Euro as a sign of value and of cultural identity', in William Uricchio (ed.), *We Europeans? Media, Representations, Identities*, Chicago: Intellect Books, pp. 123–41.

Fornäs, Johan (2012), *Signifying Europe*, Bristol: Intellect.

Franz, Barbara (2007): 'Europe's Muslim youth: an inquiry into the politics of discrimination, relative deprivation, and identity formation', *Mediterranean Quarterly*, 18:1: 89–112.

Frenzen, Niels (2011), 'Italian appeals court acquits 2 Tunisian fishing boat captains who rescued migrants in 2007', *Migrants at Sea Blog*, 29 September, <https:// migrantsatsea.org/2011/09/29/italian-appeals-court-acquits-2-tunisian-fishing-boat-captains-who-rescued-migrants-in-2007> (last accessed 12 May 2017).

Friese, Heidrun (2008), 'The limits of hospitality. Lampedusa, local perspectives and undocumented migration', presentation at Migration Working Group, EUI, Florence, Italy, 13 Feb, <https://www.eui.eu/Documents/RSCAS/Research/MWG/200708/MWG2008-02-13Friese.pdf> (last accessed 21 August 2017).

Friese, Heidrun (2012), 'Border economies: Lampedusa and the nascent migration industry', *Shima: The International Journal of Research into Island Cultures*, 6:2: 66–84.

Gardner, Anthony (2015), *Politically Unbecoming: Postsocialist Art against Democracy*, Cambridge, MA: MIT Press.

Gebauer, Mirjam, and Pia Schwartz Lausten (eds) (2010), *Migration and Literature in Contemporary Europe*, Bern: Peter Lang.

Gill, Stephen (2003), 'A neo-Gramscian approach to European integration', in Alan W. Cafruny and Magnus Ryner (eds), *A Ruined Fortress? Neoliberal Hegemony and Transformation of Europe*, Lanham, MD: Rowman & Littlefield, pp. 47–71.

Giorgi, Gabriel, and Karen Pinkus (2006), 'Zones of exception: biopolitical territories in the neoliberal era', *diacritics*, 36:2: 99–108.

Glissant, Édouard [1990] (1997), *Poetics of* Relation, Ann Arbor: Univesity of Michigan Press.

Goddard, Michael (2006), 'We are time: Laibach/nsk, retro-avant-gardism, and machinic repetition', *Angelaki: Journal of the Theoretical Humanities*, 2:1: 45–53.

Goldsworthy, Vesna (1998), *Inventing Ruritania: The Imperialism of the Imagination*, New Haven: Yale University Press.

Graebner, Seth (2005), 'Remembering 17 October 1961 and the novels of Rachid Boudjedra', *Research in African Literatures*, 36:4: 172–97.

Gram, Ole (2007), 'Escape artists: Germany, fortress Europe, and the situationist reinscripting of travel', *Cultural Critique*, 65 (Winter): 188–215.

'Greek bank staff strike over deaths' (2010), *Morning Star*, 6 May, <http://www.morningstaronline.co.uk/news/layout/set/print/content/view/full/90030> (last accessed 10 August 2013).

Grosz, Elizabeth (2008), *Chaos, Territory, Art: Deleuze and the Framing of the Earth*, New York: Columbia University Press.

Groys, Boris (2008), *Art Power*, Cambridge, MA: MIT Press.

Gržinić, Marina (2008), 'Euro-Slovenian necrocapitalism', *Transversal: Multilingual Webjournal*, <http://eipcp.net/transversal/0208/grzinic/en> (last accessed 15 May 2017).

Habermas, Jürgen, and Jacques Derrida (2003), 'Unsere Erneuerung. Nach dem Krieg: Die Wiedergeburt Europas' [Our renewal. after the war: the rebirth of Europe], *Frankfurter Allgemeine Zeitung*, 31 May, <http://www.faz.net/aktuell/feuilleton/ habermas-und-derrida-nach-dem-krieg-die-wiedergeburt-europas-1103893.html> (last accessed 21 August 2017).

Habib, Imtiaz (2008), *Black Lives in the English Archives, 1500–1677: Imprints of the Invisible*, New York: Routledge.

Hamilakis, Yannis (2002), 'The other "Parthenon": antiquity and national memory at Makronisos', *Journal of Modern Greek Studies*, 20:2: 307–38.

Hammond, Andrew (2004), *The Balkans and the West: Constructing the European Other, 1945–2003*, Aldershot: Ashgate.

Hansen, Peo (2002), 'European integration, european identity and the colonial connection', *European Journal of Social Theory*, 5:4: 483–98.

Hardt, Michael, and Antonio Negri (2000), *Empire*, Cambridge, MA: Harvard University Press.

Hardt, Michael, and Antonio Negri (2004), *Multitude: War and Democracy in the Age of Empire*, New York: Penguin.

Hardt, Michael, and Antonio Negri (2009), *Commonwealth*, Cambridge, MA: Harvard University Press.

Hargreaves, Alec C. (2010), 'Veiled truths: discourses of ethnicity in contemporary France', in Roland Hsu (ed.), *Ethnic Europe: Mobility, Identity, and Conflict in a Globalised World*, Stanford: Stanford University Press, pp. 83–104.

Hassan, Salah, and Iftikhar Dadi (eds) (2001), *Unpacking Europe: Towards a Critical Reading,* Rotterdam: NAi Publishers.

Hayden, Robert (2011), 'EUSlavija – zajednička klica raspada', *Vreme,* 23 November, <http://www.vreme.com/cms/view.php?id=1020021> (last accessed 21 August 2017).

Hiddleston, Jane (2005), *Reinventing Community: Identity and Difference in Late Twentieth-Century Philosophy and Literature in French,* Oxford: Legenda.

Hines, Nico, and David Charter (2009), 'Hoax EU sculpture by David Černý sparks diplomatic spat', *Times Online,* 14 January, <http://www.timeson-line.co.uk/tol/news/world/ europe/article5517736.ece> (last accessed 15 February 2013).

Hooper, Karen (2006), 'On the road: Bernardine Evaristo interviewed by Karen Hooper', *The Journal of Commonwealth Literature,* 41:1: 3–16.

Horton, Andrew (1997a), *The Films of Theo Angelopoulos: A Cinema of Contemplation,* Princeton: Princeton University Press.

Horton, Andrew (1997b), '"What do our souls seek?": an interview with Theo Angelopoulos', in Andrew Horton (ed.), *The Last Modernist: The Films of Theo Angelopoulos,* Westport: Praeger, pp. 96–110.

Horvat, Srećko, and Igor Štiks (eds) (2015), *Welcome to the Desert of Post-Socialism: Radical Politics after Yugoslavia,* New York: Verso.

House, Jim, and Neil MacMaster (2006), *Paris 1961: Algerians, State Terror, and Memory,* Oxford: Oxford University Press.

Huggan, Graham, and Ian Law (eds) (2010), *Racism Postcolonialism Europe,* Liverpool: Liverpool University Press.

Human Rights Watch (2011), 'The EU's dirty hands: Frontex involvement in ill-treatment of migrant detainees in Greece', 21 September, <https://www.hrw.org/sites/default/ files/reports/greece0911webwcover_0.pdf.> (last accessed 21 August 2017).

Ianniciello, Celeste (2013), '"Lampedusa in festival": the encounter with the other', *Roots & Routes: Research on Visual Cultures,* <http://www.roots-routes.org/?p=10133> (last accessed 21 August 2017).

Imre, Anikó (2014), 'Postcolonial media studies in postsocialist Europe', *boundary 2,* 41:1: 113–34.

'Italy immigration law prompts Lampedusa rescue row' (2013), *Euronews,* 5 October, <http://www.euronews.com/2013/10/05/italy-immigration-law-prompts-lampedusa-rescue-row> (last accessed 21 August 2017).

IRWIN (2008), 'NSK Garda', *Dictionary of War,* Multitude e.V. and Unfriendly Takeover Frankfurt/Munich/Graz/Berlin June 2006 – February 2007, <http://dictionaryofwar.org/concepts/NSK_GARDA> (last accessed 21 August 2017).

Ivančić, Viktor (2011), *Jugoslavija Živi Vječno – Dokumentarne Basne,* Beograd: Fabrika knjiga.

Jagatić, Dubravko (2013), 'Mladi antifašisti: fašizam je pas čuvar kapitalizma', *Novosti*, 20 October, <http://arhiva.portalnovosti.com/2013/10/mladi-antifasisti-fasizam-je-pas-cuvar-kapitalizma> (last accessed 21 August 2017).

Jameson, Fredric (1997), 'Theo Angelopoulos: the past as history, the future as form', in Andrew Horton (ed.), *The Last Modernist: The Films of Theo Angelopoulos*, Westport: Praeger, pp. 78–95.

Johnstone, Sarah (2015), 'The Vienna hotel where refugees welcome the guests', *The Guardian*, 21 May, <https://www.theguardian.com/travel/2015/may/21/vienna-madgas-hotel-staffed-asylum-seekers> (last accessed 21 August 2017).

Jones, Erik (2007), 'Populism in Europe', *SAIS Review*, 27:1: 37–47.

Jones, Kathryn N. (2009), 'Through the kaleidoscope: memories of 17 October 1961 in novels by Nancy Huston and Leila Sebbar', in Alison S. Fell (ed.), *French and Francophone Women Facing War/ Les femmes face à la guerre*, Bern: Peter Lang, pp. 211–27.

Judah, Tim (2009), 'Entering the Yugosphere', *The Economist*, 20 August, <http://www.economist.com/node/14258861> (last accessed 21 August 2017).

Judah, Tim (2012), 'Crisis could be causing the Balkanisation of Europe', *Bloomberg News*, 26 November, <https://www.bloomberg.com/amp/view/articles/2012-11-27/crisis-could-be-causing-the-balkanization-of-europe-tim-judah> (last accessed 21 August 2017).

Jusdanis, Gregory (1991), *Belated Modernity and Aesthetic Culture: Inventing National Culture*, Minneapolis: University of Minnesota Press.

Kalyvas, Andreas (2010), 'An anomaly? some reflections on the Greek December 2008', *Constellations*, 17:2: 351–65.

Karamanić, Slobodan (2015), 'Jugoslovenski revolucionarni subjektivitet: Narod ≠ Država', lecture, International Collaborative Project 'Beznacionalnost/NationLESS', The Museum of Yugoslav History, Belgrade, Serbia, 20 June.

Kassam, Ashifa (2014), 'African migrants look down on white-clad golfers in viral photo', *The Guardian*, 23 October, <https://www.theguardian.com/world/2014/oct/23/-sp-african-migrants-look-down-on-white-clad-golfers-in-viral-photo> (last accessed 21 August 2017).

Kiossev, Alexander (1999), 'Notes on self-colonising cultures', in Bojana Pejić and David Elliott (eds), *After the Wall: Art and Culture in Post-Communist Europe*, Stockholm: Moderna Museet, pp. 114–17.

Kogan, Irena (2006), 'Labour markets and economic incorporation among recent immigrants in Europe', *Social Forces*, 85:2: 697–721.

Koopmans, Ruud, Paul Statham, Marco Giugni and Florence Passy (eds) (2005), *Contested Citizenship: Immigration and Cultural Diversity in Europe*, Minneapolis: University of Minnesota Press.

Korljan, Josipa (2010), 'Izricanje neizrecivog – upisivanje traume u romanu *Ministarstvo boli* Dubravke Ugrešić', *Mogućnosti: Književnost, Umjetnost, Kulturni Problemi*, 1–3: 126–39.

Kornetis, Kostis (2010), 'No more heroes? Rejection and reverberation of the past in the 2008 events in Greece', *Journal of Modern Greek Studies*, 28:2: 173–97.

Korte, Barbara, et al. (eds) (2010), *Facing the East in the West: Images of Eastern Europe in British Literature, Film and Culture*, Amsterdam, New York: Rodopi.

Koundoura, Maria (2007), *The Greek Idea: The Formation of National and Transnational Identities*, London: Tauris Academic Studies.

Kovačević, Nataša (2007), 'Yugoslavia, an "almost forbidden word." Cultural policy in times of nationalism – interview with Dubravka Ugrešić', *Women and Performance: A Journal of Feminist Theory*, 17:3: 299–315.

Kovačević, Nataša (2008), *Narrating Post/Communism: Colonial Discourse and Europe's Borderline Civilisation*, New York: Routledge.

Kroes, Rob (2008), 'Imaginary Americas in Europe's public space', in William Uricchio (ed.), *We Europeans? Media, Representations, Identities*, Chicago: Intellect Books, pp. 23–34.

Kurtović, Larisa (2010), 'Istorije (bh) budućnosti: kako misliti postjugoslovenski postsocijalizam u Bosni i Hercegovini?', *Puls Demokratije*, 17 August, <http://pulsdemokratije. ba/index.php?id=1979&l=bs> (last accessed 13 August 2013).

Kwei-Armah, Ai (2009), *Plays 1: Elmina's Kitchen; Fix Up; Statement of Regret; Let There Be Love*, London: Methuen Drama.

Laclau, Ernesto (2007), *On Populist Reason*. New York: Verso.

Laibach (n.d.), Optimanet, <http://www.laibach.org> (last accessed 1 May 2016).

Laibach: A Film from Slovenia/Occupied Europe NATO Tour 1994–5 (2004), film, directed by Daniel Landin and Peter Vezjak, UK: EMI Music.

Lalami, Laila (2005), *Hope and Other Dangerous Pursuits*, Chapel Hill: Algonquin Books.

Lane, Charles (2012), 'Yugoslavia's lessons for Europe's disunion', *Washington Post*, 28 May, <https://www.washingtonpost.com/opinions/yugoslavias-lessons-for-europes-disunion/2012/05/28/gJQA2YmTxU_story.html?utm_term=.bf70632574f5> (last accessed 3 June 2015).

Lazarus, Neil (2012), 'Spectres haunting: postcolonialism and postcommunism', *Journal of Postcolonial Writing*, 48:2: 117–29.

Leban, Sebastjan (2011), 'EU-visione', *The EU between Free Market and Fascism: A Reader*, Ultrainput, 3 May: 6–15, <www.ultrainput.com> (last accessed 4 June 2012).

Levinas, Emmanuel [1974] (1998), *Otherwise than Being, Or, Beyond Essence,* Pittsburgh: Duquesne University Press.

Lewis, Jonathan (2012), 'Filling in the blanks: memories of 17 October 1961 in Leila Sebbar's *La Seine était rouge*', *Modern & Contemporary France,* 20:3: 307–22.

Lionnet, Françoise, and Shu-Mei Shih (2005), *Minor Transnationalism,* Durham, NC: Duke University Press.

Lionnet, Françoise, and Shu-Mei Shih (2011), *The Creolisation of Theory,* Durham, NC: Duke University Press.

Lives Lost in the Mediterranean Sea: Who Is Responsible? (2012), Report: Committee on Migrations, Refugees, and Displaced Persons, Strasbourg: Council of Europe Parliamentary Assembly.

Longinović, Tomislav (2001), 'Internet nation: the case of cyber Yugoslavia', *Sarai Reader,* 1, 31 January, <http://archive.sarai.net/files/original/16d3d8cee722275cc9d53f62734b4725. pdf> (last accessed 21 August 2017).

López, Marta Sofía (ed.) (2008), *Afroeurope@ns: Cultures and Identities,* Newcastle upon Tyne: Cambridge Scholars Publishing

López Rodríguez, Marta Sofía (2014), 'Popular fiction, serious writing: Mike Phillips's crime novels', in José Francisco Fernández and Alejandra Moreno Álvarez (eds), *A Rich Field Full of Pleasant Surprises: Essays on Contemporary Literature in Honour of Professor Socorro Suárez Lafuente,* Newcastle upon Tyne: Cambridge Scholars Publishing, pp. 143–61.

Loshitzky, Yosefa (2010), *Screening Strangers: Migration and Diaspora in Contemporary European Cinema,* Bloomington: Indiana University Press.

Lyall, Sarah (2009), 'Art hoax unites Europe in displeasure', *The New York Times,* 15 January: A6.

Lykidis, Alex (2009), *In a State of Exception: Political Subjecthood in European Film, 1990–2008,* dissertation, University of Southern California.

Mahjoub, Jamal (2003), *Travelling with Djinns,* London: Chatto & Windus.

Mahjoub, Jamal (1997), 'The writer and globalism', IFLA Satellite Meeting Speech, Århus, 26–28 August, <http://www.lib.hel.fi/mcl/articles/mahjoub.htm> (last accessed 21 May 2013).

Marciniak, Katarzyna (2006), 'New Europe: eyes wide shut', *Social Identities,* 12:5: 615–33.

Marjanović, Ivana (2011), 'The racist regime of the (white) EU Schengen border regime', *The EU between Free Market and Fascism: A Reader,* Ultrainput, 3 May: 78–93, <www.ultrainput.com> (last accessed 4 June 2012).

Markakis, John (2012), 'Taking to the streets: a short history of Greek democracy', *London Review of Books,* 22 March: 35–6.

Maurits, Peter (2015), 'Vanishing migrants and the impossibility of a European Union', *Interventions: International Journal of Postcolonial Studies*, 17:4: 503–18.

Mazzucchelli, Francesco (2012), 'What remains of Yugoslavia? From the geopolitical space of Yugoslavia to the virtual space of the web Yugosphere', *Social Science Information*, 51:4: 631–48.

Mbembe, Achille (2003), 'Necropolitics', *Public Culture*, 15:1: 11–40.

McKenzie, Sheena (2015), 'Couple's boat rescues migrants crossing Mediterranean', *CNN*, 20 April, <http://www.cnn.com/2015/04/20/sport/boat-migrants-mediterranean-drown-moas/index.html> (last accessed 21 August 2017).

McLeod, John (2010), 'Extra dimensions, new routines: contemporary black writing of Britain', *Wasafiri*, 25:4: 45–52.

Melegh, Attila (2006), *On the East-West Slope: Globalisation, Narration, Racism and Discourses on Central and Eastern Europe*, Budapest: Central European University Press.

Melillenses (2004), film, directed by Moisés Salama Benarroch, Spain: Atico7.

Mencinger, Jože (2015), 'EU je tamo gde je bila Jugoslavija', *B92*, 5 July, <http://www.b92.net/ biz/vesti/srbija.php?yyyy=2015&mm=07&dd=05&nav_id=1011911> (last accessed 21 August 2017).

Mieville, China (2009), *The City and the City*, New York: Del Rey.

Monroe, Alexei (2005), *The Interrogation Machine: Laibach and NSK*, Cambridge, MA: MIT Press.

Montuori, Chad (2011), *Gendering Migration from Africa to Spain: Literary Representations of Masculinities and Femininities*, dissertation, University of Missouri.

Mortimer, Mildred (2010), 'Probing the past: Leila Sebbar, *La Seine était rouge/The Seine Was Red*', *The French Review*, 83:6: 1246–56.

Mouffe, Chantal (2013), *Agonistics: Thinking the World Politically*, New York: Verso.

Mufti, Aamir (2007), 'Fanatics in Europa', *boundary 2*, 34:1: 17–23.

Muñoz-Valdivieso, Sofía (2009), 'Africa in Europe: narrating black British history in contemporary fiction', *Journal of European Studies*, 40:2: 159–74.

Muñoz-Valdivieso, Sofía (2012), 'Shakespearean intertexts and European identities in contemporary black British fiction', *Changing English: Studies in Culture and Education*, 19:4: 459–69.

Nancy, Jean-Luc [1986] (1991), *The Inoperative Community*, Minneapolis: University of Minnesota Press.

Nancy, Jean-Luc [1996] (2000), *Being Singular Plural*, Stanford: Stanford University Press.

Negri, Antonio (2002), 'The multitude and the metropolis', trans. Arianna Bove, 20 November, <http://www.generation-online.org/t/metropolis. htm 2002> (last accessed 21 August 2017).

Noland, Carrie, and Barrett Watten (eds) (2009), *Diasporic Avant-Gardes: Experimental Poetics and Cultural Displacement*, New York: Palgrave Macmillan.

NSK (1991), *Neue Slowenische Kunst*, Los Angeles: AMOK Books.

NSK (n.d.), *NSK State*, Immanent-Transcendent Spirit, <www.nskstate. com> (last accessed 21 August 2017).

Nyman, Jopi (2009), *Home, Identity, and Mobility in Contemporary Diasporic Fiction*, Amsterdam, New York: Rodopi.

Ong, Aiwha (2006), *Neoliberalism as Exception*, Durham, NC: Duke University Press.

Orenstein, Mitchell A. (2008), 'Postcommunist welfare states', *Journal of Democracy*, 19:4: 80–94.

Padgen, Anthony (2002), *The Idea of Europe: From Antiquity to the European Union*, Cambridge: Cambridge University Press.

Passerini, Luisa (2002), 'From the ironies of identity to the identities of irony', in Anthony Padgen (ed.), *The Idea of Europe: From Antiquity to the European Union*, Cambridge: Cambridge University Press, pp. 191–209.

Past, Elena (2013), 'Island hopping, liquid materiality, and the Mediterranean cinema of Emanuele Crialese', *Ecozon@*, 4:2: 49–66.

Perica, Vjekoslav (2004), *Balkan Idols: Religion and Nationalism in Yugoslav States*, Oxford: Oxford University Press.

Perica, Vjekoslav, and Mitja Velikonja (2012), *Nebeska Jugoslavija*, Beograd: XX vek.

Perišić, Vuk (2011a), 'Da li je Jugoslavija morala da se raspadne?', *E-novine*, 30 June, <http://www.e-novine.com/region/region-tema/27532-Jugo-slavija-morala-raspadne.html> (last accessed 21 August 2017).

Perišić, Vuk (2011b), 'Jugoslovenski paradoks', *E-novine*, 24 January, <http://www.e-novine.com/stav/44148-Jugoslovenski-paradoks.html> (last accessed 21 August 2017).

Petrović, Tanja (2012), *Yuropa: Jugoslovensko Nasleđe i politike Budućnosti u postjugoslovenskim Društvima*, Beograd: Fabrika knjiga.

Phillips, Caryl [1987] (2000), *The European Tribe*, New York: Vintage.

Phillips, Mike (2000), *A Shadow of Myself*, New York: HarperCollins.

Phillips, Mike (2009), 'Broken borders: migration, modernity and English writing', in Frank Schulze-Engler and Sissy Helff (eds), *Transcultural English Studies: Theories, Fictions, Realities*, Amsterdam, New York: Rodopi, pp. 133–49.

Phillips, Mike (2010), 'Narratives of desire – a writer's statement', in Barbara Korte et al. (eds), *Facing the East in the West: Images of Eastern Europe in British Literature, Film and Culture*, Amsterdam, New York: Rodopi, pp. 43–7.

Pirker, Eva Ulrike (2010), 'The unfinished revolution: black perceptions of Eastern Europe', in Barbara Korte et al. (eds), *Facing the East in the West: Images of Eastern Europe in British Literature, Film and Culture*, Amsterdam, New York: Rodopi, pp. 124–43.

Ponzanesi, Sandra (2004), *Paradoxes of Postcolonial Culture: Contemporary Women Writers of the Indian and Afro-Italian Diaspora*, Albany: SUNY Press.

Ponzanesi, Sandra, and Bolette B. Blaagaard (eds) (2013), *Deconstructing Europe: Postcolonial Perspectives*, New York: Routledge.

Ponzanesi, Sandra and Gianmaria Colpani (eds) (2015), *Postcolonial Transitions in Europe: Contexts, Practices and Politics*, London: Rowman & Littlefield International.

Ponzanesi, Sandra, and Daniella Merola (eds) (2005), *Migrant Cartographies: New Cultural and Literary Spaces in Post-Colonial Europe*, Lanham, MD: Lexington Books.

Pourgouris, Marinos (2010), 'The phenomenology of hoods: some reflections on the 2008 violence in Greece', *Journal of Modern Greek Studies*, 28:2: 225–45.

Pratt, Mary Louise (1992), *Imperial Eyes: Travel Writing and Transculturation*, New York: Routledge.

Probst, Lothar (2003), 'Founding myths in Europe and the role of the Holocaust', *New German Critique*, 90: 45–58.

Pugliese, Joseph (2010), 'Transnational carceral archipelagos: Lampedusa and Christmas Island', in Joseph Pugliese (ed.), *Transmediterranean: Diasporas, Histories, Geopolitical Spaces*, Brussels: PIE Peter Lang, pp. 105–24.

Rancière, Jacques [1995] (2004a), *Disagreement: Politics and Philosophy*, Minneapolis: University of Minnesota Press.

Rancière, Jacques [2000] (2004b), *The Politics of Aesthetics*, New York: Continuum.

Rigney, Anne (2012), 'Transforming memory and the European project', *New Literary History*, 43: 607–28.

Rivera, Annamaria (2011), 'Two years of racism in Italy. Main actors and secondary players, victims and rebels', in Lunaria (eds), *Chronicles of Ordinary Racism*, Rome: Edizioni dell' Asino, pp. 6–19.

'Rođenima u Yu zabranjeno sjećanje' (2010), *E-novine*, 28 October, <http://www.e-novine.com/drustvo/41789-Roenima-zabranjeno-sjeanje.html> (last accessed 21 August 2017).

Rosello, Mireille (2002), *Postcolonial Hospitality: The Immigrant as Guest*, Stanford: Stanford University Press.

Saleh, Nivien (2007), 'Europe in the Middle East and Northern Africa: the subtle quest for power', *Mediterranean Quarterly*, 18:1: 75–88.

Sarhaddi Nelson, Soraya (2015), 'Germans open their homes to refugee roommates', *NPR*, 6 March, <http://www.npr.org/sections/parallels/2015/03/06/390968567/germans-open-their-homes-to-refugee-roommates> (last accessed 21 August 2017).

Sassatelli, Monica (2002), 'An interview with Jean Baudrillard: Europe, globalisation and the destiny of culture', *European Journal of Social Theory*, 5:4: 521–30.

Sassatelli, Monica (2009), *Becoming Europeans: Cultural Identity and Cultural Policies*, New York: Palgrave Macmillan.

Scherer, Steve, and Ilaria Polleschi (2014), 'Italy in talks with EU to share responsibility for boat migrants', *Reuters*, 8 July, <http://www.reuters.com/article/us-eu-italy-migrants-idUSKBN0FD1YL20140708> (last accessed 21 August 2017).

Schleuser: The Federal Association Schleppen & Schleuser (2007), <www.schleuser.net> (last accessed 5 July 2012).

Schleuser (2011), 'Our goal is mobility X', *Schleuser pages*, <http://www.faridaheuck.net> (last accessed 21 August 2017).

Sebbar, Leila (1999) (English trans. 2008), *The Seine Was Red*, Bloomington: Indiana University Press.

Sévry, Jean (2001), 'Interviewing Jamal Mahjoub', *Commonwealth*, 23:2: 85–92.

Seyhan, Azade (2000), *Writing Outside the Nation*, Princeton: Princeton University Press.

Siljan, Sandro (2012), 'Lexicon of Yugoslav amnesia', *Criticise This!*, 26 January, <http://www.criticizethis.org/en/category/kritike/izvodjacke-umetnosti/page/13> (last accessed 21 August 2017).

Smith, Anthony D. (1992), 'National identity and the idea of European unity', *International Affairs*, 68: 55–76.

Smolin, Jonathan (2011), 'Burning the past: Moroccan cinema of illegal immigration', *South Central Review*, 28:1 (Spring): 74–89.

'Solid Sea' Project (2002), *Documenta 11*, <www.Stefanoboeri.net> (last accessed 13 May 2014).

Soysal, Yasemin (2002), 'Locating Europe', *European Societies*, 4:3: 265–84.

Spivak, Gayatri Chakravorty (2006), 'Are you postcolonial? To the teachers of Slavic and Eastern European literatures', *PMLA*, 121:3: 828–9.

Steiner, Tina (2008), 'Navigating multilingually: the chronotope of the ship in contemporary East African fiction', *English Studies in Africa*, 51:2: 49–58.

Sternberg, Claudia (2001), 'Mike Phillips on migration, inventing Europe and his novel *A Shadow of Myself*: an interview', *ZAA*, 49:4: 385–93.

Štiks, Igor (2014), 'Bosnia presents a terrifying picture of Europe's future', *The Guardian*, 17 February, <https://www.theguardian.com/commentis-free/2014/feb/17/bosnia-terrifying-picture-of-europe-future> (last accessed 21 August 2017).

Stojanov, Dragoljub (2012), 'Shall EU survive? EU on the verge of Balkanisation: the impact of economic theory and economic policy on the future of EU', <http://euroacademia.eu/ presentation/shall-eu-survive-eu-on-the-verge-of-balkanization-the-impact-of-economic-theory-and-economic-policy-on-the-future-of-eu> (last accessed 21 August 2017).

Stoler, Ann (2011), 'Colonial aphasia: race and disabled histories in France', *Public Culture*, 23:1: 121–56.

Suárez-Navaz, Liliana (2004), *Rebordering the Mediterranean: Boundaries and Citizenship in Southern Europe*, New York: Berghahn.

Subversive Festival (2008–17), <www.subversivefestival.com> (last accessed 10 June 2015).

Taras, Ray (2008), *Europe Old and New: Transnationalism, Belonging, Xenophobia*, Lanham, MD: Rowman & Littlefield Publishers.

Tempelman, Olaf (2012), 'Yugoslavia syndrome threatens EU', *VoxEurop*, 15 October, <http://www.voxeurop.eu/en/content/article/2873351-yugo-slavia-syndrome-threatens-eu> (last accessed 21 August 2017).

Terraferma (2011), film, directed by Emanuele Crialese, Switzerland: Frenetic Films.

Terraferma Presskit (2011), <http://www.frenetic.ch/films/857/pro/terra-ferma-presskit-de.pdf> (last accessed 21 August 2017).

Tibi, Basam (2010), 'The Return of ethnicity to Europe via Islamic migration? The ethnicisation of the Islamic diaspora', in Roland Hsu (ed.), *Ethnic Europe: Mobility, Identity, and Conflict in a Globalised World*, Stanford: Stanford University Press, 127–57.

Todorov, Tzvetan (2008), 'European identity', *South Central Review*, 25:3: 3–15.

Todorova, Maria (1997), *Imagining the Balkans*, Oxford: Oxford University Press.

Todorova, Maria (2015), 'Re-imagining the Balkans', in Srećko Horvat and Igor Štiks (eds), *Welcome to the Desert of Post-Socialism: Radical Politics after Yugoslavia*, New York: Verso, pp. 85–101.

Tournay-Theodotou, Petra (2011), 'Reconfigurations of "home as a mythic place of desire" – Bernardine Evaristo's *Soul Tourists*', in Helga Ramsey-Kurz and Geetha Ganapathy-Doré (eds), *Projections of Paradise: Ideal Elsewheres in Postcolonial Migrant Literature*, Amsterdam, New York: Rodopi, pp. 105–21.

Ugrešić, Dubravka (2005), *The Ministry of Pain*, New York: HarperCollins.

Ugrešić, Dubravka (2008), *Nobody's Home*, Rochester, NY: Open Letter.

Ugrešić, Dubravka (2014), *Europe in Sepia*, Rochester, NY: Open Letter.

Unfair Fair (2008), <http://unfairfair.blogspot.com> (last accessed 17 August 2017).

Unfair Fair Catalogue (2008), Rome: 1:1 projects.

Uricchio, William (ed.) (2008), *We Europeans? Media, Representations, Identities*, Chicago: Intellect Books.

Vambe, Maurice T. (2012), 'French genocide in Algeria: the role of memory in artistic representation of colonial violence in the novel, *The Seine was Red* (1999)', *African Identities*, 10:3: 221–41.

Van't Klooster, Noortje (2012), *Lampedusa: Tourism and Migration*, MA thesis, Utrecht University.

Velikonja, Mitja (2010), *Titostalgija*, Beograd: XX vek.

Veličković, Vedrana (2010), 'Balkanisms old and new: the discourse of Balkanism and self-othering in Vesna Goldsworthy's *Chernobyl Strawberries* and *Inventing Ruritania*', in Barbara Korte et al. (eds), *Facing the East in the West: Images of Eastern Europe in British Literature, Film and Culture*, Amsterdam, New York: Rodopi, pp. 185–203.

Veličković, Vedrana (2012a), 'Melancholic travellers and the idea of (un)belonging in Bernardine Evaristo's *Lara* and *Soul Tourists*', *Journal of Postcolonial Writing* 48:1: 65–78.

Veličković, Vedrana (2012b), 'Belated alliances? tracing the intersections between postcolonialism and postcommunism', *Journal of Postcolonial Writing*, 48:2: 164–75.

Verstraete, Ginette (2010), *Tracking Europe: Mobility, Diaspora, and the Politics of Location*, Durham, NC: Duke University Press.

Virno, Paolo (2004), *A Grammar of the Multitude: For an Analysis of Contemporary Forms of Life*, New York: Semiotext(e).

'Vremeplov kroz svakodnevicu druge Jugoslavije' (2013), *Politika*, 14 July, <http://www.politika. rs/sr/clanak/263732/Vremeplov-kroz-svakodnev-icu-druge-jugoslavije> (last accessed 20 August 2017).

Waterfield, Bruno (2007), 'Barroso hails the European "empire"', the *Daily Telegraph*, 11 July, <http://www.telegraph.co.uk/news/world-news/1557143/Barroso-hails-the-European-empire.html> (last accessed 20 August 2017).

Williams, David (2013), *Writing Postcommunism: Toward a Literature of East European Ruins*, New York: Palgrave Macmillan.

Wilterdink, Nico (1993), 'The European ideal: an examination of European and national identity', *European Journal of Sociology/Archives Européennes de Sociologie*, 34: 119–36.

Wilson, Kevin and Jan van der Dussen (eds) (1995), *The History of the Idea of Europe (What is Europe?)*, New York: Routledge.

Wolff, Larry (1994), *Inventing Eastern Europe: The Map of Civilisation on the Mind of the Enlightenment*, Stanford: Stanford University Press.

Wolfreys, Julian (2004), *Occasional Deconstructions*, Albany: SUNY Press.

World Conference against Racism, Racial Discrimination, Xenophobia and Related Intolerance: Declaration (2001), United Nations, <http://www.un.org/WCAR/durban.pdf> (last accessed 13 May 2014).

Young, Stephenie (2010), 'Yugonostalgia and the post-national narrative', in Bob Brecher (ed.), *The New Order of War*, Amsterdam, New York: Rodopi, pp. 89–110.

Zarycki, Tomasz (2014), *Ideologies of Eastness in Central and Eastern Europe*, New York: Routledge.

Zielonka, Jan (2007), *Europe as Empire: The Nature of the Enlarged European Union*, Oxford: Oxford University Press.

Zinaic, Rade (2015), *A Materialist Critique of Critical Balkanologies*, dissertation, York University.

Žižek, Slavoj (1993), 'Es gibt keinen Staat in Europa', <https://www.nettime.org/nettime /DOCS/1/staat.html> (last accessed 30 May 2017).

Žižek, Slavoj (2002), *Welcome to the Desert of the Real: Five Essays on September 11 and Related Dates*, New York: Verso.

Žižek, Slavoj (2008), *Violence: Six Sideways Reflections*, New York: Picador.

Žižek, Slavoj (2014), 'Shoplifters of the world, unite', in Slavoj Žižek and Srećko Horvat (eds), *What Does Europe Want? The Union and Its Discontents*, New York: Columbia University Press, pp. 104–13.

Index